Boneyards of Steel

Boneyards of Steel

Exploring the World's Aircraft Graveyards

Lorraine Evans

Pen & Sword
AVIATION

First published in Great Britain in 2026 by
Pen & Sword Aviation
An imprint of
Pen & Sword Books Ltd
Yorkshire - Philadelphia

ISBN 978 1 03614 116 5

A CIP catalogue record for this book is available from the British Library.

Typeset in INDIA by IMPEC eSolutions
Printed and bound in England by CPI (UK) Ltd.

The Publisher's authorised representative in the EU for product safety is Authorised Rep Compliance Ltd., Ground Floor, 71 Lower Baggot Street, Dublin D02 P593, Ireland.
www.arccompliance.com

For a complete list of Pen & Sword titles please contact:

PEN & SWORD BOOKS LIMITED
47 Church Street, Barnsley, South Yorkshire, S70 2AS, England
E-mail: enquiries@pen-and-sword.co.uk
Website: www.pen-and-sword.co.uk

or

PEN AND SWORD BOOKS
1950 Lawrence Rd, Havertown, PA 19083, USA
E-mail: uspen-and-sword@casematepublishers.com
Website: www.penandswordbooks.com

FSC
www.fsc.org
MIX
Paper | Supporting responsible forestry
FSC® C013604

Bring Back the Tornado!

Margo Baxter, Spanner Flight Crew, Ted Coningsby Squadron, Scotland, UK

Contents

Author's Note

When I first made public my intention to pen a book on aviation graveyards, the response was, well, less than enthusiastic from certain quarters. Comments ranged from 'oh how boring' to 'you must be off your rocker' (actual quote). What they didn't know at the time was my enthusiasm for aviation, in particular military aircraft, as I had successfully kept that part of my disposition hidden. But growing up on the flight path to Heathrow Airport and watching Concorde fly past the end of the garden five days a week, ordinarily at 17.10 pm, well, it leaves an impression. As does the Tornado fighter jet, particularly the GR4 variant, which appeared to 'stalk' my every move when I relocated to the Scottish Highlands. As likely as not, it was only a matter of time before my interest bubbled to the surface.

I first wrote about aviation boneyards/graveyards in *Burying the Dead – An Archaeological History of Burial Grounds, Graveyards and Cemeteries* (Pen and Sword, 2020), where several kind reviews, such as 'I particularly love the section on metal boneyards, train planes and automobiles left to rot in quiet corners of the world' as well as 'I especially loved the "*Boneyards of Steel*" chapter as I've always enjoyed visiting (when possible) or reading about vehicle graveyards', gave me the confidence to engage in the subject matter further. Albeit, I will admit, I did somewhat underestimate the task at hand; more on that later. As one can imagine, with an ever-increasing timeframe, and finite word count, it has been impracticable to discuss specific matters in depth. As such, topics included in the book will be expanded upon via my personal website and www.crashsiteorkney.com

Finally, I would like to add that every effort has been made to contact all relevant copyright holders, to whom I am eternally grateful. However, at the end of the day I am only human, and if an error or omission has been made, I apologize most profusely.

Lorraine Evans, Orkney 2025

Lorraine Evans can be followed at www.lorraineevans.com

Acknowledgements

I would like to express my gratitude to the following people for their invaluable support and assistance; to my publishers, Pen and Sword, in particular to my Commissioning Editor, Jonathan Wright, for his continual faith, and Olivia Camozzi; my old editor extraordinaire, Kate Bohdanowicz, without whom this book would never have come to fruition, and my current editor, Kerri Landis, with whom it has been a pleasure to work with; to Fran Flett Hollinrake and Andrew Hollinrake, for their support and longs chats; fellow aviation enthusiast and archaeologist, Carl Thorpe; Kevin Heath of ARGOS (Aviation Research Orkney & Shetland), for our seven-hour-plus tea drinking sessions, whilst discussing aviation mishaps; Elwyn R of Mach Loop fame; Former RAF Squadron Leader and ex-Tornado GR4 pilot, Tim Davies (Fast Jet Performance); Mark Hillier of Spitfires.com; Jamie Dibble and staff at Navy Wings; Royal Navy Fleet Air Arm; Sergeant Robert Warren of the Joint Casualty and Compassionate Centre; Jason Phillips, Chris Stock and staff at The Goldfish Club; Helen Webb Aviation; Dr Tom Horne; Jon Berry at CADW; Ministry of Defence; British Royal Air Force; staff at the RAF Air Historical Branch; RAF Museum Hendon; staff at the National Archives, Kew; Imperial War Museum, London; Battle of Britain Memorial Flight, RAF Coningsby; Dr George Simkiss; Lincolnshire Aviation Heritage Centre; Simply Spitfires; Jim Petty; Davis-Monthan Air Base, Pima Air and Space Museum, Commonwealth War Graves Commission; Historic England; to Ted, Nikos, Claire, Spanner Flight Crew, and Ted Coningsby Squadron members for their assistance, with a special shout-out to the following peeps for their advice and support: Daniel Walker, Margo Baxter, Christine Barnes, Nick Ward, Carol Lee, Julie Beard, Mick T; Military Aviation Channel. I would also like to extend my appreciation to those folk on various social media platforms who have offered their advice and knowledge unquestionably. I am most grateful.

List of Illustrations

Preface

The study of aviation graveyards is a much-maligned area of death research. The final resting place of sizeable non-organic flying beasts is routinely overlooked, yet it is still, in every respect, a graveyard and deserves to be recognized as such. From an extensive desert necropolis to a war-torn underwater mausoleum, very little of the world remains untouched by aviation graveyards; in fact, one could argue that the entire planet is just one huge aviation graveyard and less has been written about these remarkable sites. With a significant percentage still languishing in 'Top-Secret' military facilities, hidden behind barbed wire-fences and gated perimeters, it is hardly surprising. Nonetheless, advancements in technology have enabled those with an adventurous spirit, armchair or otherwise, to peel back these layers of secrecy and take a sneaky peak at the skeletal remains of once aeronautic marvels, the findings of which are astonishing, and often bizarre.

The meanings attached to death vary from one society to another, as does the disposal of the dead, which tells us much about how people perceive themselves and the world around them. It is no different for dead aircraft. For instance, here in the United Kingdom, when decommissioned aircraft reach the 'end of the road', they are, often, thrown onto a trash heap, awaiting the inevitable visit from an aviation death-dealer (i.e. scrap merchant). Whereas in the bygone Soviet Union, and associative Eastern Bloc countries, instead entire fighter jets, specifically the MiG variant, were often utilized as individual commemorative headstones—yes, entire aircraft—for former fighter pilots. Many of these independent MiG fighter jets can still be found proudly cemented to a sturdy pole, in some out-of-the way village square.

I took the decision, quite early on, to move away from the more traditional aviation crash site approach, especially regarding those aircraft that had been shot down and/or crashed during the Second World War.

In truth, there are many excellent books out there on this specific topic, see Select Bibliography, often written by those who were there at the time, digging out the remains, documenting the histories etc., so I do not feel it would be to anyone's benefit if I simply rehash what has already been told. It should be said though that anyone attempting to research the subject today, at a high level, will soon face streams of inconsistencies in descriptions of the same events in different books. One of the more interesting aspects of graveyard hunting is trawling for clues in the National Archives, in Kew, Surrey. *Boneyards of Steel* was no exception. However, during the research process it quickly became apparent that the task at hand was immense; for example, there are literally tens of thousands of Second World War Operational Record Book entries to decipher, hampered in no part by yours truly veering off on some tangent when something exciting caught her eye. If I had a pound for every time I exclaimed 'Oooooo a Dakota in Mogadishu!' I'd be a very rich woman indeed. Furthermore, the research process was not helped by the RAF abandoning the process of documenting an aircraft's serial number and/or engine number on its official RAF record card as the war continued. Consequently, looking for information linking lost airfields with aircraft burial pits at the end of the Second World War has become a separate project, one of which I hope to join forces with other aviation devotees in the not-too-distant future. If anyone reading this would be interested in participating, or has any information regarding aviation burial pits, not mentioned in Chapter 3, please do feel free to make contact. I would be delighted to hear from you.

By choice, I have chosen to focus on the mortuary/deposition aspect of aircraft death, to explore those areas which may not be immediately apparent to the reader. By utilizing said framework, I was able to uncover some rather compelling archetypes, such as entire fighters jets buried under the desert sands of Iraq; an underwater spacecraft cemetery located in the middle of nowhere; aircraft burial sites in Belize, South America, belonging to drug cartels; and a Coach fashion boutique sited in the interior of a decommissioned Boeing 747 passenger aircraft. That is not to say that the subject of crash sites is not discussed. Chapter 5, 'Lest We Forget', paints a picture of the distinct commemorative variations found within this category. Finally, the topic of resurrection is briefly touched upon, a unique aspect of aviation heritage, it could be argued, and one I hope to expand upon in future publications.

Postscript - Unbeknownst to me, only two months after I completed *Boneyards of Steel*, and submitted the manuscript to my publisher, I would acquire/take the helm of a once active, but defunct aviation archaeology group, namely A.R.G.O.S (Aviation Research Group Orkney & Shetland). Since then, my life has become a whirlwind of aviation gravesites, and in only a few short months we have successfully identified the specification of a disputed Spitfire wreck, completed the fascinating and somewhat amusing tale of Boulton Paul Defiant DR886, with assistance from The Goldfish Club, and I am currently liaising with the Ministry of Defence in regard to an undocumented Seafire crash. I am sure you can appreciate that knowing what I know now, *Boneyards of Steel* may have taken a slightly different path. A.R.G.O.S. is now very much active, both on land and at sea, the aims of which are to re-assess old data and utilize new technology in identifying potential aviation gravesites, implementing the highest professional archaeological standards throughout. A dive team is being assembled, and targets are being identified for 2026/27. Reports/findings will be open sourced, either via the A.R.G.O.S. website or other internet platforms. Let the adventures commence!

All US dollar/euro amounts are followed by an up-to-date corresponding value in British pounds (as of April 2026).

Chapter 1

Where Planes Go to Die

My initial foray into the world of aviation graveyards came about purely by chance, many years ago, whilst taking an afternoon stroll through Glover's Wood, adjacent to the village of Charlwood, Surrey. Located not far from Gatwick Airport, it is one of the largest areas of woodland in the Surrey Weald, but remarkably, it is also the site of a bizarre aviation graveyard. It is littered with iconic military aircraft, including a few sea harriers; a couple of Sepecat Jaguars, which I have subsequently discovered have been shipped to Selby in Yorkshire; several Sea King helicopters; and other abandoned transport. Providing a fascinating glimpse into British wartime history, the graveyard is privately owned by the Wright family, according to a search at Companies House, and although it sits behind a secured gated facility, the aircraft can clearly be viewed through the fence next to the woodland path. It would not be the last aircraft graveyard I would find hidden behind some barbed wire fence.

Before we commence, I would like to discuss terminology. Throughout the following chapters you will see the use of such terms as 'boneyard', 'graveyards', 'cemeteries', 'necropolis', 'burial grounds', 'gravesites' and such alike. Whilst similar in nature, there are subtle differences between the phraseology. A boneyard, for instance, is a term that has come to represent specific locations where aircraft are sent to when they have outlived their usefulness or have reached their natural end-of-life. Predominantly located in desert-type regions, boneyard facilities provide a range of services, including aircraft storage, maintenance, recycling, and scrapping. Often there is no set time limit as to how long an aircraft will remain, intact, at such a facility. Some are fortunate enough to be 'resurrected', to live another day, whereas others can remain in situ for decades. I tend to view boneyards as the aviation equivalent of 'God's Waiting Room', a place where aircraft dwell until they meet their fate.

On the other hand, an aviation graveyard/cemetery etc. is simply a place where aircraft are left to decompose, often in a haphazard manner. There is no set location. I have found aircraft dumped in a field in Romania, in an underground hangar in Albania, by the side of a busy road in Thailand, and on an unused taxiway in the Democratic Republic of Congo. The list is endless. Some are privately owned, others are not; there is no official storage, and none such aircraft receive any kind of upkeep or maintenance. As a colleague once said, they are left 'to undergo destructive dissolution'. A related subject is that of the 'open-air' museum, which normally comprises several preserved and well-maintained aircraft, displayed outdoors in an insightful manner, enabling the viewing public to get alongside their aircraft icon. This, however, is not always the case. A popular trend in less affluent countries is to simply stretch an old rope around some decaying aircraft in a field, alter their epithet from 'junk' to 'exhibit' and then charge visitors to view said wreckage. This does not equate to an open-air museum in my eyes. It is an aviation graveyard that has simply upgraded its designation. However, this is just my opinion, to which I know many will disagree. Consideration will also be given throughout to individual aircraft commemoration that exhibit a defined burial/final resting place, often associated with conflict, as seen in Chapter 5, or an extraordinary 'end-of-life' situation. So, without further ado, let us examine how the boneyard phenomenon came to be.

On 7 May 1945, at the Supreme Headquarters, Allied Expeditionary Force (SHAEF) in Reims, France, the German Armed Forces High Command signed the unconditional surrender of all German forces in Europe to the Western Allies. This was followed a few months later, on 2 September 1945, by the formal surrender of Japanese forces in the Pacific. After six long years of conflict, the Second World War had finally come to an end. Following the cessation of hostilities, the United States, as with other Allied nations, had a problem; that is, what to do with the huge numbers of surplus aircraft that were no longer needed. For the United States, the challenge was considerable. Around 295,000 aircraft had been manufactured for the war effort; records show that of that number 21,583 (7.34 per cent) were lost in the United States in test flights, ferrying, training accidents etc., and 43,581 were lost en route to the war and in overseas operations. That left a surplus of some 150,000 aircraft.[1] By 1944, the US Foreign Economic Administration began a programme to scrap obsolete, damaged and/or surplus military aircraft that were based overseas. There was no financial incentive, or the time, to bring them back to the United States, so they were consequently buried, bulldozed or sunk at sea. But what about the remaining stock? Thought was given to storing a substantial number of the aircraft, but it soon became apparent that the expense to do so was simply too great. As such, the War Assets Administration (WAA), together with the Reconstruction Finance Corporation (RFC), established thirty depots, predominantly in the desert regions of the south-west, to store, sell or dispose of any remaining aircraft. Incidentally, it would not be until late 1963 that all military aircraft storage and disposition centres would be consolidated into a single entity located at the now infamous Davis-Monthan. Their goal was to dispose of over $9,900,000,000 worth of aircraft, £7,315,258,500 in today's money, and before long $8,000,000 (£5,911,000) worth of military planes was being scrapped every day.[2] Here are just a few of the chosen thirty sites.

Kingman Army Airfield

Established as an Aerial Gunnery Training Base at the start of the Second World War, the Kingman Army Airfield, in Arizona, one of the Army Air Corps largest airfields, became a chosen disposal site for surplus aircraft. Offering huge open spaces, optimal environmental conditions for aircraft storage, and three runways, one of which was 2,073m (6,800ft) in length, the RFC designated Kingman as 'Sales Depot No. 41', and by October 1945, as many as 150 planes per day were being flown into the site, parked and processed. The operation was so labour intensive that, to accommodate the large numbers of employees, tent cities were erected on site. The disposal process involved the 'cremation' of as many aircraft as possible, as quickly as possible, with three huge operational furnaces working around the clock. The US federal government contracted out this process to Martin Wunderlich, of Wunderlich Contracting Company, Jefferson City, Missouri, who paid the government $2,780,000, (£2,054,183) for 5,437 of the aircraft stored at Kingman Field.[3]

So, how does one 'cremate' an aircraft? The process involves first removing anything of value, such as aircraft radios, oxygen equipment, manuals etc., then draining the fuel from the aircraft, before slicing the main airframe into smaller pieces and tossing the parts into the furnace, the flames liquifying around seventy per cent of the aircraft into small ingots. The Wunderlich contract at Kingman was a huge success and resulted in the recovery of significant resources: 20,865,249kg (46 million lb) of aluminium; 2,721,554kg (6 million lb) of aluminium from engines; 2,267,962kg (5 million lb) of aluminium propellers; 9,525,440kg (21 million lb) of steel; 6,056,6591 (1.6 million gallons) of aviation fuel; 969,0651 (256,000 gallons of oil).[4]

A total of 85 reconnaissance aircraft, 615 fighters, 54 light bombers, 266 medium bombers and 4,463 heavy bombers were disposed of. These 5,483 aircraft scrapped by Wunderlich at Kingman generated $7.5 million (£5,542,183) in gross income. Some of the most iconic aircraft ended their days in these cremation furnaces, including the B-17, B-24, B-25, B-26, Consolidated B-32, P-38, P-63 and A-20 aircraft, as well as brand-new aircraft from various assembly lines.[5] Today, the site is a Federal Aviation Administration (FAA)–approved Part 145 repair station and storage facility, where both Kingman Airline Services and Jet Yard Solution operate an active storage facility for commercial jet, turbo-prop and corporate aircraft.[6]

Walnut Ridge Arkansas

With three 1,524m (5,000ft) runways, a huge apron covering over 63 acres (254,952sqm), four large hangars, and a base engineering building, Walnut Army Airfield, located in northeast Arkansas, was an ideal site for surplus aircraft storage. Between 1945 and 1946, an estimated 10,000 to 11,000 warplanes were flown to Walnut Ridge for either storage, sale or disposal, including 65 of the military's 118 Consolidated B-32 'Dominator' heavy bombers—many had come straight from the assembly line in Fort Worth—as well as large quantities of Curtiss P-40 Warhawk fighters, which were lined up ready for the cremation furnaces.[7]

Altus Army Airfield

Between 1945 and 1953, Altus Army Airfield, in Oklahoma, would serve as a boneyard for thousands of the surplus military aircraft. Operating as an Advanced Flying School since early 1943, approximately 2,500 aircraft were stored, sold or scrapped there after the Second World War, including B-17, B-24, B-25, P-38, P-40, P-51 and P-47 aircraft. Most of the B-17s sent to Altus for storage were brand-new 'G' models right off the assembly line, which not only created a strong buyer's market, but also saved them from the furnaces. Embarrassingly, the famous *Memphis Belle*, honoured in 1943 as the first B-17 heavy bomber to complete the then-mandatory twenty-five missions, was found languishing at Altus, awaiting disposal. Thankfully, she was saved from the furnace flames before the unthinkable occurred and has now been restored to her former glory.[8]

Clinton Naval Air Station

Located 24km (15mi) southwest of Clinton, near the town of Burns Flat in Washita County, Oklahoma, Clinton Naval Air Station was originally established in 1942 as a training station for naval aviators. After the war, it served as a boneyard for US Navy aircraft. By April of 1946, over 8,800 military planes were stored at Clinton, mostly F6F Hellcats, FM Wildcats and TBM Avengers. Whilst some were sold to private individuals or companies, the majority were dismantled and cremated in two on-site furnaces, one of which was rented by Sherman Machine and Iron Works of Oklahoma City, who successfully transformed the cremated aircraft remains into much-needed scrap metal. The base was closed in 1969. Other post-Second World War naval storage and reclamation facilities were located at Naval Air Station (NAS) Litchfield Park near Phoenix, and NAS Norfolk in Virginia. At one point, more than 5,000 aircraft were left in storage at Litchfield Park. After the Korean War, this number was brought down to 2,500. In 1965, the Defense Department decided to consolidate military aircraft storage, with 800 aircraft sited at Litchfield moved to Davis-Monthan, the rest earmarked for disposal. Today, Litchfield is called the Phoenix Goodyear Airport and is the home airport for several private companies offering aircraft storage and maintenance.[9]

Cal-Aero Field 'Ontario' California

Located east of Los Angeles, near Chino and Ontario, California, the Cal-Aero Field, also known as 'Ontario,' initially began life as a civilian aviation school, established before the Second World War, and later contracted by the AAF to train pilots. After the war, the RFC commandeered the site for boneyard duties, recognizing that the surrounding agricultural area around the airfield would be an excellent storage location for surplus military aircraft. Nearly 1,900 aircraft would be transferred to Cal-Aero, including the Curtiss C-46 Commando, Boeing B-17 Flying Fortress, B-24 Liberator, P-40 Warhawk and the P-38 Lightning, amongst others, of which about 500 were sold and the rest disposed of in the furnaces, one of which was operated offsite in Norco, CA, by Sharp & Fellows Contracting. Another storage facility and boneyard were located at China Lake, California. Many of the B-29s in there were destined for target practice, although a couple of much-loved Superfortresses were saved, including *FiFi*, *Peachy*, and *Doc*. Today, no more aircraft exist at the former China Lake aircraft boneyard.[10]

Oxnard Field

Built in 1928, and named after James G. Oxnard, a New York entrepreneur, Oxnard Field served as the home of commercial aviation in Albuquerque, New Mexico, from 1928 to 1929, before it closed in 1948. After the end of the Second World War, it too became a designated boneyard, receiving over 1,500 old aircraft onto its unpaved runways, such as the B-24 Liberator and B-17 Flying Fortress bombers, as well as P-38 and P-51 fighters. Most of the aircraft were sold or disposed of on site, reclaiming some 4,535,924kg (10 million lb) of aluminium. Oxnard would later become part of Kirtland Air Force Base.[11]

Not many aircraft escaped the cremation furnaces; a few were initially earmarked for preservation, such as the B-29 *Enola Gay*, which dropped America's first atom bomb on Japan in the Second World War. By June

1947, the War Assets Administration had virtually completed its job of disposing of some 65,000 aircraft.[12]

Which brings us to the largest boneyard in the world today, and the site that most people are familiar with—Davis-Monthan. Named after Lieutenants Samuel H. Davis and Oscar Monthan, two Tucsonans and First World War pilots who died in separate military aircraft accidents, Davis-Monthan Air Force Base is located around 11km (7mi) southeast of downtown Tucson, Arizona. Housing 11,000 airmen from thirty-four unique mission partners, which support six combatant commanders worldwide, it is perhaps more famous for being the official home of the 309th Aerospace Maintenance Regeneration Centre (AMARC), the sole aircraft boneyard and parts reclamation facility for all excess military and government aircraft. With the area's low humidity, between ten and twenty per cent; low annual rainfall; hard alkaline soil, known as 'caliche', whereby the soil is baked so hard that aircraft can be safely parked without needing tarmac or concrete stands; and an altitude of 777m (2,550ft), which aids natural preservation: Davis-Monthan is the perfect choice for a major boneyard storage facility.[13]

Initially, Davis-Monthan AFB was one of the smaller storage bases, mainly used for the storage of the Boeing B-29 Superfortresses and C-47 Skytrains, but from the mid-1940s, as the larger bases closed or relinquished their major storage mission, including Kelly AAF, Texas, Pyote AAF, Texas, and Tinker AAF, Oklahoma, the primary responsibility for aircraft disposal was handed over to Davis-Monthan AFB. On 10 January 1946, the first of 300 C-47s arrived at Davis-Monthan for long-term preservation, joined in May 1946 by more than 600 B-29 Superfortresses and an additional 200 C-47 Skytrains. Some were preserved and returned to action in the Korean War; others were scrapped.[14] From here, however, the numbers would steadily increase. For example, in 1953, a large number of North American T-6D and T-6F Texans arrived at the boneyard from various operational, non-training units, as would twenty-seven Boeing B-29A Superfortresses, which were part of a batch of eighty-seven B-29A's loaned to the British Air Force under the Military Assistance Program, returned for storage from the United Kingdom. The Royal Air Force had used the B-29 as a four-year, stop-gap measure to provide the United Kingdom with a strategic bomber capability before their chosen platform, the English Electric Canberra, could enter service.[15] In 1954, over 100 Boeing B-29 Superfortresses arrived at the boneyard, assigned to reclamation purposes, whereas in 1955, over 170 North American T-6D, T-6F and T-6G Texans arrived, together with a number of North American B-26B, B-26C and TB-26B Invaders, 150 Republic F-84E Thunderjets, and over 200 further North American T-6 Texans. In February of 1956, the first Convair B-36 Peacemaker aircraft arrived at Davis-Monthan AFB for disposal; the entire fleet of 384 Peacemakers would ultimately be dismantled, except for 4 remaining B-36 survivors saved for air museums.[16] By late 1963, the secretary of defence directed the consolidation of all military aircraft storage and disposition centres into a single entity located at Davis-Monthan. This facility became the Military Aircraft Storage and Disposition Center (MASDC) in February 1965, an early incarnation of AMARC, culminating with the immediate transfer of over 800 Navy aircraft from the Navy Storage Depot at Litchfield Park. Following the United States withdrawal from Vietnam in 1973, the boneyard facility reached an all-time high capacity with a total of 6,080 aircraft sprawled across the desert terrain.[17]

As with other US boneyards, Davis-Monthan had three civilian smelters in operation, under contract to the Air Force, to effectively cremate unwanted aircraft. One was operated by Aircraft Associates and was going full blast, tasked with disposing of predominantly B-50s and 265 B-29s, whereas the other two were owned by Page Airways and Marpak, and they concentrated their efforts on the 230 acres full of B-36 carcasses.[18] Alongside smelting operations, the guillotines were also working overtime, cutting up aircraft wings and fuselages into easily handled pieces to be fed into the smelters. Probably the most dramatic disposal process that came to pass was the B-52 fleet reduction, to meet the terms of the Strategic Arms Limitation Treaty (SALT), a series of bilateral arms control agreements (1972–79) between the United States and the Soviet Union, aimed to limit the production and deployment of strategic nuclear weapons. Hundreds of the giant B-52 bombers were towed to a clear piece of desert floor, where a huge guillotine was used to chop off the wings and then the fuselage into pieces. The parts were then piled up neatly in a stack and left in place for months, to allow Soviet satellites to verify their destruction.[19]

Those aircraft not destined for the ovens were subsequently stored in the desert, the procedure of which was rather basic during the early days. To start with, upon arrival the aircraft's serial number would be noted, together with its general condition, and the equipment onboard would be registered. After which the aircraft would be towed out to an allocated desert location, lifted onto wooden blocks, to take the weight off the tyres, and simply left there. Every so often the aircraft would be inspected for corrosion or damage. This was followed, in 1947, by attempts to cocoon aircraft in a form of plastic sealant, reported to be seven times stronger than rawhide. Implemented by the Fort Pitt Packaging Company, these early attempts were not a success, with many of the coverings ballooning and cracking from climatic expansion.[20]

Today, the process has somewhat advanced, and those planes destined for storage undergo a procedure not dissimilar to that of Ancient Egyptian mummification! First, all ejection seats, guns, cockpit equipment and classified hardware are removed. The aircraft is then carefully washed with fresh water to remove any organic residue and allowed to dry. The fuel system is protected by draining it, refilling it with lightweight oil, and then draining it again, leaving a protective oil film. Once dry, the plane is wrapped in a substance called Spraylat—short for sprayable latex—a two-stage sealing process covering gaps and holes and generally blocking the intrusion of moisture or wildlife, thus reducing the degradation of the aircraft in the desert heat. The bottom coat is black, but the topcoat is white, which reflects the sun and helps to keep internal temperatures low. The Spraylat also must be applied before 10.00 am; after that, as the atmospheric temperatures rises, the material simply won't stick to the plane. Finally, the aircraft is towed to its designated 'storage' position.[21]

Some aircraft were fortunate to avoid the cremation furnaces and embalming process altogether and leave the desert boneyard intact. In 1950, almost two-thirds of the cocooned B-29s returned to service, with eighty-seven loaned to the British Royal Air Force, as previously mentioned. A few years later several B-26s would depart for Brazil, whilst 180 T-6G trainers were sold to the French Government. Peru received two B-57s, ten C-45 Hs and two B-26s, with a further eight B-26s sent to Guatemala. Other aircraft were donated to towns and civil defence operations for display or training purposes. Under educational provisions, the G.I. Bill of Rights purchased 17,000 primary and advanced training aircraft; and 3,000 large and medium transport aircraft, including 550 C-47 Skytrains, 20 C-54 Skymasters and 12 twin-engine Lockheed freighters were sold to companies in a developing air cargo transportation industry.[22] In fact, as I write, ten DC-10's have just gone up for auction at the Davis-Monthan site.[23]

In June 1966, Colonel I.R. Perkins became the new commander of the Davis-Monthan boneyard and offered another avenue whereby those aircraft marked for disposal could escape their fate. First, he arranged for the transfer of several museum-type aircraft in the boneyard to be moved to an area near the perimeter fence, where they could be viewed by the public. He was also the driving force behind the adjacent Pima Air & Space Museum, which opened its doors to the public on 8 May 1976. With the Air Force graveyard, a matter of a few hundred yards away, the museum is guaranteed an inexhaustible supply of exhibits for the foreseeable future.[24]

So, what does the storage concept entail? Well, most fighter aircraft need around fifty hours of labour to be prepared for storage; it's eighty hours for helicopters because a box must be built to protect their rotor heads. Big aircraft such as the B-52 can require up to 300 hours for decommissioning. Each aircraft deposited at the boneyard site is divided into a specific type: Category 1000 refers to an aircraft preserved so that it can be recalled to duty and fly again if required. This is called 'inviolate' storage, meaning no parts can be pulled from these aircraft without official authorization. Only some ten per cent of the aircraft in the boneyard are kept in Category 1000 condition. Category 1500 refers to aircraft previously fully preserved. Those aircraft in Category 2000 are used for spare parts and are often referred to as 'can birds'. Both Type 1000 and 2000 aircraft, after in-processing, will be given a treatment of Spraylat. Category 3000 aircraft are considered 'temporary' visitors to the boneyard; they consist of planes in good condition that are likely to be redeployed. Consequently, they receive the most care and attention; every thirty days their engines are run, they are towed to lubricate their bearings, and their fluids are serviced. Category 4000 are generally the oldest aircraft in the Boneyard and are likely to be scrapped for parts or in some cases donated as museum pieces.[25]

Aircraft can be moved to different categories and even return to duty after decades standing in the desert heat. A B-52H Stratofortress *Ghost Rider* S/N 61-1007 was restored back to flight status by boneyard personnel, along with maintenance crews from Barksdale, Minot and Tinker Air Force Bases. In February 2015, it successfully flew to Barksdale AFB, at a speed of 250 knots, after seven years in storage.[26] Another B-52H, S/N 60-0034, *Wise Guy*, was also restored and returned to active service in the Air Force in March of 2021. The record for an aircraft returned to flying status after extended storage was an F-4 brought out of Type 2000 status and reconditioned to be a target drone after more than twenty years in the desert.[27]

Large commercial aircraft have a limited lifespan, approximately twenty-five years according to industry calculations. Regardless of whether this natural expiration date has been reached, or the aircraft is required to be temporarily taken off flying status, as occurred in the recent global pandemic, when the time comes, such aircraft must be stored in an environment that is conducive to preservation. Two large aircraft boneyards exist in California today—the Southern California Logistics Airport (SCLA) and the Mojave Air & Space Port—that provide the user with the necessary end-of-life solution. SCLA is in Victorville, California, about 145km (90mi) northeast of downtown Los Angeles. It is nestled on the former site of the George Air Force Base, and is home to Southern California Aviation, a vast transitional boneyard facility for commercial aircraft. Featuring a precision instrument runway of 4,587m (15,050ft) and a secondary runway length of 2,785m (9,138ft), it has the ability to accommodate the largest aircraft flying today, from Boeings to Federal Express, and can offer a range of aviation-related facilities ranging from aircraft end-of-life to maintenance and repair programmes. SCLA is also a popular destination for the movie and television industry. Dozens of movies, television episodes and commercials have been filmed at the locale over the years, ranging from *Oceans 11* (2001), *Jarhead* (2005) and *The Fast and the Furious: Tokyo Drift* (2005) to episodes of Top Gear US and Roadkill.[28]

With only one of a handful Convair 990 Coronado aircraft in existence, together with a McDonnell Douglas F-4D Phantom jet guarding the entrance, the Mojave Air and Space Port, located approximately 153km (95mi) north of downtown Los Angeles, serves a variety of aviation and space industries. First opened in 1935 as a small, rural airfield serving the local gold and silver mining industry, today, with its dry, desert climate, spanning over a vast arid area, it has become a popular and well-used boneyard storage facility for commercial airliners, such as Boeing and Airbus. Its most consistent customer is Qantas Airlines, who prefers to send its 'deceased' aircraft to the Californian desert rather than its own homegrown boneyard in Alice Springs, Australia. Their last ever Boeing 747 VH-OEJ, nicknamed *Wunala,* was delivered to the desert of Mojave, arriving on 24 July 2020. They also make use of the boneyard facilities at SCLA, in Victorville. As with the latter, Mojave too has provided a prime location for both film and TV production, which include such classics as *Hot Shots!* (1991), *Waterworld* (1995) and *Die Hard 2* (1988), as well as episodes of *NCIS*, *S.W.A.T.* and *MythBusters*. Prices range from $1,500 (£1,108) for a location permit to $10,000 (£7,391) for a runway fee and include access to the boneyard, the boneyard hangars, and associated wreckage.[29]

To complete our brief foray into America's desert boneyards, the once clandestine nature of Pinal Airpark may interest a few. Located 13km (8mi) northwest of Marana, in Pinal County, Arizona, it was one of the most secure and secretive airfields in the world—the home to America's Foreign Intelligence Agency, the CIA, and its covert operations throughout the Vietnam War. It was the primary facility of Intermountain Airlines, a CIA 'front' company which was used to supply covert operations, the most famous of which is often referred to as 'Air America'. As the Economic Development Director and Site Manager Jim Petty explains:

'The CIA operated flights in and out of the airfield throughout the Vietnam War. The grounds were secured by patrols and motion sensors (the latter are still scattered around the field, atop 4-foot-high rusty stakes). Those entering required a security clearance'.[30]

Some of Air America's operations during the Vietnam War included the infiltration and exfiltration of US personnel, the provision of direct and indirect support to US Special Forces, and the conducting of photo-reconnaissance missions on Viet Cong activities. In addition to these standard tasks, there were also rumours that Air America was directly involved, and profiteered, from drug smuggling activities, namely in the transportation of opium and heroin, during the civil war in Laos. This allegation has apparently been supported by former Laos CIA Paramilitary Operations Officer Anthony Poshepny, of the 'Special Activities Division', plus former Air America pilots, and other people directly involved in the war.[31]

Since then, Pinal Airpark has cleaned up its act, for want of a better phrase, with the County Public Works Department responsible for its daily management and development. As Jim Petty stated: 'the Airpark lately was described as a "Diamond in the Rough"—I am happy to say the diamond that is the Airpark is starting to be polished.' Covering an area of 6sq km (1,508 acres), with a single 2,101m (6,893ft)-long runway, four helipads, and a capacity for more than 500 aircraft, it has become a popular boneyard destination for retiring commercial aircraft. Customers include Delta Airlines, who sent most of their fleet of Boeing 747s to Pinal upon their retirement; Brazilian carrier Variglog, whose cargo planes are visible through the boneyard's perimeter fence; as well as some very old TWA stock. In fact, some aircraft haven't even moved from the boneyard since their arrival some thirty years ago.[32]

'Everyone sees the old passenger jets and think they've been parked out here forever, slowly wasting away. That's somewhat true, for some aircraft. But although some aircraft have been there for three decades or more, others have arrived almost directly from the factory.' - Jim Petty

Unlike other boneyards, Pinal Airpark is open to the public and limited tours are available.

Smaller civilian and less-regimented graveyards do exist in the United States, such as the 120 acres (.5sq km) of random aircraft decomposing in farmers' fields in Rantoul, Kansas, adjacent to Dodson International. Another example was White Industries Aircraft, in Bates City, Missouri, one of the oldest suppliers of parts to the general aviation and commuter airlines. Founded in 1956, the 170-acre (.7sq km) site comprises around 2,800 planes, in various stages of decay, also lying dormant in fields. Said company, however, was recently acquired by BAS Part Sales, Greely, Colorado.[33]

As with the United States, throughout Western Europe and beyond, at the cessation of the Second World War, the huge numbers of surplus aircraft that were no longer required was an issue that needed to be addressed. This also included the remains of aircraft that had been shot down during combat. Here in the United Kingdom, as well as in related military bases abroad, the British authorities had a monstrous task to undertake considering the vast number of aircraft that left the production line throughout the Second World War, from just under 8,000 in 1939 to over 26,000 in 1944. Making allowances for those aircraft that became casualties of the war, this still leaves thousands of aircraft surplus to requirement. Compared to the United States, the United Kingdom did not have the necessary land capacity to maintain vast boneyard-style facilities, let alone a suitable climate, so what became of the aircraft? Unfortunately, the available data is somewhat sparse. Just snippets here and there; for instance, a reference to a scrap merchant returning an end-of-life Spitfire back to the RAF in disgust once he discovered its history. Having contacted the RAF Air Historical Branch for assistance, I was surprised to discover that, unlike the scenario in the United States, there were no kept records or data on the subject matter. Nor did they know of anywhere else said information might be held/obtained. Their archive does hold Aircraft Movement Cards (A.M. Form 78s), but no documentation stating as to what explicitly happened to individual aircraft after the war—i.e. were they buried, were they scrapped, did they enter the cremation furnaces etc. It remains somewhat of a mystery.[34] Discussions with the RAF Museum also drew a blank, and combing for evidence through thousands upon thousands of operational logbook entries in the National Archives, as mentioned in the Introduction, is an ongoing process. A typical entry will read as follows: '57 Repair and Salvage Unit, Middle East; based in North Africa then Italy and disbanded in January 1945. Includes five photographs of Wellington aircraft being salvaged (RSU).'[35] Despite this, I have been successful in gathering numerous unsubstantiated reports of 'my grandfather/father took apart and buried (insert aircraft of your choice). More on this matter will be discussed in Chapter 3.

Outside of the United States, located in Alice Springs, Northern Territory, Australia, Alice Springs Airport is Asia-Pacific's very first aircraft boneyard. Opened in 2014 and operated by Brisbane-based Asia Pacific Aircraft Storage Ltd (APAS), the 110 hectare (1.7sq km) site, located on the opposite side of the main runway terminal, was chosen due to its climate suitability, an arid desert environment characterized by an average year round humidity of approximately twenty-five per cent, low rainfall, and low-lying in situ vegetation providing additional dust suppression qualities.[36] Other factors included a significant existing infrastructure, excellent transport links and a capacity for major expansion:

> 'Our target market is clearly the Asia Pacific region', owner Tom Vincent says. 'It's simply because it's the ease of access we present to that target market. We're five hours from Singapore. We've got the correct climatic conditions and the right environment for protecting the aircraft. And Asia-Pac is forecast by both Boeing and Airbus to be the highest growth region in the world.'[37]

According to the company website, the primary objectives of APAS Ltd are as follows: Focussing on storage: providing convenient storage in the region, with rapid reintroduction and redeployment opportunities; maintenance, with tailed aircraft storage maintenance programmes; parts out, selective parting options or full aircraft decommissioning; end-of-life services, where decommissioning services can fully dispose of residual aircraft components.

At first, business was slow, and it took almost three years for the boneyard to attract its first customer, an Embraer EMB 120 Brasilia twin-turboprop commuter airliner: 'to see the first aircraft come in is quite a milestone and we're looking forward now to seeing many more'. Initially, it was challenging for the operator to find airlines and aircraft leasing companies willing to overlook the Mojave Desert in California and Arizona's 840-hectare (8.4sq km) Pinal Airpark in favour of Alice Springs, but soon the Embraer would be joined by a Boeing 737 from Nauru's Our Airline, a Qantas 767, and four Airbus single aisle planes from Tigerair, Singapore. By 2016, its first European registered aircraft, an Airbus A330-300, had arrived.[38]

In an ironic twist of fate, it would be the COVID global pandemic that enabled the boneyard to come to the fore. With airlines scrambling to find somewhere to store or park their aircraft, the Alice Springs facility became a favourable option for many of the world's leading airlines; both Singapore Airlines and Cathay Pacific are among the airlines that sent much of their grounded fleet there, to the extent that by September 2020 the capacity had almost reached breaking point. APAS were forced to announce they would commence the storage of aircraft at a new site, Toowoomba Wellcamp Airport, two hours inland from Brisbane, Queensland.[39] It is perhaps fitting that the first Cathay Pacific pandemic-era aircraft to be stored at Alice Springs was also the last one to leave, almost four years after it arrived.[40]

Although nothing resembling the scale of above, Europe does have a couple of boneyards that are worthy of mention. The first is located at Teruel Airport, Spain, which has the prerequisite dry climate that makes it suitable for long-term storage of aircraft, together with an appropriately sized runway that is 9,268m (5.7mi) in length. Constructed as a storage and recycling facility for airliners, it functions as an industrial-aeronautical facility, with parking that can accommodate the largest of airliners.[41] It is also a base for TARMAC Aerospace, formed in 2007, as a European Union Aviation Safety Agency and FAA Part 145 MRO company involved in aircraft storage, aircraft maintenance, and recycling. With its headquarters in Tarbes, and further facilities in Toulouse and Paris-Vatry, France, the latter a former NATO base, it can accommodate 280 airliners at any one time, dispersed among the four facilities. Customers include Boeing, Bombardier, and Airbus, amongst others. In fact, TARMAC was responsible for the recycling of seventy-five per cent of the world's Airbus A340s. Interestingly, in 2022, it signed a memorandum of understanding with Airbus and the city of Chengdu, China, for the launch of an aircraft boneyard-style management service in China.

'TARMAC Aerospace offers aircraft & engine owners and operators parking space for more than 280 aircraft and 120 engines in Europe. We can accommodate all types of aircraft from regional to A380 types. TARMAC Aerosave's mission is to preserve and maximize the asset value during its storage period by applying rigorous Maintenance tasks.'[42]

As an aside, even though China does still send several of its retired aircraft to the deserts of Arizona, over a decade ago China Aircraft Leasing Group Holdings Ltd announced that they would be investing $2 billion (£1.5 billion) to build the country's largest plane disassembly plant in Harbin, known as China's Ice City, which is unusual, considering boneyards are typically located in arid, desert regions. Since then, Harbin has become a significant location for aircraft maintenance, disassembly, and recycling.[43]

Cotswold Airport, located 11km (7mi) to the southwest of the old Roman town of Cirencester, is a private aviation airport here in the United Kingdom. It was originally a Royal Air Force station, known as RAF Kemble, and was home to the Red Arrows aerobatics team until 1983, when they moved to RAF Scampton. The station was then utilized by the United States Air Force (USAF) as a maintenance facility, before it was returned to the Ministry of Defence on 31 March 1992.[44] All military flying ceased at Kemble Airfield in March of 1993, and in September 2009 Kemble changed its name to Cotswold Airport, becoming one of Europe's largest boneyard facilities and home to Air Salvage International, a privately owned company, operating since 1997. With 9,290sqm (100,000sq ft) of climate-controlled storage at its disposal, parking for up to fifty narrow or twenty wide bodied aircraft and a 2009m (9,591ft) runway capable of accepting large airliners, such as the Airbus A380, it has become well-renowned for its aircraft storage, maintenance and/or parting out.[45] Air Salvage International is one of the founding members of the Aircraft Fleet Recycling Association, the aim of which is to raise commercial value for end-of-life aircraft, and according to its official pitch 'it handles 10% of the global disassembly market annually'.[46] Comprising a series of taxiways and aprons, ASI is located at the so-called 'Belfast W/E' end of the airport; the latest Google Earth imagery depicts a graveyard of several aircraft, in varying degrees of decay, including a large Boeing 727, awaiting their fates. A similar facility can be found in the Netherlands, at Twente Airport, located approximately 4km (2mi) outside of Enschede in Overijssel. Called 'Aircraft End-of-Life Solutions', the name rather imparts its objectives, the company partners with airlines such as Airbus, Boeing, KLM, Lufthansa, TNT and others.[47] Another company worth mentioning is EirTrade Aviation, located at Ireland West Airport Knock, a 'global aviation asset management and trading company headquartered in Dublin, Ireland, with facilities/representation across Europe, the United States and Asia', who state that they can 'disassemble an engine in 20 days'.[48]

From humble beginnings at the end of the Second World War, the boneyard phenomenon, today, has become a multi-billion-pound industry with hundreds, if not thousands, of salvage/recycling companies fighting to get a fair share of the action. As an example, the boneyard at Mojave

Air and Spaceport, California, is believed to be surrounded by at least sixty individual scrapping companies.[49] It is not a surprise, therefore, that such a lucrative business in aircraft body parts can also court controversy. In September 2024, Australian Rex Airlines was accused of stealing four Saab aircraft from the Kingman Boneyard, Arizona, in 2020. The accuser, an American leasing and maintenance firm, Jet Midwest, claims the airline stripped the planes for parts, including engines and propellers, and later scrapped the airframes despite not having paid for the aircraft in full. Court documents claim that Rex Airlines told spare parts provider 340 Aviation Services to 'cut the wings off the airframes and to scrap the airframes', taking some of the profits from the sale of the parts. Parts of the aircraft were later identified as languishing in an Indonesian storage facility. The same documents show that Jet Midwest originally sued Rex for $7.2 million (£5,323,140), plus legal costs, but the case was later thrown out of court by New South Wales Supreme Court Justice James Stevenson, as by the time Jet Midwest had submitted their claim for theft, Rex Airlines had rather conveniently gone into liquidation. With such huge financial gains to be made, similar scenarios are bound to follow.[50]

Leaving the subject of boneyards, for the time being, and shifting focus onto aviation graveyards, one site that may be familiar to readers can be found in Albania, at the Kucove airfield, around 65km (40mi) south of Tirane. Brought to the public attention in 2011 via the popular BBC TV programme *Top Gear*, the mountainous site was first constructed in 1952 by the People's Socialist Republic of Albania, with a little Soviet assistance, and remains one of the largest airfields in Albania. It was also home to the remains of over seventy of the most iconic fighter jets of the Soviet era, including the famous MiG-15, MiG-17 and MiG-19 jets, many of which were left slowly crumbling away on the tarmac, their silver-grey paint faded by the elements, their glass canopies broken and open to all weathers. In 2004, the Albanian government announced plans to scrap the necropolis, to modernize the facility for attaining NATO membership, and to raise the necessary funds to update its military infrastructure. It, therefore, decided to sell off some of the aircraft. Receiving strong interest from aviation collectors and museums alike, the first series of jets went to a public auction, with the opening bids initially set at 1.1 million lek, just over £9,600 ($13,300) quickly having to be raised to 1.9 million lek £16,600 ($23,000) 'It was a surprise for us', Defense Minister Mimi Kodheli told The Associated Press, noting 'a rush' of interest from prospective bidders in the United States, Germany, France and Italy. Ilirjan Kola, 61, who flew the Albanian Air Force MiG-15 to MiG-19 jets from 1976 until 1991, said the planes were always so expensive to operate. 'MiGs were so costly', he was quoted as saying. 'A twin-engine MiG-19 consumed 52 litres of fuel a minute. With a normal flight of 30–40 minutes, imagine the expense ... Better that they had sold them before.' In August 2018, the Prime Minister of Albania, Edi Rama, announced via Facebook that NATO would be investing more than 50 million Euros (£43,610,750) to assist in the modernization of the site.[51] A few months later, in October 2018, it was announced by Reuters that the old MiG graveyard would become an official NATO airbase. On 4 March 2024, the air base was officially inaugurated, and has since hosted NATO Balkan air-policing, NATO flight operations and Albanian Air Force operations.[52]

The abandonment of aircraft left rusting upon the tarmac is a common feature of old Cold War airfields. The collapse of the Soviet Union was a hasty affair, with little or no time to arrange for the removal of manpower, let alone military hardware. As such, forsaken aircraft can be found strewn throughout old Eastern Bloc countries. Some graveyard sites are located on the doorsteps of major cities, in plain view, whereas others are hidden away from prying eyes. Commencing with the Russian Motherland, it is not just the Siberian wilderness where some of Russia's most desolate aircraft graveyards are located. In the country's capital, stunning skyscrapers once stood next to derelict air bases, such as the Khodynka Aerodrome, located a few kilometres north-west of Moscow city centre. Opened in 1910, it was the birthplace of Russian aviation and centre of Soviet-era aircraft design and manufacturing and the site of the first ever Russian international flight, in May 1922. After 1941, Khodynka became a storage facility for disused aircraft, in addition to the site of the Russian National Aviation Museum.[53] When the museum closed in 2003, aircraft such as the Mikoyan-Gurevich MiG-25, Yakovlev Yak-25, Mikoyan-Gurevich MiG-21, Sukhoi Su-17, as well as a collection of Mi-2 and Mi-8 helicopters, were left out in the open to rot. The land housing the museum and much of the adjacent aerodrome was sold off and redeveloped into several high-rise residential developments. What happened to the aircraft is still unclear, but it is believed the majority were moved to the administrative district of Lukhovitsy.

The world of the 'urban explorer' can be somewhat shady, to say the least, with participants often trespassing onto private property. Over the past decade many boneyards have been discovered by such enterprising groups and whilst I do not condone such illegal behaviour, especially concerning those who cause wanton damage to machines just for a few likes on social media, #Loser, one cannot deny, at times, such efforts can produce pure gold. I am reminded of the exploits of British writer Darmon Richter who, many years ago, would often partake in such activities for research purposes. His 'adventures' in Moscow, especially his photographic production, is a delight to see. For example, whilst exploring an abandoned satellite communications facility, 'somewhere in a forest around an hour away from the capital', he unexpectedly stumbles across an aviation gravesite that had most certainly not been on their radar, excuse the pun:

> 'Nearby, on the outskirts of the complex, we stumbled quite by accident across a fleet of rusting aircraft tucked away between the folds of a chain-link fence. Gutted chassis, broken propellers, twisted, sagging wings; landing gear in many cases lost beneath the oncoming foliage. The graveyard featured a range of fighter jets – amongst them the skeletons of a snub-nosed MiG 21, and nearby, the sleek, twin-engine MiG 29.'[54]

I am still trying to trace the whereabouts of said fighter jets as we speak, as they no longer appear to be evident. It is possible that some were transferred to the Central Museum of the Air Forces at Monino, located approximately 38km (24mi) from Moscow. The site was an operational military base from 1932 to 1956, and even though the 'museum' opened in 1960, the area was still off-limits to civilians throughout the Soviet era. Many of Moscow's abandoned military aircraft found their way here.[55]

Not all urban explorers have an overriding desire to leave their creature comforts for the great outdoors, with many preferring more desk-bound adventures. All made possible by the implementation of Google! In the year

2022, Google Maps made available to the public a series of satellite images taken over Russian territory, and it did not take long for the eagle-eyed spotter to uncover yet another Moscow district cemetery, this time based at Zhukovsky International Airport in Oblast, home to Russia's Gromov Flight Research Institute. And what a cemetery, with the hulks from every era of Soviet jet-age strewn across its concrete parking aprons.[56] I fully appreciate that Google's satellite imagery may not be entirely accurate, and can be months, more often years, out of date. However, comparing the images that went viral in 2022 to today, 2025, there are some noticeable differences/absences within the cemetery, with some planes moved from their initial observed position. One example is the Tu-144, the 'Concordski', the Soviets' answer to the British-French-made Concorde, which now sits on a different concrete apron. Flying briefly in the 1970s and 80s, it could carry a total of 140 passengers, although apparently it never did reach Mach 2 in flight (approx. 1,400mph or 2,250kph). It was also believed to be the only commercial passenger jet built with ejection seats, for the pilots that is, not for the passengers. Sixteen Tu-144s were produced, with the entire fleet collectively flying fewer than 3,000 hours before being retired; one was briefly brought out of retirement as a flying test bed for NASA.[57]

Opposite the Concordski appears to be a 'fighter row' with what looks to be at least one example of nearly every Russian MiG aircraft ever fielded, from the 1950s-era MiG-21 to the hyper-fast MiG-25 and MiG-31. Away to the Concordski's right, parked under a row of trees, is the most comprehensive section of fighter jets, all in various stages of disrepair. The line includes a Yak-28, the Russian Navy's version of a Harrier jet, capable of vertical take-off. It is surrounded by several versions of the Su-27, one of the most modern fighters in the world, including a real gem: the black-painted, experimental, forward-swept-wing Sukhoi Su-47 Berkut, which clearly stands out in the satellite image. Remarkably, only one was ever built. The Buran-class space shuttle, the Soviet's answer to the US space shuttle, does not appear to be visible on the aprons; but out on a wide-open stretch of grass, near the airport's main runways, is a giant VM-T Atlant transporter aircraft, a converted bomber that was created to carry the Buran on its back. The giant, teardrop-shaped cargo pod where the shuttle would be sited is unmistakable. To the left of where the Buran once stood are the skeletons of two massive Mi-26 Halo helicopters, blades removed, whilst away to their north, alongside a number of non-descript hangars, sits one lonely MiG 1.44, a delta-wing fighter and the only known prototype of Russia's first attempt to take on the US Advanced Tactical Fighter (ATF). Apparently, it only flew twice, making its maiden flight in February 2000, nine years behind schedule, and later cancelled that very same year. Other discernible planes, such as the Tu-160 Blackjack and Tu-95 Bear bombers, are evident, although both have obviously seen better days, and there appear to be several other additions to the graveyard since the original satellite pictures went viral, albeit they are difficult to accurately identify.[58]

One can only imagine the extent of aviation graveyards that once littered Russian territory, like Ugolny Airport on the outskirts of eastern Siberia. Once the heart of the USSR's terrifying bomber fleet, all manner of airborne firepower was kept here, from Tupolev Tu-95 Bears to supersonic Tu-22M Backfires, all patiently waiting for the word from their Russian masters to attack the hated West. The order never came, the military base was deserted, and the aircraft were simply left behind to rot. Many fell victim to the harsh Siberian climate, whilst others were left in aircraft hangers slowly decaying in their concrete tombs. A similar fate befell the Vozdvizhenka Air Base, located some 97km (60mi) north of Vladivostok, in far-eastern Russia, and only 64km (40mi) from the Chinese border, where a rusting graveyard of twenty Backfire bomber carcasses were dumped.[59] Some aircraft have become additions in so-called 'open-air' museums, often on the site of old military airfields. Although, in these instances, the term 'open-air museum' is often just semantics. Whereas such museums here in the United Kingdom, for example, may have the odd one or two of each plane variant on display, Russian examples can have literally hundreds if not thousands lined up, some in better shape than others. Having taken a look at some recent photographs of such an aviation resting place, which shall remain nameless due to confidentiality, a friend, who is an old aircraft maintenance engineer and far more knowledgeable on Soviet aircraft than I am, reliably informed me that it wouldn't take too much effort to get said bombers airworthy again!

It is difficult not to draw attention to the aircraft cemeteries that once existed in Ukraine, such as the one at Poltava Airfield, located approximately

8km (5mi) northwest of the city centre. During the former Soviet Union era, it was the site of a military flight training school where some of the best pilots in the communist state were trained. But with the demise of the USSR, many warplanes were subsequently transferred to Kazakhstan. This was followed in 2006 by the disbandment of the only heavy bomber aviation division in the whole of Ukraine. The remaining aircraft at Poltava, which included the Tu-160, then the most powerful aircraft on Earth, the first Soviet supersonic bomber Tu-22, Mikoyan-Gurevich MiG-21 fighter, Tupolev Tu-16 bomber, and the Sukhoi Su-24, amongst others, were thus abandoned, destined for the scrap heap.[60] Until May 2007, that is, when a group of enthusiastic pilots turned to the local authority with an audacious plan to breathe new life into the aircraft cemetery by reclassifying the site as an 'open-air' museum. Even then, it was still nigh-on impossible to gain access to view the aircraft; this would only be made easier a decade later.[61] Today, however, with the ongoing conflict in Ukraine, whilst there have been claims of missile strikes causing damage, the extent of that destruction, particularly to the cemetery aircraft, is unclear and often disputed. Having sifted through endless pages of 'official' aviation records regarding the current situation, I could only find details of a Mi-24 gunship helicopter destroyed by a Russian 9K720 Iskander cluster munition strike on Poltava Air Base on 2 July 2024.[62] I should also add that another Ukrainian military site, Shyroke Airfield, a few kilometres from the eastern city of Zaporizhzhia, once too had an impressive aviation cemetery, with over 100 flying variants ranging from L-29 Dolphin fighter jets to a handful of Mi-2 helicopters. Their current situation is also unknown.

So, what became of other Soviet graveyards? Here are just a couple of examples of the fate that befell some of them.

1) When Kyrgyzstan gained independence from the Soviet Union, in 1991, around sixty Soviet aircraft, from helicopters to full-size airliners, were left to die on ramps at the eastern end of what is now Manas International Airport in Bishkek. Whereas behind Osh International Airport, in an overgrown field, there appears to be a small aviation graveyard containing around a dozen Yak-40s and several AN-2s that have certainly seen better days.[63]

2) The Baltic Sea state of Latvia was part of the Soviet Union from the Second World War to 1991, and it has a fine example of an old Cold War aircraft on display at Riga Airport. Again, referred to as a 'museum'; in truth, according to a recent site visit by a colleague, it really isn't anything more than a loose conglomeration of dead aircraft dumped in a field. It exists because of one man, Victor Talpa, its founder and manager, and has a wide range of MiGs, Tupolevs and Antonovs, as well as a rather large Mil Mi-6 helicopter in its 'collection'.[64]
3) Minsk, the capital of Belarus, once had a designated aviation graveyard—if the existing photograph of a Belarussian workman I recently found, shown cutting up a plane, is anything to go by. I would go as far to say that this was arguably the fate of many Cold War aircraft, the resulting scrap metal providing a valuable resource for impoverished post-Soviet states. Another cemetery site is simply referred to as 'Rassokha', and it was regarded as the largest aviation graveyard of both military and civilian craft in Belarus. I say Belarus, as some sources say that Rassokha refers to a village in the Chernobyl Exclusion Zone, on the Belarus border, the site of a large quantity of mechanical hardware that was abandoned after the world's worst nuclear disaster. After the clean-up process commenced in 2006, all aircraft were deactivated, sawn apart and smelted. Rassokha, itself, closed its doors in 2012, and all that remains are a few pieces of scrap metal dotted here and there.[65]
4) In Moldova, there doesn't appear to be a singular renowned aircraft graveyard/boneyard. Albeit, at the aerodrome of Vadul lui Vodă, formerly a Volunteer Society for the Assistance to the Army, Aviation and Navy site, there sits the remains of an An-2, together with some old warplanes.[66] The final resting place of a MiG-21UM, in the hamlet of Seminovca, is currently atop a monument commemorating wartime pilots, as is a MiG-17F, firmly attached to its pedestal in Cahul, in southern Moldova. Similarly, a MiG-19P has been cemented on top of a plinth on the outskirts of Floreşti, located on the river Răut.[67]
5) In Uzbekistan, the old Tuzel airfield, near Tashkent, has been slowly developing into a business airport over the past few years. Even so, former military aircraft such as the Su-17UM-3, the Su-17 and the An-12 still leave their mark. Whereas a satellite image of Termez

Airport, near the Afghan border, taken a couple of years ago, depicts a cemetery of former United States-bought Afghan military helicopters and planes, abandoned by Afghan forces as the Taliban advanced.[68]

6) In the Almaty region of Kazakhstan, near the village of Samsy, there appears to be a graveyard of old civilian aircraft, reported to be in private ownership. At the Baikonur Cosmodrome, situated in the Kazakh Steppe, two Buran space shuttles have become entombed in a filthy, dilapidated hangar. One of them is nicknamed *Ptichka* ('Birdie'), and it was supposed to have flown the second Buran mission. In fact, it was more than ninety per cent ready for lift off when the Buran project was oddly cancelled in 1993. The other model was used for ground tests and was not designed to fly. A third shuttle was destroyed in 2002, when a hangar collapsed on top of it.[69]

The larger East European communist countries, often referred to as the Eastern Bloc, particularly those with a sizeable air force, exhibited close historical and cultural connections to the Soviet aircraft industry, so it is not unusual to find identical types of fighter jets and bombers, as listed above, still/once languishing in similar necropoli. For instance, near the Hungarian village of Nagygyimót, in a field at the southern end of Pápa Air Base, there exists a graveyard of around thirty ex-Soviet aircraft, which include a variety of MiG-21 fighters and several Su-22 fighter-bombers. Currently owned by the Hungarian Air Force, they are in a poor state of preservation, as their engines have been filled with concrete to make them unusable. The result is that several of the aircraft are now sinking into the ground due to the added weight.[70] Just outside Burgas Airport, at the southern end of Bulgaria's Black Sea coast, you will find a small graveyard of retired aircraft, predominantly civilian, that has been recently classified as an 'open-air museum'; whereas several abandoned military aircraft can be viewed at Krumovo Air Base, on the south side of Plovdiv Airport, at what is the now the Bulgarian Museum of Aviation.[71] Zruc Senec Air Park, in the Pilsen region of the Czech Republic, is a rather peculiar privately owned graveyard consisting of both military and civilian aircraft, in various states of preservation. Created by aviation enthusiast Karel Tarantík, who began salvaging planes in 1990, the Air Park decided to open to the public in Christmas 1992, with a Soviet Mil Mi-8 helicopter and a Ilyushin Il-14FG the first aircraft on display.[72]

In Serbia, behind the Belgrade Aeronautical Museum, there is a remarkable aviation graveyard housing a multitude of aircraft once operated by the former Yugoslav Air Force, Serbian Air Force and Serbian State Security. At the end of the Balkan Wars (1991–1996), all parties involved were subject to the 'Florence Agreement on Sub-Regional Arms Control', an accord to reduce, monitor and control the size of military assets, to prevent further hostilities. Dozens of Soko J-21 Jastreb, NJ-21 Jastreb and J-22 Orao 1 aircraft, once operated by Serbian forces, were taken out of service and dumped here.[73] Interestingly, although this site is now operated by the museum, the area housing the Serbian aircraft is strictly off-limits to the general public and can only be viewed from the main museum building. Party to the same cease fire restrictions, in Croatia, bar the odd plane found rotting in a field, at the beginning of 2025, many of their old military aircraft, including a MiG 21, Bis 112, the Mil Mi 24 helicopter and the anti-aircraft gun M55 A4 20/3, went on a display at a new memorial park in Kapela, near Bjelovar, in honour of the Croatian Air Force and air defence.[74]

When all is said and done, even after all these years, secrecy still surrounds former Soviet states and Eastern Bloc countries; therefore, the extent to which aviation graveyards once existed will probably never truly be known. Ultimately, in some remote areas, particularly around former Soviet military bases, there will always be the odd decommissioned aircraft, no doubt more, slowly decomposing, a forgotten relic of a bygone era.

For those who prefer their aircraft a little more on the larger size, a few commercial graveyards in Africa are worth a mention. The nation of Nigeria has been plagued with aircraft graveyards over the past few years, with CH Aviation, a Swiss-based firm that specializes in data and information gathering for global aviation operators, estimating that Nigeria now ranks higher than Germany, United Kingdom, Argentina, and Malaysia as the top country with highest number of retired aeroplanes, totalling an impressive sixty-nine per cent of the world's unserviceable aircraft.[75] Benin City Airport is one such example where, in a forgotten corner of the airfield, the grounded planes of the now obsolete Okada Air have been left to expire. Established in 1983, the airline's operational hub was based at Benin Airport, but by 1997 Okada Air was facing severe financial difficulties and hence the business collapsed. Its core fleet of BAC-111s, once the pride of Nigeria, now lie abandoned, their vast decaying hulks clearly visible on Google Earth.[76] A similar scenario exists at Al Murtala Muhammed International Airport in Lagos, although the aircraft have been slowly disassembled over the past decade. Other African graveyards include one at Goma Airport, in the Democratic Republic of Congo, where the children affected by the country's devastating civil war have very little else to do but to play among the carcasses of abandoned commercial airliners dumped on the airport runway, whilst another small aircraft graveyard can be found at Lanseria Airport, in South Africa, located to the northwest of Johannesburg. Here, the skeletons of once forty, now it appears there are under ten, commercial aircraft, including the likes of a Boeing 727, are dumped in a field by a derelict runway.[77] As we shall see, in today's throwaway climate, this sight is not altogether uncommon.

Chapter 2

Aviation Archaeology

No study of aircraft graveyards can truly commence without a brief discussion about aviation archaeology and some of the controversies surrounding it. Public awareness and interest in the subject matter have increased exponentially over the past couple of decades, not only through commemorative events, but also through a wide-ranging number of TV documentaries and programmes. Some examples include the recovery of a Wellington bomber from the waters of Loch Ness, filmed by the BBC, as well as three separate Time Team archaeological excavations of aircraft between 1999 and 2008. Channel 4 TV has covered the search for Douglas Bader's Spitfire, as well as Guy Martin documenting a two-year Spitfire restoration project, which had been buried on a French beach for decades. More recently BBC2 has given us the *Dig WW2* programme, whilst National Geographic's *Air Crash Investigation* programme has become progressively popular. For pure military aviation adrenaline, one also must give a shout-out to Channel 4's recent *Top Guns: Inside the RAF* documentary series.

'Aviation archaeology' is a multi-faceted term, the meaning of which can differ to whom you ask. For example, a quick peek at the Aviation Archaeological Investigation Research website defines aviation archaeology as 'primarily the locating and documenting of old air crash sites', whereas author and founding member of the Lancashire Aircraft Investigation Team, Nick Wotherspoon, states that it covers 'almost any form of research into or collecting of artefacts connected with the history of aviation'. In the United States, The International Group for Historic Aircraft Recovery define it as 'a study of the physical, historical and ethical treatment of aviation artefacts', whereas aviation expert Dirk Spennemann of Charles Sturt University, Australia, defines the term as the 'field that addresses both the archaeology of single airplane wrecks and the archaeology of the support structures of aviation'.[1]

The term 'aviation archaeologist' can also be deemed somewhat misleading, as from the outset the activity was dominated by groups of enthusiastic 'amateurs', who were 'short on sanity but saturated with enthusiasm',[2] with professional archaeologists largely ignoring the subject matter entirely. Although I will admit I have no love for this phraseology, as many of these 'amateurs' were highly skilled individuals. As such, moving forward I prefer to use the term 'avocational archaeologist', which is defined as 'persons engaged in archaeological research, but who lack formal, university training in archaeology and are not employed in the discipline as their primary means of income'.[3] I would also put forward the argument that the collective growing interest in aviation archaeology from a professional standpoint, particularly here in the United Kingdom, coincided with the recognition of 'conflict archaeology' as an accepted academic discipline within in its own right.

The history of aviation archaeology dates to the 1960s, when several enthusiasts began to take an active interest in the scattered remains of aircraft from the Second World War. Whether they be inexpert souvenir hunters, or more serious prospectors of valuable military artefacts, searching for aircraft wreckage in the 1960s required only enthusiasm and the landowner's permission. With the release of several war-related films, including the *Battle of Britain* in 1968, together with the RAF Air Historical Branch allowing researchers to troll through their accident and aircraft record cards, whereby hundreds of new crash sites came to life, in the 1970s there was a rapid growth in the excavation of downed military aircraft, with individuals coming together to form groups, in order to share the costs of excavation and to provide a band of skills for research, recovery and preservation. Before long, the aviation recovery movement had spread rapidly throughout the United Kingdom, largely unchecked, leading to the movement being collectively labelled by some as 'relic hunters and grave robbers'.[4] In 1973, the Ministry of Defence (MoD) announced that they had abandoned all claim to crashed planes and that any items of official interest had been recovered. They later revised this position, issuing their first 'Notes and Guidance' to recovery groups, which declared the following: All RAF wrecks remained Crown property; enemy aircraft were captured property surrendered to the Crown; the MoD were acting agents for US authorities; and that any excavation without official permission was illegal interference with Crown property.[5] Sadly, these edicts were largely ignored by the aviation movement and excavations continued unabated, that is until several incidents involving the discovery of human remains and unexploded bombs, together with a spate of bad publicity, forced the British Government to pass into law the Protection of Military Remains Act 1986, which is still in place today.[6] Let us take a closer look at what said Act entails.

The Protection of Military Remains Act 1986

The Protection of Military Remains Act 1986 is: 'An Act to secure the protection from unauthorised interference of the remains of military aircraft and vessels that have crashed, sunk or been stranded and of associated human remains; and for connected purposes.' It makes no difference to where the remains are sited, whether that be lying on the surface or underground. All military aircraft crash sites in the United Kingdom, its territorial waters, or British aircraft in international waters are protected, and it is an offence under this act to tamper with, damage, move or unearth any items at such sites, unless the MoD has issued a licence authorizing such activity. Legally, no penetration below 45cm (18in) is permitted without a MoD licence. Anyone wishing to recover a military aircraft or excavate a military aircraft crash site in the United Kingdom is, therefore, required to obtain a licence from the Joint Casualty and Compassionate Centre (JCCC), part of the Defence Business Services (DBS). Likewise, a licence is also required to excavate any military aircraft crash site in the United Kingdom, irrespective of whether the aircraft was in the service of the British, American, German or other nation's armed forces. For example, crashed US military aircraft and their equipment remain the property of the US government, but the MoD acts on behalf of the US authorities. Applications to recover American aircraft, therefore, are required to be made to the JCCC. Outside the United Kingdom, in international or British territorial waters, the Protection of Military Remains Act 1986 no longer applies and the excavation of crash sites of British aircraft are subject to the laws of the country concerned. However,

MoD policy is to discourage disturbance of such sites unless necessary, in respect of host government approved activities, like land reclamation or construction.[7]

The licence procedure is a lengthy process, with some rather important caveats. Before one can be issued, applicants are required to provide detailed research on the aircraft they wish to recover to the JCCC, such as the location of the aircraft and the fate of the crew. A licence will be issued for one year only and will authorize activity within the defined area only, as specified on the application. Therefore, licence holders will need to apply for a new licence if they wish to continue working on an excavation into a second year. A licence will not be issued to anyone under the age of eighteen. The MoD reserves the right to deploy its representatives to witness any excavations approved under the Protection of Military Remains Act 1986.[8]

Permission from the respective landowner/occupier is also deemed a prerequisite. Once the necessary permission has been granted, full liaison with the landowner/occupier is required to ensure the minimum of inconvenience and damage to their property. In the case of aircraft remains being sited on Crown Land, permission must be obtained from the appropriate government department. Where aircraft recovery takes place within the boundaries of a National Park, or an area designated as being one of outstanding natural beauty (both of which, in the main, comprise of land which is privately owned), the greatest of care and consideration should be taken to ensure that the site is left in a tidy condition once the excavation has ceased. Local councils may impose additional requirements or limitations in respect of archaeological activity within their area of jurisdiction, particularly if the crash site is in an area where other historical artefacts may be disturbed. Applicants for a licence under the Protection of Military Remains Act 1986 should therefore check with the council or local sites and monuments records officer in advance, or at the same time, as applying for a licence from the MoD.[9]

As is the norm with any archaeological excavation of a gravesite, health and safety is a priority; for example, the shoring of ditch walls to prevent collapse/proper use of machinery etc. However, the excavation of aircraft comes with a unique set of variables, in particular unexploded ordnance (ranging from bombs to small arms ammunition) that remain in the crash site. For instance, a crashed B-17 bomber exposed by the sea on the coast of Kent, in 1998 to 1999, became the target of unauthorized individuals who dug out the wreckage in advance of the official excavation, scattering live ammunition throughout the site, which ended up in the possession of local children![10] If unexploded ordnance/ammunition/pyrotechnics are discovered, all authorizations granted by the licence are automatically suspended and the police must be informed immediately. On no account should an individual/group interfere with suspected live ordnance. The police will then contact The Joint Service Explosive Ordnance Disposal (EOD) Operations Centre, who will arrange for a team from either the Royal Air Force or Royal Engineers to safely dispose of said ordnance. A licence will not be issued if significant amounts of unexploded ordnance (bombs) are believed to be present at the site.[11]

Another sensitive issue regarding the excavation of an aircraft grave/crash site is the possibility of human remains being found. If it is known or suspected that there might be human remains at the site, a licence will not be issued. If human remains are found, the MoD has full authority to suspend the excavation and designate a third party to complete the excavation as necessary. If, despite the taking of precautions, human remains are discovered, all authorizations granted by the licence are automatically suspended. On no account are the remains to be touched, and they should be always treated with due respect. After all, the site, for all intents and purposes, is a war grave. The discovery must be reported immediately to the MoD, the local police and thereby the local coroner. The MoD will take all the necessary steps to trace and notify the next-of-kin, or other relatives, and in no circumstances is a recovery group to act in this respect. Any breach of these conditions will normally lead to revocation of the licence. The presumed identity of the aircrew should not be divulged to anyone in advance of an inquest.[12]

Any items of personal property, such as watches, rings or wallets etc., recovered from a wreck site remain the property of the individual, and must be surrendered to the JCCC, who will endeavour to return such items to any surviving relative. Other items recovered, such as official documents/records, remain the property of the Crown, this also includes items recovered from crashed British aircraft outside the United Kingdom (for which a licence is not required). On expiry of the licence, or completion of the excavation if earlier, licensees are required to file a report to the JCCC, listing all items found and, if appropriate, request transfer of ownership. Although the latter is not always assured in practice, ownership of, for example, parts of the aircraft may be transferred to the licensee.[13]

Should the MoD later discover that not all items recovered were declared to the JCCC, or that items were recovered or disposed of contrary to the terms of the Protection of Military Remains Act 1986, the licensee or individual concerned will be liable to prosecution. In fact, failure to follow any of the terms and conditions described above could result in the entire enterprise becoming an unlawful interference with a protected site, as defined in the Protection of Military Remains Act 1986, and could lead to civil or criminal proceedings. A link to the full MoD guidelines can be found in the Notes and References section.[14]

The JCCC has a corresponding organization within the US military, that it often works closely with in respect to USAAF aircraft that lie buried within the United Kingdom, although its remit is far more proactive, with US Congress decreeing that every American casualty will be accorded the right to be repatriated and buried in US soil. This responsibility is assigned to the Joint POW/MIA Accounting Command (JPAC) which conducts global search, recovery, and laboratory operations to identify unaccounted-for Americans from past conflicts. Located on the island of Oahu, in Hawaii, and employing more than 400 joint military and civilian personnel, JPAC continues its search for more than 83,000 Americans still missing from past conflicts.[15]

With such legal protections in place, you would naturally assume that any remaining air crash sites would be safe from the activities of unsavoury individuals. I'm sad to say that is not the case. A friend, and fellow archaeologist, Carl Thorpe, from the Cornwall Archaeological Unit, recently brought to my attention the excavation of a Spitfire he was personally involved with during the summer of 2017, on Frythens Farm, located just outside St. Erth, in Cornwall. It was at this location, on the evening of 24 March 1942, that Squadron Leader Daniel Cremin Distinguished Flying Cross (DFC) RAF and Sergeant William Norman

Royal Australian Air Force (RAAF) of 66 Squadron were involved in a mid-air collision during a night flying exercise. Both their respective Spitfire Mk V aircraft plummeted to the ground in adjacent fields, and burst into flames upon impact.[16] Sadly, both pilots were killed and an RAF recovery crew is believed to have salvaged what remained of the bodies and their aircraft, as neither the Operations Record Book, nor the RAF Casualty Files, detail the recovery of the bodies, or contain any descriptions of the human remains recovered from the crash sites. An eyewitness to the events, Edna Hocking stated:

> 'In 1941/2 I lived on Tregethes Farm, St. Erth. At 10.30 one night we heard the collision of two planes. Two Spitfires had crashed and fallen into the field of the next farm called Frythens. I've no idea how this crash occurred. Both pilots were killed and their bodies put in the barn overnight. It was awful and the police were out in the dark looking for parts of the bodies.'[17]

In 2012, a metal detectorist and Second World War enthusiast, named only as Mr Strick, located and illegally investigated one of the crash sites, without a MoD licence, digging a hole 1m (3.2ft) deep and removing several aircraft parts. These apparently included a substantial amount of Perspex from its cockpit canopy, an empty 20mm cannon cartridge, pieces of Bakelite, copper cabling and copper-alloy objects, a collection of corroded ferrous fragments, a high-pressure pipe coupling, pieces of twisted Duralumin, hose couplings, buckles, pieces of corroded aluminium alloy and electrical capacitors. He also recovered a burnt penny, which he assumed had derived from the pilot's pockets.[18] It is believed that Mr Strick donated these artefacts to the wartime museum at the former RAF Davidstow base, in Camelford, Cornwall, later self-publishing an e-book about the finds. Albeit when it came time for the Cornwall Archaeological Unit to submit their final report, strangely said finds were not readily available for inspection, let alone recorded or catalogued at a professional level of detail, thus hampering the identification of exactly which Spitfire said artefacts derived from.[19]

Unbelievably, this is not the end of the story. For only a few years later, in 2017, another Second World War researcher, named as Mr Palmer, also carried out an illegal excavation without a licence, this time in the vicinity of the northern aircraft wreck site, where he unearthed human remains. Although he reported his finding to the local police, who immediately informed the Cornwall coroner, it is unclear to this day if Mr Palmer removed any artefacts from the crash site prior to him contacting the authorities.[20] Understandably, the tenant farmer has now been advised by the authorities that he should not sanction any further investigation of this site in the absence of a JCCC licence, albeit it is unlikely that any such licence would be granted.[21]

So, what fate befell the two individuals, you may ask yourself, who, under the Protection of Military Remains Act 1986, broke the law by illegally excavating both crash sites and removing what booty they uncovered? Well, in truth, nothing! I have here in my hands a Ministry of Defence Police response, Ref: eCase: FOI 2019/08485, dated 19 August 2019, to a Freedom of Information Act 2000 request by a concerned individual (name has been omitted to protect their identity).[22] The application states:

> 'Recent changes in policy affecting the issuing of licences under the terms of the Protection of Military Remains Act (198) for the possible disturbance or intentional excavation of military aircraft crash sites in the UK have been justified by the JCCC by referring to the illegal disturbance of the partial remains of Acting Squadron Leader Daniel Edward Cremin, D.F.C. at Frythens Farm, St. Erth, Cornwall, by known individuals - an action which the JCCC in its guidance on the subject quite clearly states would make such individuals liable to prosecution under the Act. As this incident was quite clearly illegal activity under the terms of the Protection of Military Remains Act (1986), the details of which being well documented and accurately recorded and in the public domain (see: Frythens Farm, St. Erth, Cornwall: archaeological excavation of a WW2 Spitfire crash site, Report No: 2017R051, published by The Cornwall Archaeological Unit). Could you please outline the

> rationale behind the MoD's decision not to take any legal action against the individual concerned please?'[23]

The MoD Police Secretariat and Freedom of Information Office replied as follows:

> 'As a result of a scoping enquiry conducted by the Ministry of Defence Police into the case referred to in your request for information, it was determined that there was insufficient independent evidence to indicate that any criminal offence §had been committed. The only evidence was an account that had been published on the internet.'[24]

Perhaps one of the worst examples of conduct from so-called 'aviation enthusiasts' I have read about occurred after the tragic death of Red Arrows display pilot, Flight Lieutenant Jon Egging, whose jet crashed into a field near the River Stour in August 2011. He had just thrilled the masses on the seafront at Bournemouth as part of a full Red Arrows team display. The weekend after the tragedy the crash site, close to Throop Mill, became awash with people, hundreds of them in fact, if the reports are anything to go by, each one trying to grab themselves a piece of the wrecked plane. One local resident, Mr Young, stated: 'I have seen people clambering all over the fences onto the Malmsbury Estate to get a piece of the plane.'[25] He even witnessed one person with a metal detector scouring the field and another posing for a picture with items from the crash that he had uncovered. It later transpired that one individual even attempted to sell parts of the downed jet on eBay![26] A spokesman for Dorset Police said at the time that officers from the Criminal Investigation Department (CID) were investigating a number of incidents after receiving reports that on 25 August people were seen with metal detectors and shovels at the crash site. A police spokesperson said: 'The warning is anybody found to be taking parts of the aircraft should be aware it is RAF property, and they are committing theft.'[27]

Another appalling example occurred more recently, during the summer of 2021, when local Kent metal detectorist and coastal warden, Tony Ovenden, witnessed an individual stripping parts from a protected B-17 bomber plane, located in Sandwich Bay, Kent, before physically loading the parts into a trolley and carting them away.[28] The aircraft in question had been on its first mission, heading to Solingen in Germany, when it plummeted into the bay in 1943. Thankfully, the ten-man crew survived the crash. Ovenden immediately reported the incident to Kent Police with Services Archaeology and Heritage Association branding the looter 'disgraceful and illegal'.

'Witnesses saw an individual in the water wearing a wetsuit trying to remove parts of the aircraft. It is alleged that excavating equipment was used to remove part of the infrastructure of the aircraft. Closer inspection of the B17 indicated that it had been systematically stripped. The fuel tanks have gone, fuel pipes and wiring also missing. There was evidence of tools being used to hack away at the right wing.'[29]

The professionals, it seems, can also be caught out on occasions, as documented by Andy Brockman, archaeologist and author of *The Buried Spitfires of Burma - A 'Fake' History*, when he discovered that work on an alleged crash site of a Second World War Lancaster bomber, shown in the first episode of a controversial new Channel 5 TV series about metal detecting, *Digging for Treasure—Tonight*, may have been in breach of the UK Protection of Military Remains Act 1986.[30] The programme in question, which was first broadcast on 26 August 2022, shows pre-recorded segments about the work of a Mr Paul Edwards, who describes researching the crash of a Pathfinder Force Lancaster QF-Q EE105 aircraft of 97 Squadron, which was shot down over Norfolk on the night of 24 August 1943. In these segments, Edwards is depicted metal detecting in the field where the aircraft is thought to have crashed, proclaiming finding so-called 'hot spots' with his metal detector, and recovering what appears to be a spent machinegun bullet from the site of the bomber crash. He is then shown directing a ground-penetrating radar (GPR) survey of the suspected site. After these particular segments, the programme then returns to one of its presenters, Dan Walker, who proceeds to show off a number of artefacts supposedly recovered from the crashed aircraft, including pipework, a manufacturers' instruction plate and, most significantly, elements of parachute harness which, the programme claimed, were last touched by mid-gunner Flight Sergeant John Kraemer, of the RAAF, whose remains were found in the wreckage.[31]

However, an investigation in 2022 by thePipeLine, an informative website owned by Brockman, and the Services Archaeology and Heritage Association, showed that the MoD, and specifically the JCCC, had been unable to confirm, at the time, the existence of a currently valid licence to search for and recover artefacts from the crash site of EE105, namely the Lancaster bomber in question, including by use of a metal detector. A licence under the Protection of Military Remains Act 1986 was issued in 2006, but there is no record of any artefacts being reported as found to the JCCC. In fact, the most recent application for a new licence to investigate the crash site of the Lancaster aircraft was apparently turned down by JCCC. Understandably, this calls into question the provenance of the artefacts shown on *Digging for Treasure—Tonight*.[32]

The MoD was certainly concerned enough, and commenced their own investigation, a spokesperson stating to thePipeLine:

> 'I can confirm that we have seen the programme and have approached Daisybeck Studios for comment and made them aware of POMRA. We are currently awaiting a response from them to clarify the circumstances surrounding the recovery of the artefacts shown.'[33]

A recent foray into a popular 'aviation archaeology' Facebook group made for depressing reading, and I came away feeling somewhat dumbfounded and exasperated. For context, the very first group post I came across depicted a selection of pillaged metallic objects from a protected air crash site, said hiker and aviation enthusiast had visited said site in his weekend off, followed by another post from an individual showing off images from a wrecked Spitfire, including the aircraft's propellor blade. If this wasn't galling enough, the comments underneath were maddening, with numerous expressions of 'great images', 'wonderful job', 'good on ya' etc. Only one individual had the courage to put his head above the parapet and point out that it was illegal under the Protection of Military Remains Act 1986 to commit such wrongdoings. This poor person was crucified, receiving a barrage of insults, abuse, and even one threat of physical violence! Alas, this is all too common nowadays. Throughout the research process for this book, I have come across a plethora of individuals who see nothing wrong with illegally stealing parts from wrecked aircraft or desecrating legally protected war graves. I have even seen evidence of some breaking into secured premises and removing the winter protections off treasured heritage aircraft, thus potentially damaging the craft, all for a few clicks and likes on their respective social media outlets. They show no remorse for their actions, in fact the opposite, and they will openly mock and/or threaten those who bring them to task about their irresponsible and, often, illegal behaviour. What can I say? Unfortunately, we now live in an age of 'entitlement'. An age where certain individuals believe it is perfectly acceptable to belittle the bravery and sacrifice of those men, and women, who died in the very aircraft they defile. Regrettably, by their actions, they are also sullying the reputations of genuine avocational aviation enthusiasts.

Taking this into consideration, I was intrigued to discover just how many people had been prosecuted under the Protection of Military Remains Act 1986. In his 2014 PhD thesis entitled 'Phased Aviation Archaeology Research [PAAR]: Development and application of a standardized methodology to Second World War aircraft sites in Scotland', archaeologist Terence Christian followed a similar train of thought and discovered that data relating to prosecutions was limited. In fact, what data was available showed the Protection of Military Remains Act 1986 to be little enforced, as we have already documented on the aforementioned Frythens Farm incident in Cornwall, despite the recognition that cases are undeniably heritage crimes. In total, Christian found only three aircraft cases, including a prosecution in 2002 for the illegal excavation of a Hawker Tempest, which resulted in the offender receiving a twelve-month suspended sentence; in 1996, a member of the public was cautioned in relation to the illegal excavation of a Spitfire in Kent.[34] Considering the sizeable number of military air crash sites here in the United Kingdom, together with an obvious limited political will to police them, what is the current state of play, so to speak, when it comes to more recent criminal transgressions/cautions/prosecutions, as the legal protections of such sites is wholly inadequate? At the time of writing, I have submitted several Freedom of Information Act 2000 requests to both the MoD Police Secretariat and Information Office and the JCCC regarding the matter. It will be interesting to read their responses.

Although vast numbers of wrecked aircraft had been excavated since the 1960s, and relics removed, virtually none of this has been recorded in any professionally recognized archaeological format, apart from the taking of private photographs. In fact, no long-term, systematic study pertaining to the removal of material from historic aircraft wreck sites exists. In recent years, some avocational archaeologists have made concerted efforts to see their work documented in book form, to which we are eternally grateful, or via informative websites and magazines, and although this may help to rectify previous oversights, they are no substitute for formal archaeological site reports.[35] In the late 1970s, the British Aviation Archaeological Council (BAAC) was founded, to which many established and valued avocational aviation groups declared their allegiance; albeit, at the time of writing, their website has not been updated since February 2024, and their last Facebook post also dates to 2024. BAAC is self-described as 'the official national body in the United Kingdom for aviation archaeologists and researchers of historic aircraft crashes', and encourages its member groups to 'research the background of each incident, display relics in the context of their local history and to commemorate those who, all too often, died in the crashes'.[36] Similar to the Council for British Archaeology (CBA), a United Kingdom–wide educational charity that helps champion and promote participation in archaeology, the BAAC is also a charity, with no official government support, that follows a five-fold purpose: 1) To establish and maintain ethical standards; 2) To provide a forum for discussion; 3) To provide advice for member groups; 4) To liaise with national and international bodies; and 5) To promote the preservation of aircraft relics and relevant historical documents.[37] Yet unlike the CBA, which conforms to recognized Institute of Field Archaeologists standards and practices for the conservation, management and the study of any archaeological resource, in a study of several BAAC affiliated avocational aviation groups, Dr Terence Christian found the BAAC's approach to be somewhat deficient in this particular area. He states:

> 'BAAC documents reveal support of ethical standards that are in contrast to mainstream archaeology. Despite its professed goal "to establish and maintain ethical standards" (BAAC 2000a),

> consultation of the BAAC Code of Conduct reveals a document which advises actions which irreparably destroy archaeological information. In addition, the BAAC's ineffectiveness as a unifying organisation is evident in the methodological problems observed in avocational research, many of which are due to a lack of strict accountability to, and a lack of guidance from, a larger archaeological organisation.'[38]

Christian also discovered that much of the avocational aircraft archaeology community had not followed the precedent set by professional archaeology projects, especially during those early years. Very few, if any, had adhered to a standardized archaeology methodology, the approach of each group differed from site to site, with photographs and site plans showing very little accuracy or in many cases, non-existent. He also found that avocational aviation archaeologists consistently did not: a) georeference finds, features and trenches; b) employ standard methodological procedures, including the use of vertical and horizontal controls; or c) produce a record of work undertaken.[39] Christian is not alone in his criticisms, as respected avocational historic researcher and author, Alan Clark, from the Peak District Air Accident Research Team, also laments the lack of research designs within avocational aviation archaeology, in an open written piece in *Aviation Archaeologist,* a magazine published, ironically, by the BAAC.[40] One area, however, where the BAAC guidelines do parallel professional archaeology is in the recommendation that pre-field investigation archival research be undertaken.[41]

An example of just how poor nonstandard excavation methodology can be is aptly demonstrated by the excavation of a 1975 Supermarine Spitfire Mk. IX PT766, undertaken by the now-obsolete South Wales Historic Aircraft Preservation Society (SWHAPS). A subsequent investigation and recovery effort in 2009 by the Marches Aviation Society found that the SWHAPS had dug the wreck site only to recover the Spitfire engine, nothing else. Having excavated a large haphazard hole, the aircraft remains were dragged out and, once the engine was recovered, the remaining Spitfire parts were unceremoniously dumped into the backfill. It was even reported by one of the SWHAPS dig participants that a leading wing edge of the Spitfire had to be forcibly pushed back down into the hole, so that it did not continue to pop back up![42] Not entirely filled with confidence, I decided to look into other avocational group 'reports', also dating from before the Protection of Military Remains Act 1986 came into force, and found a number of concerning statements, ranging from 'the best method of discovery was to clamber in the mud until your foot contacted metal, then, using one foot as a lever, try to prise it loose' to 'using a piece of a wing as a sledge to move larger pieces across a lagoon'.[43] Oh and, of course, not forgetting in reference to the use of a digger versus a stubborn piece of crash site detritus 'roaring to full power he wrested violently, causing the entire marsh for yards to undulate'.

Tensions between the professional and avocational community, in a them versus us scenario, can even arise amongst the very best of folk working in the field. This occurred during the 1999 *Time Team* three-day excavation of a B-17 wreckage located in Reedham Marsh, Norfolk. In the official site report, Tim Taylor recalls a profound methodological disagreement between the *Time Team* archaeologists on one side and the avocational aviation volunteers on the other. He states:

> 'Already the differences in working methods between the aviation excavators and TIME TEAM archaeologists were beginning to clash. To the excavators, it made no sense to dig carefully around the remains with small trowels or to record each layer carefully as the archaeologists, led by Phil [Harding], were doing. At this rate, they said, we would find nothing significant in the three days available—a sad waste of an opportunity and, more to the point, of the availability of the large machines on site, which could move mountains and were required to move spadefuls. The archaeologists disputed this, saying that there was no way of knowing what had been found so far. The fact that the enthusiasts had done so many other excavations of aircraft did not really prove anything because they had always tackled their sites so roughly. If they had used archaeological methods, they might have drawn different conclusions. It was important to discover the context of what we had found so far and only then decide what to do next. Despite the archaeologists' best intentions, some shortcuts were being made by those working on the site.'[44]

It should be said that the generalized bedrock of professional archaeology training does not include the specialized aircraft-specific knowledge to be found in avocational aviation groups. To their credit, had it not been for the activities of such groups, many air crash sites would now be permanently lost under new buildings, new roads or simply be forgotten. In addition, much of what/has been excavated in the past now forms the bedrock of many a fabulous museum, such as Tangmere Military Aviation Museum, in Chichester, Lincolnshire Aviation Heritage Centre, East Kirby, and Norfolk and Suffolk Aviation Museum in Flixton, to name but a few. In their defence, and as Christian observes, the avocational archaeologist's dedication to cataloguing the historical context of aviation wrecks sites most certainly provides valuable information to both avocational and professional archaeologists alike:

> 'Avocational groups excel in conducting background research. The collation and publication of historical research, via organisations' websites, online forums, popular publications and books provide aviation archaeology with data sets often beyond the scope of professional projects and budgets. Many organisations focus on a specific locale and maintain databases and dossiers for wreck sites in the surrounding region.'[45]

In truth, as eyewitnesses to events grow old and die, whether you agree with their methods or not, it should be recognized that had avocational enthusiasts not pursued their interests when they did, the opportunity to connect aviation excavations with living memory, and thus documentary history, would simply have been missed.

Legislation Outside of the United Kingdom

Outside of the United Kingdom, archaeological legislation in Northern Ireland, for example, works in conjunction with the United Kingdom–wide Protection of Military Remains Act 1986, and elevates all buried aircraft remains to the status of 'archaeological objects. In addition, there is a further requirement to comply with the Historic Monuments and

Archaeological Objects (NI) Order 1995. Thus, anyone wishing to excavate/retrieve an aircraft out of the ground in Northern Ireland will require two licences. Throughout The Troubles conflict in Northern Ireland, which lasted for almost thirty years, the vast majority of aviation heritage was understandably forgotten by most, albeit a few local community groups, such as the Ulster Aviation Society, who endeavoured to safeguard and document both wartime and general aviation history during this time.[46]

Unsurprisingly theatres of war, throughout Europe, possess very strict laws with regards to digging crash sites/downed military aircraft, although this was not always the case. A recent conversation with an ex-curator of an eminent national war museum informed me that in France, particularly during the 1970s and 1980s, it was not uncommon for treasure hunting folk to plough their way through crash sites in search of elusive, yet highly desirable Nazi/Luftwaffe memorabilia. If human remains were stumbled upon, they were often simply placed into a sack and deposited at the local 'poste de police'. Times have, thankfully, changed, and France now has very strict laws with regards to such illicit behaviour, throughout the Western Front and other related battlefields, as does Germany under their Monument Protection Act. In fact, I was intrigued to discover that much of the European legislation with regards to air crash sites coincided with the prohibited use of metal detectors. Which is not surprising considering a) the illicit use of metal detecting is an ongoing worldwide heritage problem and b) aircraft consist of metallic parts, so metal detecting and aircraft enthusiasts are intrinsically linked. As would be expected, detection on heritage sites is prohibited throughout most European countries, with a licence or special permission required in other areas. There are some interesting caveats; for instance, it is rumoured that in Latvia, a country renowned for the illegal appropriation of Second World War military memorabilia, both national and local authorities keep a list of every relic hunter in their area. In Greece, the illicit use of metal detectors on air crash sites comes with a jail term of between ten to twenty years—whereas metal detecting on several beaches in Italy is strictly controlled by the mafia![47]

In the United States, whilst no combat missions were flown across their skies, hundreds of military aircraft were lost in training accidents, weather-related crashes, and other mishaps. All such incidents were investigated by the military, and any human remains were recovered, but this subsequently left hundreds of aircraft to decay far from the beaten path, often perched on inaccessible mountain tops, in remote deserts or deeply submerged in lakes and territorial seas. As such, aviation archaeology in the United States followed a somewhat different path to that in the United Kingdom, and though United States–based avocational aviation archaeology groups exhibit variations in both objectives and inadequate methodologies, similar to those found in United Kingdom–based organizations, most US groups were/are proud exponents and dedicated to the hobby of 'wreck chasing'. Examples of such groups include the X-Hunters Aerospace Archaeology Team, Oklahoma Wreckchasing, Arizona Wrecks etc.

From the beginning, wreck chasing activities developed along two parallel tracks. One was dominated by amateurs, motivated by personal satisfaction and/or performing a public service. The other was populated by treasure hunters searching for parts or entire aircraft that could be used for restoration projects. The latter often had a financial incentive attached.[48] Such exploits were reshaped in 1995 by the creation of the website *Wreckchasing.com,* by aviation journalist Nick Veronico, which at its height was receiving over 100,000 hits per month. Despite 'building a community for people who are interested in wreck chasing', and purposely not publishing any geographical coordinates of crash sites, to protect them from being overrun by looters, it wasn't difficult for people to discover where such sites were located.[49] Before long, air crash wrecks were being uploaded to YouTube for all and sundry to see. As archaeologist and biological consultant Ryan Gilmore stated: 'you can easily reverse engineer what they did to get to these locations, and before you know it, those wrecks are pretty much gone.'[50]

The first studies in the United States referring to aircraft as 'archaeological artefacts' were published in the early 1980s, and by the early 2000s, professional aviation archaeology was a designated body. Unfortunately, the conservation ethos that underpins the academic discipline of archaeology soon locked horns with the so-called 'warbird community', who preferred the 'recovery and restoration' approach. Inevitably, such tensions led to a backlash against the then-commonplace practice of raiding aircraft carcasses for parts to be displayed in museums or used to build flyable aeroplanes stitched together from a mix of original, repurposed, and brand-new components.

'Instead of recovering military airplanes, aviation archaeologists now argue that the wreck sites themselves are worthy of preservation. Yes, they say, airplanes are invaluable artifacts. But at the same time, the changes they've undergone due to pilferage, erosion, and other natural forces are significant elements of the historical and cultural record.'[51]

One leading and widely respected United States–based organization, worthy of mention, that has overcome these concerns and successfully achieved a somewhat healthy balance between the two opposing factions is The International Group for Historic Aircraft Recovery [TIGHAR]. Founded in 1985 by former air crash investigator Richard Gillespie, and based in Pennsylvania, Gillespie, the group tends to focus its efforts on submerged aircraft and recovering intact wrecks. I first came across the organization whilst researching the 'Maid of Harlech', a Lockheed P-38 Lightning fighter aircraft, presumed to be USAAF serial number 41-7677, that was found sunken on a beach in Wales. According to their monthly journal, which is free to download via their website, it states that TIGHAR's activities include: Investigating aviation and aerospace historical questions and mysteries through archival research, forensic data analysis, and archaeological expeditions; Producing papers, publications, and videos to further the foundation's educational mission; Providing expert historical and archaeological research to government agencies for evaluation of cultural resources related to aviation/aerospace; Advocating for accuracy, integrity and professionalism in the field of aviation historical investigation; and the preservation of the material culture of flight. Famed for their search in the disappearances of both aviator Amelia Earhart and American conductor and musician Glen Miller, TIGHAR are also known for their use of both professional archaeologists and avocational volunteers in their ventures, thus bridging the gap between both competing parties. Moreover, they have also developed their own rapid recording methodology, based upon crash investigation techniques, whilst employing standard archaeological methodologies during their surveys and excavation.[52]

Locating and Excavating an Aircraft Wreck

The archaeological study of historic aircraft can usually be divided into three categories: accidental discovery, avocational excavations and professional projects. Accidental discovery is the means by which the limited professional archaeological study of historic aircraft wrecks are generally made, usually during new construction or infrastructure improvement activities.[53] A smaller percentage of accidental discoveries are by individuals, or groups, pursuing recreational activities, for example, the discovery of the aforementioned 'Maid of Harlech', in Wales, was made by a family spending a relaxing day at the beach.

Locating a crash site from scratch is a skilled affair. Many crashes become deeply buried in soil or marshland, usually buried 2 to 4m (6 to 13ft) below ground level. Having fallen from a height as far as 4,572m (15,000ft) and crashing into the ground at a speed of 966kmph (600mph) or more, it is hardly surprising. Additionally, the engines may also have been ticking over at 3,000 revolutions per minute, (or fifty times a second), so it is not unexpected that many aircraft self-imploded upon impact.[54] As such, recovery teams, whether that be RAF Maintenance units or private contractors, rarely had the manpower, time or suitable machinery to extract engines in this condition. In marshy soil extraction was even more limited, as aircraft engines would naturally sink to a much deeper level. To give an example, on 25 November 1940, a two-man recovery team from A.V. Nicholls & Co, a Brighton-based company engaged to assist No.49 Maintenance Unit, the unit principally responsible for aircraft recovery in the south-east, set out to retrieve the remains of Spitfire II P7386, which had crashed at Sandwich on 14 November. Having found the engine at a depth of just over 6m (20ft), a painstaking effort was then made to pull the engine out from its earthly tomb. Despite working on it until 27 November, flooding foiled any attempts at extraction and the job was eventually abandoned, the engine is believed to still be in situ.[55] Unlike your usual ancient treasure finds, crashed aircraft can weigh a great deal; for instance, the Merlin III engine's stated dry weight was about 625kg (1,375lb). Although rarely found in a single piece, the deadweight of the central block and its internals is considerable; lifting this from a depth of

5m (16.4ft) in a marsh is no mean feat and one which requires engineering skills not normally needed on conventional archaeological sites.[56]

Identifying components from wrecked aircraft can also be somewhat challenging, as the vast majority of finds from wartime air crash sites consist largely of piles of scrap metal. A few components are obvious, such as an aircraft propeller, but identifying fragments of piping, hydraulics, airframe actions and shattered pieces of engine casings can be problematic. Notwithstanding, years of ploughing and general surface movement often brings small artefacts to light, such as fragments of airframe, components, spent bullet cases etc., with hedgerows and ditches often providing a surprisingly rich harvest of finds. Often, these smaller objects will yield manufacturing stencils, parts numbers or quality inspection stamps.[57]

The various materials used in the manufacturing process also have a bearing on the rate of aircraft survival. Magnesium was valued for being the lightest known commercial metal but was 'very liable to corrosion'. For example, the excavation of a P-51 Mustang, which crashed near its base at Duxford in 1944, discovered that most of the metal alloys had corroded into blue oxide. In fact, 1940s magnesium alloys had a propensity to decompose almost immediately, even in service, let alone in the ground, despite the addition of other metals, such as aluminium and zinc, to inhibit this defect. By way of illustration, magnesium alloy was widely used in the fabrication of Spitfires—on their control column handles, air frame rivets and so on—and what often survives is just a pile of unrecognizable powder, if that. It is, therefore, not surprising that today, aircraft dating to the Second World War are maintained with components remanufactured in modern materials.[58] Another issue to consider is the velocity patterning. For example, high velocity crashes produce their own unique markings. A high-angle, high-velocity impact generates a deep crater with a short, but wide, scatter of material, fanning outwards from the point of impact. A high-speed, low-angle impact creates a shallow elongated trench. Because the aircraft involved in a high-speed, low-angle crash tends to skip along the ground, the heaviest of the material settles furthest from the initial point of contact.[59] Similarly, the presence of munitions on board can complicate the artefact scatter pattern, especially if the munitions explode upon impact, as two related deposits of material exist: the first being the site of the initial aircraft impact, the second, the explosion scatter. This is an archaeologically recognizable phenomenon referred to as 'Bombturbation'.[60] In short, digging up aircraft can be extremely dangerous to the uninitiated. As Ian McLachlan states in his book *Final Flights: Dramatic Wartime Incidents Revealed by Aviation Archaeology*:

> 'I have already mentioned the risks from ammunition, and anti-tetanus jabs make sense before cavorting in quagmires. When workings are deep, it is wise to monitor cracks developing in the bank and have stepped edges, reducing the risk of collapse. Excavations can become engineering projects, plant hire is expensive, and insurance cover may be necessary.'[61]

Today, wrecks of military aircraft are becoming increasingly rare. In *Out of the Blue: Assessing Military Aircraft Crash Sites in England, 1912–45*, dating to 2002, V. Holyoak highlights that out of the 576 aircraft known to have been lost over the United Kingdom during the Battle of Britain, at least 250 had been the subject of some form of archaeological intervention. Over the past two decades, this number has substantially increased.[62] A question I am often asked is that, considering we already know a significant amount of information regarding crash events, especially of downed Second World War aircraft, surely their recovery/excavation is pointless? I beg to differ. Recent excavations have demonstrated that records from avocational excavations are often fragmentary, at best, with plans, if available, plagued with inaccuracies. As archaeologist Guy de la Bédoyère observes *in Battles Over Britain: The Archaeology of the Air War*:

> 'The Battle of France and the Battle of Britain are not as precisely documented as one might think, the standard of recording varied as the war progressed. We have already seen that a trotted-out procession of historical events does not automatically bear up to close scrutiny. Details of individual crashes are also not straightforward and doubt surrounds many of them.'[63]

A prime example of this is the 2011 excavation of a crashed Spitfire XT-K X4273, shot down over London during the Battle of Britain, killing its pilot, Robin MacGregor Waterston. Directed by Tracy Spaight, archaeologist and co-author of *Burma's Buried Spitfires: A 'Fake' History*, rather than simply searching for any remaining artefacts, the wreck site was fully excavated to a very high archaeological standard, in the same way as an air crash would be investigated by an Air Accident Team. This forensic archaeological examination discovered that the demise of Waterston's Spitfire was somewhat different to what had previously been believed; for instance, it had not impacted deeply into the ground, as initially thought, which made sense of some of the contemporary eyewitness accounts and recorded memories of the incident collected over many years.[64]

Another example is the 1999 Time Team excavation of the Spitfire P9373, from 92 'East India' Squadron, which was shot down in 1940 near Wierre-Effroy, France, during the battle for Dunkirk. Flown by Sergeant Paul Klipsch, who died in the crash, until the excavation nothing more was known of the precise circumstances surrounding the downing of the Spitfire, apart from the fact it occurred whilst attacking a significant number of German aircraft. However, in the professional post-excavation research, conducted by air crash investigator Steve Moss, a rifle calibre (7.92mm) hole in the door was discovered, possibly marking the entry point of a bullet that killed Klipsch, thus causing his Spitfire to fall to its death.[65]

The Future of Aviation Archaeology

Today, aviation archaeology is starting to raise some big questions. There is now an increasing recognition among archaeologists that we need a more sophisticated approach to the study of aviation, whereby an individual wrecked aircraft is not only viewed as an archaeological artefact, but also as an expression of the culture which created and used it. The Spitfire is a perfect example of this way of thinking. Not only was it a superbly designed fighting aircraft but, for us British, it has also become a symbol of national pride and identity. In *Military Aircraft Crash Sites: Archaeological guidance on their Significance and Future Management*, published in 2002, Historic England states:

> 'Crash sites have significance for remembrance, commemoration, their cultural value as historic artifacts and the information they contain about both the circumstances of the loss and the aircraft itself.'[66]

Similarly, some archaeologists are questioning whether some aircraft should be recovered at all, much less restored using modern components. A prime example of the complexities of 'what is to be done with it' is the 1976 discovery of a Wellington bomber, deep in the waters of Loch Ness, Scotland. Found by a team of American researchers who had travelled to Loch Ness in search of the infamous Loch Ness Monster, Nessie failed to put in an appearance this time around; what the team did not expect to find, some 60m (197ft) below the surface, was a Vickers Wellington bomber aircraft, N2890, that had plummeted into the water in 1940. The Wellington has a remarkable pedigree. It is the only British bomber built continuously throughout the Second World War, with over 11,000 such aircraft emerging from the production line. However, by the 1970s, there was only one known complete Wellington in existence, which made the discovery of N2890 paramount. Between 1980 and 1984, following several remotely operated vehicle (ROV) surveys of the underwater site, it was apparent that the Wellington had suffered several damaging incursions by both souvenir hunters and/or recreational divers, yet remained surprisingly intact. In 1984, the Loch Ness Wellington Association Ltd was founded, its aim being to raise much-needed funds to recover the aircraft.[67]

The following year, in 1985, Vickers Wellington N2890 was ultimately recovered from the loch, albeit not without incident, as both the front nose and the rear aft of the wings broke free during the lifting process. Even so, the cold, icy waters of Loch Ness proved an ideal environment for sustaining not only the fuselage, but also several organic items, which under normal circumstances would not have survived, such as the navigator's logbook, a couple of leather helmets and even some of the upholstery. In fact, when the Wellington's rear taillight was reconnected to a battery, it was still found to be working! Having transported the bomber to Brooklands Museum, in Weybridge, Surry, discussions soon became rather heated as to what now should be done with her. Two opposing, and very distinct, viewpoints quickly emerged. On one side you had those who believed that the aircraft's remains should be cleaned, lacquered and put on display as an 'exploded airframe', whilst those on the other side were in favour of N2890 being put back to how she was found in 1976. Interestingly, a quick search into the archives at Brooklands reveals that the Museum was well aware they would receive criticism for adopting the latter approach but, as stated in their 'Definite Restoration Policy', they were determined not to return the Wellington to an 'as-new' condition. In the words of one of the original Wellington design team: 'We'd have to put in so many new pieces to get it airborne that it would no longer be identifiable as N2890.' Parts were kept wherever possible, unless they were too badly damaged, as was the case of the central fuselage, whereby a 20m (66ft) section of another Wellington's aircraft fuselage, in use at the time as a farmer's shed, was appropriated. Creation of other parts were permitted, but only as a last result, and only if they were required for the structural integrity of the aircraft. By treating N2890 as a valuable archaeological artefact, rather than focussing on whether to get her airborne or not, Brooklands Museum successfully achieved a favourable 'middle ground' between the competing demands of archaeology, which normally dictates that excavated material to be kept in an 'as found' condition, and those aircraft enthusiasts who wish to reconstruct aircraft to an overall 'as-new' condition.[68]

A question often asked is, would the public be better served if wrecked aircraft were preserved where they lie as solemn memorials to the air crews who flew them? It is an intriguing thought but, as mentioned previously, with no political will to police such sites, how would they remain protected from the activities of persistent 'ne'er-do-wells'? Another worrying trend that has reared its ugly head over since 2024, is the physical disposal of aircraft from major museum collections in favour of computer-generated technology. Obviously, I will refrain from naming and shaming, but this course of action I find both incomprehensible and deplorable. Alas, it appears the new generation of 'museum curators' have little interest in genuine artefacts. Underwater archaeology specialist and museum professional, Megan Lickliter-Mundon, recently stated:

> 'Right now, these are objects of the very recent past, but one day, there will be no more flying vintage aircraft. So, I think that a lot of the university-archaeology mindset is to anticipate the future and get guidelines in place for how to treat these objects in 100 years, 200 years, 300 years.'[69]

Perhaps not dispensing with your flying vintage aircraft, in the first instance, would be a start . . .

Underwater Archaeology

To end the segment, I would like to briefly touch upon the subject of underwater aviation archaeology. The topic will be explored in greater detail in Chapter 4. Water covers more than seventy per cent of the Earth's surface, yet the subject of underwater aviation graveyards is an area of history that has received little attention by mainstream archaeology. Although the amount of academic research on submerged aircraft has vastly increased over the last decade, there is still a large body of knowledge that is reliant on non-academic sources. In parallel to land-based aviation archaeology, legal constraints to protect aircraft grave sites underwater are present, albeit their effectiveness is open to question. The first is the United Nations Convention on the 'Law of the Sea' 1982, which was the final result of a decade-long process to establish some form of consensus between nation states on their 'rights' and 'responsibilities' on the high seas, with so-called 'sovereign immunity', classified in Section 10, Article 236 (UNCLOS), as pertaining towards any 'warship, naval auxiliary, other vessels or aircraft owned or operated by a State and used, for the time being, only on government non-commercial services'.

At first glance, aircraft entombed underwater would, therefore, have some form of protective rights. Unfortunately, a proviso states that to receive such protections, the aircraft should have been underwater for at least 100 years, which precludes many important archaeological sites. Albeit Article 2 (9) does state that proper respect should be given to all human remains located in maritime waters, which is a very real possibility within aviation archaeology.[70]

In short, the responsibilities for protecting underwater aircraft sites appear to lie with independent sovereign nations, the importance of which, we shall see, vary from country to country. For example, Italy has very robust legislation in protecting its heritage, underwater or otherwise, with a few aircraft in the waters of Sicily, casualties from the Second World War, officially listed as protected.[71] Whereas in the territorial waters of Malta, another major underwater Second World War aviation heritage site, the aircraft wrecks here, of which there are many, are not protected to the same degree. Albeit, in the 1990s, the formation of the Malta Aviation Museum Foundation, together with the use of modern scanning equipment to record and map any aircraft wrecks around the waters of Malta, was a positive step forward. The ban on all fishing, bar surface fishing, by Malta's Marine Maritime Authority, has also aided efforts.[72] It should be emphasized once more that all underwater aircraft wrecks in United Kingdom waters fall under the Protection of Military Remains Act 1986.

Historically speaking, submerged aircraft have had more of an economic value rather than academic worth, viewed as valuable material to scavenge, like that of shipwrecks, and an increase in sea activities, such as recreational diving, has left a gap in our understanding of this submerged heritage. As with any underwater site frequented by divers, there is always a danger of damage, intentional or otherwise, as well as theft. Again, in Malta, a popular tourist destination for divers, the disappearance of armaments from several submerged aircraft would indicate that 'souvenir hunters' have been active, thus ignoring the 'look and don't touch' sentiments expected. Fundamentally, the lack of ethics and absence of rules in such situations, as with many land-based aviation sites, really does need to be addressed. In short, all aviation archaeological emplacements deserve to be treated with greater reverence and respect.

Chapter 3

A Traditional End

Whilst many aircraft graveyards remain above ground, there are some that follow, shall we say, a more 'traditional' path and have been designated a subterranean ending. One such graveyard was stumbled upon by accident in Iraq during the early stages of the Second Gulf War (2003–2011). In April 2003, having captured the Al-Asad Airbase in Western Iraq, Australian forces, together with members from the Special Air Services Regiment (SAS), unearthed more than fifty Soviet-era fighter jets buried deep in the sand, including the high-performance MiG-25 Foxbat, a high-speed interceptor renowned for its exceptional speed and altitude capabilities. The aircraft were typically buried in large pits or concealed under camouflage nets, making them difficult to detect from the air during coalition bombing campaigns.[1] A few months later, in August 2003, the operation was repeated, when American troops discovered even more MiG-25s, and Sukhoi Su-25s ground-attack jets, interred under the sand of the vast Al-Taqaddum Airfield, located some 74km (45mi) west of Baghdad. Each aircraft was in remarkably good condition, considering its surroundings, albeit minus its wings. These were not found buried within the complex.[2]

Despite existing intelligence hinting at 'things buried in the desert', it still came as a surprise to those in charge of military operations. As the former Defence Secretary Donald Rumsfeld stated: 'We'd heard a great many things had been buried, but we had not known where they were, and we'd been operating in that immediate vicinity for weeks and weeks and weeks…12, 13 weeks, and didn't know they were there.'[3] Why the then leader of Iraq, Saddam Hussein, chose to bury his country's fighting aircraft in the middle of the desert is not certain. After all, before the invasion of Iraq by America and its coalition partners, Iraq had one of the largest air forces in the region. He no doubt concluded that his Iraqi units were simply no match for the superiority of the invading US/coalition forces, and thus chose to bury his aircraft, saving them for future use.

In a similar vein, in November 2011, twenty-three RAAF F-111 aircraft, a popular all-weather attack fighter capable of low-level penetration of enemy defences, were interred in the Swanbank landfill site, just outside the city of Ipswich, in Queensland, a year after their operational career had come to an end.[4] Affectionately known as 'The Pig' in Australian military circles, the F-111C version had been the stalwart of the RAAF since 1973. Although a few of the aircraft did survive the cull, some were preserved and are now on display in various aviation museums throughout Australia; others were dispatched to RAAF air bases dotted around the country; the remaining stock, minus their wings and tail, were entombed below ground.[5] For aviation enthusiasts, the decision was not a popular one, but it was a stipulation of the deal between the Australian military and the United States when acquiring the F-111s that they be securely disposed of upon their retirement. As Gregg Gray, former senior non-commissioned officer (SNCO), US Air Force, explains:

> 'The fuselages were constructed out of bonded panels, and that bonding used asbestos, this is why it was deemed prudent to bury them. Trying to recover the materials was not cost effective, and it was full of hazards requiring a very comprehensive facility and PPE to even attempt. So, it was decided to bury them to take away the possibility of exposure to asbestos.'[6]

An equivalent scenario occurred in 2019, when two Mil Mi-24 Hind helicopters were unearthed at a similar landfill facility in Darwin, buried under hazardous waste, more than 330km (205mi) from their former home at RAAF Tindal Base near Katherine, Northern Territory.[7] The aircraft were among four Russian military helicopters bound for Papua New Guinea, in the mid-1990s, as part of a $49.9 million (£37.5 million) deal between the Papua New Guinea government and a UK military company called Sandline International. However, the aircraft did not arrive in Papua New Guinea due to an international diplomatic scandal known as the 'Sandline Affair'; the Papua New Guinea government engaged Sandline

International to supply mercenaries and military equipment to eliminate secessionist leaders on Bougainville Island, an autonomous region of Papua New Guinea, and thus repossess its vast and highly lucrative Panguna copper mine. In the ensuing fallout, Australia unwittingly found itself the owners of two Mil Mi-24 Hind helicopters.[8]

Details of this newly acquired consignment were initially kept secret from the public, and any attempts to sell the aircraft were stalled by complications, as it was unclear who were, in fact, the legal owners of the aircraft. For almost two decades, the helicopters remained at RAAF Tindal Base, there was even some suggestion of transferring them to the Darwin aviation museum for public display, but this never came to pass. In the intervening years, the aircraft started to decompose rapidly and were found to be riddled with asbestos. Disposal was the only option. 'A few years ago, we had a couple of shipping containers turn up here that were required to be buried,' stated Nik Kleine, Waste and Capital Works Executive Manager, City of Darwin. The two Mil Mi-24 Hind helicopters are now buried under Shoal Bay.[9]

Australia's fondness for burying obsolete aircraft does not end here, as illustrated in February 2024, when a photograph of twenty-seven dismantled MRH Taipan helicopters, awaiting burial, was leaked to the press. A year earlier, the entire fleet of ninety was permanently grounded after a fatal crash in the Whitsunday Islands, Queensland, killed four of the crew onboard.[10] When questioned, Defence Industry Minister Pat Conroy told reporters that the Taipans were no longer in flying condition and would require a huge amount of time and money to get them airworthy: 'The best value for money option for the Commonwealth was to sell the spare parts and dispose of the rest of the asset.'[11] This decision has not proved popular with those on the other side of the political divide, and has rekindled frustrations over the Australian government's decision to bury the aircraft underground rather than donate them to Ukraine, with some Army veterans and engineers, who once worked on the fleet of Taipan helicopters, offering to rebuild the aircraft so that they can be sent to aid the war effort. Nonetheless, as one qualified observer noted: 'If Australia was not capable of keeping the MRH to a flying status that enabled even the minimum acceptable flying rates of effort to keep aircrew competent, what chance does a country at-war, with limited people and resources have?'[12]

For years, there had been rumours of Second World War Nazi aircraft buried somewhere in Midwest America. The site suspected was a nondescript airfield in Seymour, Jackson County, Indiana, a small outcrop of land, equidistant between the city of Indianapolis and Louisville, Kentucky. Known as the 'Crossroads of Southern Indiana', before the war, the area comprised a collection of family-owned farms producing enough food and grain to live by, until May 1942 when the US Army Air Corps, the precursor to the USAF, took up residency less than 5km (3mi) from the city and immediately commenced negotiations with twenty-seven local farmers to buy out their land. The farmers agreed, and soon this newly acquired parcel of land became Freeman Army Airfield.[13] Named after Captain Richard Freeman, a graduate from West Point, the United States Military Academy, an aviation pioneer and native of Indiana, who was killed in a B-17 crash near Lovelock, Nevada, in February, 1941, Freeman Field would become an advanced twin-engine training field, one of hundreds used to train aircrew personnel in preparation for war. With four 1,701m (5,580ft)-long by 30m (100ft)-wide paved runways and nine taxiways built for trainee aircraft cadets to use, it was a pivotal stop on the way to flying larger bombers and cargo aircraft after basic flight training had finished.[14]

In 1945, as the war in Europe was nearing its end, under a directive from the Commanding General of the Army Air Forces, H. H. Arnold, that an airfield be found and used as a repository and testing centre for 'enemy aeronautical equipment', Freeman Field was placed under the direct command of the Air Technical Service Command, its mission to receive, recondition, evaluate, and store at least one of every item of enemy aircraft material. Rebranded a Foreign Aircraft Evaluation Centre, in a programme entitled Operation Lusty, over eighty German enemy aircraft, captured from the Third Reich, found their way to Freeman Field to be taken apart, flown and studied. At the same time, in a separate venture named Operation Paperclip, many of the German scientists and engineers who built these machines were commandeered to reverse engineer the technology for the newly emerging US Air Force and later, NASA.[15]

The variety of captured German aircraft that found its way to Seymour is quite staggering. Apart from conventional stuff like the Focke-Wulf Fw-190, Junkers Ju-88s, and even a radar-equipped Heinkel He-129 night fighter, there was the mostly wooden mono-jet Heinkel He-162 Volksjäger, the so-called 'People's Fighter', the iconic Messerschmitt Me-262 twin-engine jet fighter, as well as the Messerschmitt Me-163 Komet, a rocket interceptor with a hellish chemical power source. Furthermore, the Arado AR 234 'Blitz', the world's first operational jet bomber, also spent time in Indiana after the war. As did the Flettner Fl 282 'Kolibri', Germany's equivalent to the Sikorsky Hoverfly and the Dornier Do-335, the fastest twin-engine piston aircraft of the war. The Horton Ho-229, a vaguely B-2 bomber-shaped, wing jet fighter arrived on base by August 1945, as did the Wernher von Braun's V2 ballistic missile. This is in addition to several warehouses full of captured Luftwaffe equipment.[16]

With the end of the war, activities at Freeman Field were gradually shut down; testing at the base did not conclude until October 1946. Soon after, the base was transferred to the WAA, the government agency tasked with liquidating excess military assets. Whilst several of the German planes were saved for museum displays, many were scrapped. The remnants of the remaining aircraft, which were scattered around in large hangars, were loaded into trucks, taken to various places around the airfield and buried in a series of pits.[17] The land was then sold to the City of Seymour for just $1 (£0.74), with the caveat that the military could take it back if war ever broke out again.

Since those days, many people have come forward to talk about their experiences at Freeman Field, either witnessing the dumping of aircraft and/or parts or being directly involved in their burial. The first significant recovery effort, in the early 1990s, was headed by Second World War aviation buff Charlie Osborn, under the moniker of Blue Sky, but nothing of note was uncovered.[18] There was no further activity until 1995, when aircraft mechanic Lex Cralley, founder of Salvage I, based in Princeton, Minnesota, who has a passion for preserving the Second World War aviation history, obtained permission from the Aviation Board of Freeman Field to try again. With a different search methodology from those who tried before, which included the use of ground imaging radar, Cralley was confident he would uncover the buried aircraft. Yet again, in August 1995, after an extensive search nothing was uncovered. Over the next several months other areas of the airfield site were searched but the buried German aircraft remained elusive.[19]

It wasn't until early 1997 that Freeman Field began to reveal its secrets, with the first solid evidence of buried aircraft parts discovered; albeit all were of American manufacture. By this time, Cralley had teamed up with Dallas Tohill, an aircraft historian who worked at Tidewater Tech, an aviation maintenance school located in Norfolk, Virginia, who also managed its own historic aircraft restoration facility. It would be Tidewater Tech who provided much of the funding for the next adventure.[20] With a new search now in motion, this time the team moved to a different area of the airfield, learning from their previous mistakes. Even so, with over 8sq km (2,100acres) of ground to cover, it was, as Cralley stated, 'like looking for the proverbial needle in the haystack'. Nonetheless, after three days of digging small exploratory holes, they finally uncovered an aircraft engine cylinder head, only 91cm (3ft) below the surface. Continued digging produced a further hundred-cylinder heads, from a variety of aircraft, together with several large wooden props inscribed with German writing. Several propeller blades were also uncovered; some were clearly from a German Focke-Wulf Fw 190, whilst two came from a Beechcraft AT-10.[21] After several years of painstaking and sometimes frustrating research and exploration, the existence of buried German aircraft parts at Freeman Field had finally been proven.

Regrettably, as no whole aircraft, or major structures, had been found, Cralley and his team decided to abandon their operations just after 1997. It wasn't until almost a decade later, in 2009, that Seymour native David Gray, a career pilot and Second World War historian, would form the group known as the Freeman Field Recovery Team (FFRT) and commence a new investigation.[22] Having obtained permission to excavate from the relevant authorities, and with full backing of the Freeman Army Airfield Museum, the team underwent a new approach, this time focussing on archive material and firsthand witness accounts. In doing so they believed that they had discovered the whereabouts of the missing aircraft, identifying approximately a dozen potential dig sites. Having caught the attention of the National Geographic channel, a film crew was dispatched to Freeman Field to film the FFRT in action. For those interested, the show *Diggers*, aired in March 2014.[23] Today, Freeman Field is the city airport, comprising an industrial park housing over sixty businesses, combined with a large expanse of farmed agricultural land. It also has a small museum, opened 1997, dedicated to preserving the history of the cadets who trained there during the Second World War.

Almost eighty years since they last took to the skies, in 2013, eight British Hawker Hurricane fighter aircraft, dating to the Second World War, were uncovered in a forest near the Ukrainian capital, Kyiv.[24] Often overlooked by the more popular and faster Spitfire, the single-seater Hurricane was a very capable aircraft, the first in the United Kingdom to fly over 483kph (300mph), and was used in every theatre of the war, even on warships. Designed by aeronautical engineer Sydney Camm, the Hurricane was responsible for shooting down more than half of the enemy aircraft destroyed during the Battle of Britain in 1940, not the Spitfire; their contribution to victory over Nazi Germany should never be overlooked.

'The Hurricane was a strong, easy to fly machine', stated Oleks Shtan, a former airline pilot who led the Kyiv excavation, 'It was stable as a gun platform and suitable for inexperienced pilots.'[25]

So, how did these eight remarkable aircraft end their final days buried in a forest in Ukraine? According to BBC news, the buried aircraft were among 3,000 Hawker Hurricanes sent to the Soviet Union after 1941 under what is often referred to as the 'Lend-Lease Programme', a programme whereby the United States would 'lend or lease' vital war supplies, which included military equipment, food and petroleum products, to any nation deemed vital to the defence of the United States, in essence to the United Kingdom and the Commonwealth, the Soviet Union, France, the Republic of China, and other Allied nations of the Second World War. Passed on 11 March 1941, materials delivered under the act were supplied at no cost, to be used until returned or be destroyed, the latter preventing repayment. In this case of the Kyiv Hurricanes, the United States had purchased a significant number of Hurricanes from the United Kingdom, which were subsequently transferred to the Soviet Union, with the understanding that the Soviets would repay the United States for any aircraft that remained intact at the end of the war. However, no repayment was forthcoming as the Soviets had cunningly stripped the Hurricanes of their internal parts and dumped their metallic bodies into the forest ravine, a tactic used by the Soviet Union, and others I might add, to avoid reimbursement of monies owed.[26]

There had always been rumours of aircraft buried on the outskirts of Kyiv, according to a statement from Ukraine's Oleg Antonov State Aviation Museum, in Kyiv, but if an unexploded wartime bomb had not been discovered, and diffused, in the forested ravine, then the Hurricanes may have remained undetected for years. By chance, explosive experts, checking the area for further ordnance, found their underground remains. The wreckage of the fighter aircraft has now been excavated by volunteers and donated to the aviation museum.[27] As Oleks Shtan said,

> 'It is very rare to find this aircraft in Ukraine...It's very important for our aviation history because no Lend-Lease aircraft have been found here before.'

Formal burial within a cave system was a traditional means of interment for humans throughout prehistory, from some of the earliest graveyards of mankind, to today's Toraja kinsfolk who inhabit the island of Sulawesi, in Indonesia. Although its popularity has waned throughout time, what one doesn't expect to come across when exploring such ritualistic practices is the sight of an aircraft within a similar system. Yes, surprisingly, the humble cave has entombed many aircraft, such as the remains of a feared German bomber, a Dornier 217.ZA, found some 1,000m (3,280ft) into a French cave in the Pyrenees.[28] Designed to carry heavy loads, the Dornier 217.ZA was utilized on both the Western and Eastern Fronts either as a strategic bomber or a reconnaissance aircraft, directing ground attacks and anti-shipping strikes in Normandy and the battles of the Atlantic. It is an intriguing find. According to documentation, in July 1944 two Dornier bombers became lost on their return to base and subsequently collided over the Pyrenees mountains. The Germans had stationed many of their Dornier fleet outside the French city of Toulouse, from where they conducted bombing raids on Allied forces. The eight crew members died instantly, and fearing German reprisals, the local people decided to bury the wreckage of the planes by throwing them down a nearby 100m (328ft) cave, to hide any evidence of their existence.[29] Speaking in the nearby village of Sacoue the then mayor, Yvette Campan, who has lived there all her life, remembers her grandparents talking about how scared they were when the two bombers crashed and seeing the crews' bodies scattered over a wide area. The last thing they wanted was to attract attention. Even now, there is no local ceremony to mark the recovery of the wreckage. As Campan stated: 'the Germans were the enemy after all. If it had been a British plane that was being salvaged it would be a different story.'[30]

For decades after the war, the whereabouts of the German aircraft remained a closely guarded secret within the local community. That is, until one plucky explorer, Gilles Collaveri, who had heard the rumours regarding long-forgotten German bomber aircraft, asked a local cave investigative group to help him search the bottom of a cave he had found deep in the forest. They agreed to assist and, sure enough, at the base of the cave they stumbled upon the charred metal sections of one of the lost Dorniers. Months of bureaucratic back and forth followed, before the French authorities gave the necessary permissions for the Dornier to be retrieved. After which, Collaveri, together with a group of approximately fifty archaeologists and historians, began the difficult task of lifting the remains out from the cave. Employing a network system of makeshift cranes and harnesses, they slowly began to lift the wreckage up through the narrow passageway, which included parts of the wing, ammunition, remains of an oxygen tank and a cockpit part, complete with German instructions.[31] Although well preserved, reconstruction of the aircraft, with so few parts, was not a possibility. Thus, most of the remnants were shared between museums in southern France and Berlin.

Continuing with the war theme, as mentioned in the opening chapter, what befell thousands of decommissioned aircraft, after serving in the Second World War, has always been a conundrum. That they were destroyed is beyond doubt. It is the specific manner of their destruction, and by whom, is where the confusion lies. At the beginning of 2025, I was fortunate to speak to a 94-year-old RAF veteran, whose mind, I must say, was as sharp as a tack. He was responsible for repairing damaged aircraft, Spitfires, Hurricanes but predominantly Mosquitoes, and he told me that there were possibly thousands of aircraft buried around old Second World War airfields, as he had witnessed many being buried after the war had ended.[32] This conversation set in motion in what I can only describe as a 'treasure hunt', searching for any clues, whether that be eyewitness testimony, rumours, hearsay, gossip etc., to gain further information. Despite an extraordinary volume of 'I know someone who knew someone who knows someone who was there', scenarios that transpired, I did glean a few intriguing titbits.

In Canada, there are many airfields, apparently, where both Harvards and Cornells have been buried in pits at the end of the runway. If the land has subsequently been utilized for agricultural purposes, parts are often dug up when ploughing. In the United States, at the old Sanford Naval Station, there is/was a burial pit supposedly filled with aircraft remnants and a helicopter.[33] I have also read similar claims to P-38s buried in the old US airbase at Clark Field, in the Philippines, particularly near the Sacobia river area.[34] In fact, upon receiving their closure notice, it was extremely common for old US military bases to bury any surplus items, from old desks to aircraft, in large open dumps at the back of the base. Bruntingthorpe Aerodrome, Leicestershire, was a former RAF base during the Second World War. The station was opened November 1942 as the home of No. 29 Operational Training Unit RAF, operating the Vickers Wellington. After the war, the base was utilized by the USAF, with plans to convert the site into a Strategic Air Command bomber base, for the new Boeing B-47 Stratojet medium-range nuclear bomber. Today, the site is privately owned and is currently the largest vehicle test track facility in the United Kingdom. Set in 670 acres, there is a mixture of open land, either laid to tarmac or concrete, combined with expanses of open grassland and large areas of woodland. According to an employee of the owners, after the USAF left the base, they dug one enormous pit somewhere on the site and buried anything that was surplus to requirement, including aircraft sections. Some years later, a group of ex-USAF servicemen returned to the site with metal detectors to try and find the burial dump—they failed.[35]

The Fleet Air Arm offloaded many of their destroyed wartime aircraft into landfill sites, such as RAF Balado Bridge, in Perth and Kinross in Scotland. Being a RAF base, it is probable that the RAF utilized said dumpsite too. The large wartime burial dump at Stansted, left behind by the USAF in 1945, was partially excavated in the 1980s and was found to contain various damaged parts removed from B-26 Marauders, notably side panels exhibiting bullet damage, armoured glass from the tail fin position and kit bags full of leather flying clothing.[36] During construction work at RAF Fairford, parts from a B-47 Stratojet were discovered buried in a pit on the southeast corner of the base. These included the lower tail section and twin-engine pods, complete with outrigger struts. It is believed that the parts belonged to aircraft 305BW B-47E 52-0255, which had been delivered to Fairford in 1959 for ground instructional use and then scrapped in late 1963. Apparently, the pit also contained a number of USAF vehicles.[37] I have also read that when enlarging the boundary of Chino Airport, California, workmen unearthed a pit containing A-20, P-40 and P-47 aircraft parts.[38] Also, several Gipsy Moth engines were unearthed at former RNZAF Taieri, near Dunedin, New Zealand, in the early 1990s.[39] There are also rumoured to be numerous Corsairs, Venturas, and P40s buried under the runway of Hamilton International Airport in Canada.

At RAF Colerne, in Wiltshire, where from 1940 to 1955 RAF Fighter Command units were based, aircraft that had been parked there after the war were supposedly buried in situ, as the plummeting aluminium prices rendered them unprofitable as scrap.[40] Whereas in Dalgety Bay, Rosyth, Scotland, thousands of aircraft instruments were burnt and then buried on site. I recently read an account of one individual who, weeks after the end of VJ Day, went around demolishing piles of Lend-Lease aircraft around Europe. Terms were hostility plus twelve weeks, after which the planes had to be paid for. As with the Soviets and the Hurricane agreement mentioned above, huge numbers of aircraft were 'written off' by 'enforced explosion', that is demolition charges, and bulldozed into a series of large burial pits to avoid repayment fees.[41] RAF engineers in Burma, whose squadrons were in the process of 'winding down', evidently either torched or bulldozed any excess aircraft before committing their remains to the earth. Another eyewitness account from a RAF Flight Engineer explains how, for eighteen months after the war ended, his responsibility was to fly aircraft from all around Europe back to Longtown, Silloth or Kirkbridge in Cumberland. Once they arrived, an official in a 'brown work overall' would climb the aircraft ladder with a clipboard and a hammer, thereby destroying all American instruments in the cockpit. The pilot would then countersign that they had been destroyed, and the aircraft would then be transported to the smelter, to be cremated, at what is now Sellafield.[42] Supposedly, there are also several unwanted B-17s buried at the end of the runway at RAF Woodbridge, as well as aircraft sections under Dawson's Plantation in Newton, a picturesque ancient woodland in Nottinghamshire, where wartime aircraft were salvaged by a maintenance units from the early 1940s through to the 1950s. At RAF Kenley, two Spitfires, TB885 and PK665, were apparently abandoned on the base dump in 1958. They were then buried but later recovered; the latter was apparently purchased by a private collector and displayed in the family garden. Until the wife objected, that is, and the Spitfire was sadly scrapped![43] One must not forget several DH9 First World War bomber aircraft that were found hidden away in the elephant stables of the Maharaja's Palace in Bikaner, Rajasthan.

Continuing with the rumour mill, a former British Leyland worker recently contacted me with claims about the old Longbridge Plant, in Birmingham, which was a shadow aircraft factory throughout the Second World War, stating that there is/was an under croft full of partially buried aircraft; the area was sealed off in 1945 when car production commenced. Whilst at RAF Edzell, in Aberdeenshire, Scotland, huge numbers of bombers were apparently destroyed here after the Second World War, estimates range from 800 upwards, some straight from the factory, by cutting them apart with chainsaws and bulldozing them into the end of the runway.[44] At RAF Detmold in Germany, later Hobart Barracks, the Army Air Corps unearthed aircraft sections dating to the Second World War, whilst clearing parts of the airfield for the construction of a new hangar.[45] Those parts found at RAF Gutersloh are displayed in a small museum. In Malta, in 1944, several aircraft parts, predominantly from Spitfires, were loaded onto a barge and dumped into the sea off Benghisa Point; many were still in their original manufacturer's packaging. Likewise, after the Second World War had ended, hundreds of military aircraft that were parked wing-to-wing along the Safi airstrip, which now forms part of Malta International Airport, were towed to Hal Far and pushed over the cliffs. Apparently, the wreckage was cleared for scrap by an Italian salvage company, albeit it is unknown how thorough a job the clean-up process was.[46] By all accounts, there are a number of Lancaster bombers buried under the sands of Egypt; whilst in Sierra Leone, in West Africa, where the British used natural cave systems for the repair and maintenance of military aircraft during the Second World War, it has been claimed that a number of aircraft were enshrined inside the caves after the war ended.[47]

This 'death and destruction' modus operandi utilized by the military is not wartime specific. I am constantly reminded of the decommissioning of the United Kingdom's Tornado fighter jet, in all her variants, as this was the particular aircraft that I waved to most mornings when living in the Scottish Highlands as they whizzed by on a low track bombing practice. It is also the jet that almost knocked me off a mountain pass whilst I was out climbing one day. I would like to add that I was at a greater height than the Tornado! It is affectionately referred to as the 'Norfolk Land Shark' or the 'Tonka' by all who love her. I was able to track down one of the scrap merchants who was employed by RAF Marham to dispose of the fighter jets. Having kindly discussed the scraping process with me, which included the burial of any leftovers on the dump sites, he then sent me some images. All I can say is, it isn't pretty. If any former Tornado pilots happen to read this, if your fighter jet's designation was either ZA472, ZA597 or ZD716, I sadly know what became of her.[48] The demise of another popular fighter jet which went down a similar route to that of the Tornado is the USAF F-14 fighter jet, or the 'Tomcat', as it is sometimes referred to, made famous by the first *Top Gun* movie. Rather than allow any spare parts to fall into the hands of the Iranian military, who predominantly still use the F-14 aircraft, the Pentagon decided to destroy the F-14 fleet by slicing them apart into small 61 x 61cm (2 x 2ft) pieces, to make sure no one would ever use the aircraft again. After that, the remaining scrap was combed through to make sure nothing useful remained.[49] Whilst a few aircraft did end their days as exhibits in various US museums, completely stripped from the inside out, the remaining few F-14s that escaped the destruction currently reside in the boneyard at Davis-Monthan. Figures 9a & 9b depict the F-14s parked here in 2007, awaiting their fate, whilst the second image, dating to 2009, depicts the removal of an F-14 on a scrap lorry.

Tall Tales

There have been persistent rumours over the years regarding all sorts of military aircraft that have been hidden or buried in some unorthodox location. One of my favourite stories features an assortment of Nazi aircraft, the feared East German secret police, the Stasi, and several airport runways frequented by Ryanair! It begins just after the fall of the Berlin Wall in November 1989, when papers found in a number of files captured from the Stasi documented the presence of Luftwaffe aircraft, bombed-up and primed to go, together with a significant amount of unexploded munitions, buried under the runways of Schoenfeld Airport, located 18km (11mi) southeast of Berlin, the main destination of low-cost airlines. Buried in bunkers between 8 and 9m (26 and 30ft) deep, experts believe it entirely feasible that, in the aftermath of the Second World War, and with Berlin littered with millions of tonnes of unexploded ordnance, the incoming Soviets would wish to do away with the armaments as quickly and efficiently as possible. As Berlin historian Karl-Heinz Eckhardt stated: 'They would have stuffed them anywhere they could - there was simply too much stuff to blow up all at once. There was a warren of massive Nazi bunkers beneath the site of the present airport that would have suited their purposes.'[50] In fact, beneath the streets of modern-day Berlin, you will find a vast warren of tunnels and shelters built during the reign of the Third Reich.

Despite the rumours the city authorities claim the airport is perfectly safe, with a spokesperson saying: 'We became aware of the bunkers in 1993, four years after the fall of the [Berlin] Wall. A check was undertaken then, and everything was determined to be safe.'[51] Nonetheless, it begs the question as to why such a statement was recorded in the Stasi state files in the first instance? The Stasi spied on almost every aspect of East Germans' daily life, as well as international espionage, and kept files on over 5.5 million people. If there were indeed aircraft buried deep under Schoenfeld Airport, the Stasi would most certainly be aware of them. Unfortunately, it may take some time before the veracity of this remarkable disclosure can be corroborated, or not. The Stasi archives were immense, holding some 111km (69mi) of files. But in the weeks before the Berlin Wall fell, Stasi agents began destroying as many of these documents as they could. Thousands were pulped, burnt, or shredded, with some 40+ million pages torn up and stuffed into sacks. Today, even though a team of archivists are attempting to piece together these fragments, it is a painstaking exercise, one which some estimate could take centuries to complete.[52] The answer to the buried Luftwaffe aircraft, and what happened to them, I fear, will never be solved in my lifetime.

Keeping with the phantasmagorical German theme, in February 2025 it was reported by the German newspaper *Bild* that historian Mirko Kühn had discovered the whereabouts of a secret underground Nazi aircraft hangar, codenamed *Alpendohle*, near Altenburg Airport in Thuringia, eastern Germany. For decades, myths have surrounded the Leinawald forest massif near Altenburg, with both treasure hunters and local historians alike speculating that the area contains the missing Amber Room, a decorated chamber comprising a series of panels crafted from 6 tonnes (6.6 tons) of amber mounted on gold-leaf walls and adorned with mosaics and mirrors, stolen from Russia, that became a secret cult site of the Nazis. According to Stasi documents, the German Democratic Republic tried to investigate the structure in 1964 but had to pull back due to an alleged leak of poisonous gas, whilst Russian tabloid newspaper *Komsomolskaya Pravda* reports that the renowned American treasure hunter Norman Scott attempted to search the area without success. Kühn claims that he identified the hangar by piecing together old aerial photographs with documentary evidence: 'There are eyewitnesses, aerial photographs, and measurements that confirm my theory,' said Kühn. With a length of over 200m (656ft), 25m (82ft) in width, and a height of 5m (16ft), Kühn believes that the site is capable of accommodating up to ten large aircraft, including the burial of dozens of unfinished jet fighters of the type Heinkel He-162, that are rumoured to have been abandoned at the site. He believes he has also identified the entrances: 'Down there is the buried entrance', he says to a *Bild* reporter pointing to the broken slope downwards, informing them that a simple excavation at one of the presumed emergency exits of the hangar could lead to the discovery of several long-forgotten aircraft, buried in time.[53]

The North Head Historic Reserve in Auckland, New Zealand, comprising one of Auckland's fourteen Tūpuna Maunga (ancestral mountains) has always been shrouded in mystery. First tunnelled by prisoners between 1885 and 1891 to protect New Zealand from Russian attack, the underground network, which stretches no more than 200m (656ft) into the rock face, is supposedly the final resting place of the first two Boeings ever built. Local folklore states that the twin Boeings were brought to New Zealand by Kiwi aviation pioneers Leo and Vivian Walsh to promote their New Zealand Flying School.[54] It was here that Royal Flying Corps pilots received their training during the First World War. More recently, ex-commercial pilot Martin Butler has dedicated two decades of his life to trying to uncover what happened to the two Boeing aircrafts, in what he refers to as 'the holy grail of aviation', and claims to have found new evidence to support his case, an update of which he publishes in his book *Tunnel Vision*. Having conducted a ground radar search with a professional geophysicist, Butler found areas in the mountain that could easily be the home to blocked tunnels and potentially the Boeing burial site: 'Every search carried out on North Head to date had major flaws', he said, admitting that though the geophysicist experts had begun the adventure with him with a 'huge amount of scepticism', they had now been won over.[55]

I can hear the collective groans from the aviation community as I write about the following so-called 'discoveries', but it is important to understand that there may be people outside the community reading this who may not have heard the following rumours or, as I have become aware during my research, have been fooled by media headlines into believing something which has yet to be proven, let alone yielded any conclusive evidence. After all, if you had just read the headline 'A warplane graveyard: 50 German Focke-Wulfs that disappeared after the Second World War are found wrapped in sheets buried under an old Turkish airport,' in the *Daily Mail* newspaper, or 'Over 50 missing warplanes found buried in central Turkey' in the *Hurriyet Daily News*, you would have a tendency to believe them.[56] Alas, not all is what it seems.

The Focke-Wulf Fw 190, a single-seat, single-engine aircraft, was one of the best fighters flown by the Luftwaffe (German Air Force) during the Second World War. Its arrival in Turkey was the result of joint Turkish-German aviation relations, which started prior to the First World War and continued with the ill-fated TOMTAŞ factory, established in a partnership with the German company Junkers, which opened on 6 October 1926 in the city of Kayseri in central Anatolia.[57] On 18 June 1941, two years into the Second World War, Turkey and Germany reaffirmed their alliance by signing a non-aggression pact. The negotiations were led by Germany's then-ambassador to Turkey, Franz von Papen, Germany's chancellor before

Adolf Hitler. A year later, financial terms were brokered between the two countries whereby in return for commodities, such as high-grade iron and chromium, Germany would provide Turkey with war supplies, including aircraft, anti-aircraft guns, tanks and spare parts. Sixty disassembled Focke-Wulf Fw 190s were shipped to Turkey initially, followed by another twelve for spare parts, a total of seventy-two aircraft.[58]

Initially flown to Bursa in northwestern Turkey, the Focke-Wulf Fw 190s were distributed to other locations, namely Sarıgazi in Istanbul and Merzifon in the central Black Sea region, before some reached the city of Kayseri. In fact, there is an interesting reference in Turkey's Aeronautical Associations *Flying Turk* magazine, dating to August 1954, where Turkish Air Force Captain Tacettin Gökdeniz comments on thirty-six Focke-Wulf Fw 190s that took part in a flight from Bursa to Kayseri in the summer of 1948. Why this specific piece of information is particularly intriguing is that all the international news outlets reporting on the 'buried aircraft' story have the Focke-Wulf Fw 190s disappearing from Kayseri in 1947![59]

Although the existence of these aircraft is highly disputed by aviation experts, who believe they were probably decommissioned and sold for scrap, efforts to find the missing warplanes began in earnest as far back as 2015, when a metal detector survey was carried out around the Kayseri airbase. According to newly surfaced documents, so the newspaper reports claim, the United States wanted Turkey to destroy all the German Fw 190A3 warplanes and force them to purchase US aircraft. In response, the Turkish authorities chose to hide the Fw 190s by burying them at Kayseri, at a depth of 5m (16ft), carefully wrapped in protective oil canvases, according to Uluhan Hasdal, an amateur aviation historian.[60] Hasdal believes if they are there, the aircraft should still be, more or less, operable: 'I call on the Kayseri Municipality to take note of this situation and to take action to recover and restore these aircraft to their former glory so that the entire world may enjoy them once again,' states Hasdal.[61] That was a decade ago. There are still no signs of the 'elusive' Focke-Wulf Fw 190s . . .

Another wild tale worthy of mention centres around a stash of as-new Spitfires buried underground somewhere around the town of rural Oakey, in Queensland, Australia, too, still reportedly in their crates.[62] Opinions vary from a high-level defence conspiracy among senior RAAF officers to a single leading aircraftman who couldn't bear to see the aircraft destroyed, so he buried them. The aircraft in question are the remnants of 656 Mark V and Mark VIII Spitfires that were delivered to the RAAF during the Second World War. They were supposedly hidden underground with spares and fuel for the re-taking of Queensland in the event a Japanese invasion forced a retreat to the infamous Brisbane Line, a proposed plan that emerged in 1942, whereby Australian forces would be withdrawn from Queensland and the Northern Territories to focus on defences in the south. The plan was ultimately rejected by the Australian War Cabinet and government.[63]

Accounts regarding the Spitfires' existence vary widely, depending on to whom you speak within the local Oakey population. RAAF records show that 544 aircraft, 232 of which were Spitfires, were flown to Oakey to be sold to a scrap metal dealer, confirmed by local Toowoomba resident, Laurie Wenham, who was employed in breaking down the aircraft prior to melting in 1948. 'I do not believe there are any hidden aircraft and various "sightings" over the years were probably parts or partial aircraft pilfered or purchased as scrap,' he was quoted as saying.[64] Yet, a lifetime Oakey resident, who did not wish to be named, claims to be a reliable witness to the burial site of at least five of the aircraft in what may have been a trial disposal near the old Federal Mine. Although he says that he did not actually see the aircraft going into the ground, he did witness contractors digging a trench and see a large crate interred inside. Some decades later, it is reported that the contactors claimed to have buried the aircraft, albeit these claims are unsubstantiated.[65]

More recently, a former Second World War airman has claimed that during an exchange of confidences in the 1950s, another airman and lifelong friend told him that he and others had hidden aircraft in a hole in the side of a hill near Oakey.[66] This version of the story centres on reports of a squadron of around eighteen Spitfires, supposedly Mk XIVs, packed away in crates, and was even reported upon in *Royal Air Force News.* The UK MoD subsequently sent a RAF Group Captain, a Wing Commander and a technical NCO to Oakey to investigate.[67] So, what is the truth?

From reports that I have read, many suggest that the underground burial theory developed in the telling and retelling of rumours that a few aircraft had been buried, hidden or dumped in a disused coal mine. After all, the area around Oakey is abundant with abandoned coal mines. Local resident Lester Reisinger, who has conducted several searches, stated: 'They're there alright, under the Oakey drive-in theatre.' The now disused theatre was built directly on top of an old mine, the Federal, and is the closest to Oakey airfield, the area Reisinger, and others, believe the Spitfires are buried. The existence of an aerial photograph, taken on 30 September 1945, clearly depicts an entrance tunnel to the Federal Mine still open, complete with a railway line entering the tunnel, together with several crates awaiting relocation to destination unknown. In 2001, local farmer and pilot David Mulckey gained permission to carry out an exploratory search of the site, to no avail. A mix-up with photographic survey identification resulted in him digging in the wrong place. 'As soon as I arrived, I realized that we were in the paddock adjacent to, not on, the correct site', said Mr Mulckey, the latter showing evidence of digging and heavy lifting even after sixty years.[68]

The story does not end here though, as more recently the Spitfire legend has gained new interest from filmmakers and aircraft enthusiasts James Carter and Karl von Moller, whose aim is to produce a documentary about their search for the buried aircraft entitled *Broken Wings*. 'In 2000, we heard some incredible stories about Spitfire aircraft buried in the ground near Oakey. 'The more we researched, the more we felt the story would make a remarkable and exciting documentary,' said Carter. Further information can be found via their website, which is worth a view. The official statement reads as follows:

> 'Broken Wings is a documentary film currently in production in Melbourne, Australia. It explores the legend that a quantity of brand-new Spitfires still in their original shipping crates, are buried somewhere around the township of Oakey in southern Queensland. Some 553 Spitfires along with Kittyhawk's, Mustangs and Boomerangs were disposed of at 6 Aircraft Depot, Oakey at the conclusion of the Second World War. James Carter and Karl von Moller, both warbird enthusiasts and film makers from Melbourne are behind the venture and it's their fascination with warbird aircraft and a desire to tell a remarkable story that's been driving this exciting project for the past 16 years.'[69]

Which brings us to the next topic, Spitfires in Burma. I can hear another collective groan! When I first began researching boneyards for *Burying the Dead*, several years ago, I distinctly remember people commenting, 'Have you heard about the Spitfires buried in Burma?' By this time, I had already begun collecting people's testimony with regards to the burial of aircraft at the end of the Second World War, so I was aware of how contentious such claims can be. But the existence of crate loads of Spitfires, in numbers ranging anywhere from twenty to 124, buried in an old RAF airfield in Burma?! I was somewhat sceptical. It appears, for good reason. However, for those unfamiliar with this particular 'saga', I will attempt to offer a simplified account.

Rumours of buried Spitfires from the Second World War have circulated since, well, the end of the war itself. As one commentator put it: 'when the Second World War came to an end in August 1945 the legends began'. But in 2012, a Lincolnshire farmer and aviation enthusiast, David Cundall, claimed he had discovered the whereabouts of numerous Spitfires buried underground in Burma, now Myanmar. Cundall was no stranger to finding missing aircraft and had tracked down the remains of many other Second World War aircraft in the 1970s and 1980s, including a Lancaster bomber that crashed in Lincolnshire in 1944. It was returning from a raid over Germany, badly shot up and on fire, when the crew was forced to ditch before they could reach the airfield. He had also found the remains of a Hawker Hurricane in Tetney Marsh, Grimsby, in 1990 and a Spitfire Mark V at Goole in Yorkshire in 1992.[70] But this new claim understandably caught the attention of the world's press. So much so that in April of that year it was reported that the British Prime Minister David Cameron had negotiated an agreement with Myanmar President Thein Sein for the recovery and repatriation of at least twenty crated Spitfires, reportedly buried at RAF Mingaladon in Yangon. A Downing Street spokesperson said: 'We are pleased to hear that contracts have been awarded, which mean that the digging up of the Spitfires in Burma can begin. We've always said that we want to see these Spitfires back home in Britain – perhaps one day even flying over the skies of Britain – and today's news brings us another step closer to that.'[71]

In January 2013, a full contingent of experts, including archaeologists, geophysics technicians, plus state-of-the-art excavators, headed for the defunct RAF Mingaladon Air Base, which is now the site of Yangon International Airport. Funded by Wargaming Ltd, after weeks of surveying, digging and exploration nothing was found (some timber had been found the year previous).[72] In fact, the archaeological team had uncovered some interesting documentation regarding RAF Mingaladon, prior to leaving for Myanmar, which 'puts a damper' on the entire buried Spitfire theory. For example, from the operations logbook, photographs, and even newsreels, they all show that on 19 August 1945, 607 Squadron disbanded at RAF Mingaladon and their Mark VIII Spitfires were transferred directly to 8 Squadron of the Indian Air Force, who flew back to India after the war with all their aircraft.[73] Furthermore, on 11 September 1945, another Spitfire squadron, quoted as being directly involved in the burials by Cundall, namely 273 Squadron, flew out of Mingaladon with all their aircraft too.[74] Archival records also showed that the RAF unit that handled shipments through Rangoon docks, 41 Embarkation Unit, only received thirty-seven aircraft in total from three transport ships between 1945 and 1946. Finally, as pointed out in a preliminary briefing by Andy Brockman, RAF Mingaladon was a combat zone for three years, and the area marked out by Cundall as the Spitfire burial site was a primary target for the RAF and USAAF bombers dropping 500 and 1,000lb (227 and 454kg) bombs, capable of dispersing significant amounts of debris on explosion penetrating some 9m (30ft) down in places.[75] With a lack of any archaeological finds, plus contradicting written accounts, Wargaming Ltd pulled their funding and left the project. Tracy Spaight, Wargaming's director of special projects, stated: 'No-one would have been more delighted than our team had we found Spitfires. We knew the risks going in, as our team had spent many weeks in the archives and had not found any evidence to support the claim of buried Spitfires.'[76]

Since this mitigating failure to find any evidence of buried Spitfires, Cundall has continued with his quest. On 8 December 2013, he apparently returned to Mingaladon with new sponsors, American firm Claridon Logistics, this time to bore holes into the ground, using a machine that 'cuts through concrete', then to lower a camera down inside. Holes were dug; no evidence of aircraft was found.[77] In 2014, whilst leaving the operations in the hands of his Myanmar partner, a local firm called Shwe Taung Paw, work continued until October 2014, when it was stated that if nothing had been found by that date, then all operations would cease for the foreseeable future. Again, nothing was found. It has remained as such to this day.[78]

Alas, Cundall's story of buried Spitfires appears to be just that: a story. His claims rest on uncheckable evidence and the reported testimony of ageing members of the British armed forces, none of whom set eyes on the crates being buried, let alone set eyes on what they were alleged to contain. This is coupled with the Myanmar survey scan evidence which categorically does not prove the presence of buried aircraft. Cundall, however, will hear none of it and claim the scans do, proclaiming as much to anyone who will listen. With limited space here, I will admit to an oversimplification of the full events. However, for those of you who would like to read more regarding this tale, I highly recommend the book *The Buried Spitfires of Burma: A 'Fake' History* written by Myanmar excavation team members Andy Brockman and Tracy Spaight, where they effectively expose Cundall's somewhat duplicitous nature.[79]

The Drugs Game

The existence of covert aircraft graveyards throughout the drug producing regions of South America is a topic little studied, let alone discussed, for obvious reasons. The fact we know about them at all is, often, purely by accident—a chance discovery by those fighting the cartels and the war on drugs. In the cat and mouse game between the Narcos and the authorities, a distinct methodology can easily be identified. In essence, the cartels purchase an unknown number of aircraft; they fill the aircraft with drugs; they have the aircraft flown to a remote area where, upon landing, they are met by a group of fellow cartels members, often in possession of heavy excavation equipment. The drugs are removed from the aircraft, a large grave is dug, the aircraft is buried within and then covered with earth. During the same time, the authorities are attempting to catch up to the Narcos and intercept said aircraft. An example of this recently played out in northern Belize, in an area called Shipyard, in the Orange Walk district, when the police unearthed the remains of a twin-engine aircraft, a suspected drug plane that they had been following. As Chester Williams, the commissioner of police explained:

> 'We mobilized and deployed our personnel to different possible landing spots across the country. This time around the plane entered our air space just around four a.m. on Sunday morning. It flew over and went north and then it went south and disappeared from the radar . . . the plane shifted and went and landed in this extremely remote area which is not even an air strip - it landed in a farm upon arrival there was no sight of the plane, but we found one excavator, one bulldozer, one tractor. We also observed a huge portion of the soil that appeared to have been freshly disturbed and several debris of what we believe was from a plane. So, we got someone who could operate the equipment, and we dug the soil that was disturbed and came across the plane that was buried . . .'[80]

A similar event occurred in Baja, California, when it was discovered that drug cartels were using a 19km (12mi)-long dry lakebed near the remote town of Todos Santos as a landing strip. Having witnessed a plane overhead late the previous evening and then seen flames rise from the vicinity at sunrise, residents alerted the municipal police to the situation. When they arrived at the site, they were met by a group of men in federal police uniforms who were dismantling, burning and burying a large aircraft, later identified as a Caravelle. Having assured the municipal police that they had the situation under control, they were allowed to continue with their business. Within hours the cargo, thought to be pure cocaine, according to US officials, with a street value at a minimum of $200 million (£148 million), had gone, as had the aircraft, buried in the lakebed, along with the federal officers, who were obviously cartel members. To this day, investigators cannot explain how the jet entered Mexican airspace without detection or diversion by federal authorities.[81]

One of the most disturbing finds occurred in 2024, according to the *LA Times* newspaper, when, during a routine morning patrol along the

Arizona-Mexico border, a retired Drug Enforcement Administration (DEA) agent, James Hawkins, stumbled upon a carefully concealed cartel plane buried in the Sonoran Desert. Expecting to find the usual cargo of drugs or weapons, what he found in the aircraft was evidence of a vast criminal enterprise extending from the Mexican federal government to the halls of Washington, D.C. The discovery of the buried aircraft and its contents would lead to the arrest of two Mexican governors, four US congressmen, dozens of high-ranking officials, and expose a $2 billion (£148 billion) web of deceit, murder for hire, and corruption.[82]

To finish this chapter, I would like to share perhaps one of the most poignant aircraft burials to have taken place in recent memory, that of United Airlines Flight 93, a domestic Boeing 757-222, one of four commercial passenger airliners hijacked by al-Qaeda terrorists as part of the 11 September 2001 terrorist attacks, which killed nearly 3,000 people. Enroute from Newark International Airport in New Jersey to San Francisco International Airport in California, Flight 93 was the last of the four planes to take off, delayed due to air traffic congestion, whilst the other three airliners crashed into the World Trade Center in New York City and the Pentagon in Washington, D.C.[83] After the terrorists took control of the flight, the passengers and crew used their phones to call their loved ones, thereby discovering the fate of the other three planes. Having discussed the situation amongst themselves, and taking a vote, the passengers and crew decided to launch a counteroffensive against the terrorists in an attempt to regain control of the aircraft. One flight attendant, Sandy Bradshaw, even told her husband, over the phone, that she was filing pitchers with boiling water for passengers to throw at the hijackers. The call ended when everyone began running up to the front of the aircraft. From the surviving open line recordings, the voice of one passenger, Todd Beamer, is clearly heard saying ‘Let’s roll’ to the other passengers.[84] Albeit extremely brave, the passengers’ attempts were futile, and Flight 93 crashed into a field in the township of Stonycreek, Somerset County, Pennsylvania, not far from Pittsburgh, killing all thirty-three passengers and seven crew members.

Generating a massive explosion upon impact which burnt for hours, the aircraft had so fragmented that pieces of wreckage were scattered 13km (8mi) from the initial point of impact. A temporary memorial was erected by visitors in the days after the impact, located on a hillside 450m (1,476ft) from the crash site, where visitors could leave flowers, flags, crosses, rosaries and other commemorative items.[85] This was followed by a slew of memorials in the succeeding years, including the official Flight 93 National Memorial, which comprises a visitor centre, a memorial plaza and grove, the 'Wall of Names', where the name of each passenger, and crew, is inscribed together with the 'Towers of Voices', a 28m (93ft) tall structure with forty wind chimes, designed to represent the lasting memory of the voices of the passengers and crew members.[86] Yet little mention is made of the event that occurred on 21 June 2018. For on this day, due to persistent efforts by the Families of Flight 93, the National Park Service (NPS) and the National Park Foundation, the wreckage of Flight 93 was transported by lorry, via a series of four shipping containers, to the crash site. Here, in a small private ceremony, at a restricted access zone on the sacred ground of the Flight 93 National Memorial, the families of the passengers and crew who perished, plus the attending first responders, watched as the remains of the aircraft were lowered into the ground, entombed forever in a purpose-built grave.[87]

Chapter 4

A Watery Burial

One of the largest burial grounds in the world is also the least explored. Water covers more than seventy per cent of the Earth's surface, yet the subject of water graveyards for aircraft is an area of history very little studied, unlike its ship/boat counterpart. This is hardly surprising when you consider that its fluid-like nature often renders the fate of the dead, organic or otherwise, unknown. Apart from 'flying boats', and the deliberate dumping of aircraft into the sea as mentioned in Chapter 3, aircraft are not obviously designed to operate within a water environment. The material makeup of an aircraft and its design are maximized for aerial operation; even the most controlled landing on water can cause catastrophic damage. Additionally, prolonged exposure to water, especially seawater, can be especially harmful, albeit the condition of an aircraft and its components after submersion in water is dependent on several factors. Included in these factors are whether the water was fresh or saltwater, the water depth, the aircraft's materials, the immediate surrounding environment in which the aircraft lies, the amount of dissolved oxygen in the water and so on.

Two factors are key in the formation of an underwater aircraft gravesite: namely the circumstances of the deposition itself and the design and composition of the aircraft. A violent, uncontrolled impact will naturally have a devastating effect, often with the complete destruction of the aircraft. A pilot attempting to ditch on water will have a slower trajectory, short of stalling, which would often cause the tail to hit the water first, possibly resulting in it breaking away.[1] Those aircraft with fixed undercarriages, such as the Japanese torpedo bomber found off the coast of New Britain, Papua New Guinea, are in danger of overturning when they come into contact with water. In deeper water, the weight of the engines on the aircraft's wings can cause the aircraft to invert on descent, whilst single-engine fighters will often descend nose first due to the force of the engine.[2] Propellers, if the aircraft has them, can also offer an insight into the circumstances connected

gure 1: Airmen from the 386th Air Expeditionary Wing give a final salute to C-130E aircraft, a purple ·art recipient, at Ali Al Salem AB, Kuwait. The aircraft had just flown its last combat mission. (USAF ıblic Domain)

gure 2: a) Boneyard - Structured, methodical layout of X24 Stored Lockheed C-5 Galaxy's, David onthan AFB (Aeroprints CC BY-SA 3.0) b) Aircraft Graveyard - Haphazard dumping ground of planes lo Weiss CC BY-SA 4.0)

Figure 3: a) B-29's Awaiting Disposal at Tinian 1946 Public Domain USAAF b) Surplus B-25's, B-26's B-17's at Ontario, California 1946 (Bill Larkins CC BY-SA 2.0)

Figure 4: Fairchild A-10A Thunderbolt in storage at Davis Monthan AFB depicting full Spraylat applicati (Aeroprints CC BY-SA 3.0)

igure 5: Abandoned Albanian fighter jets at Kucove Air Base (Robert Schleiffert CC BY-SA 2.0)

ïgure 6: Zruc Senec Air Park, Czech Republic (Quellenangabe CC BY-SA 2.0)

Figure 7: Buran Space Shuttle Test Article (Clement Vaster CC BY-SA 2.0)

Figure 8: U.S. forces use heavy equipment to pull a MiG-25R Foxbat-B from beneath the sands in Ira
Several MiG-25s and Su-25 jets were found buried at Al-Taqaddum airfield west of Baghdad. (USA
Sergeant T. Collins Public Domain)

igure 9: a) F-14 mothball at Davis Monthan Boneyard in 2007 (A.Shell CC BY-SA 4.0) b) Two years later, 2009, the F-14 is off to the 'Aviation Rainbow Bridge' (USAF Public Domain)

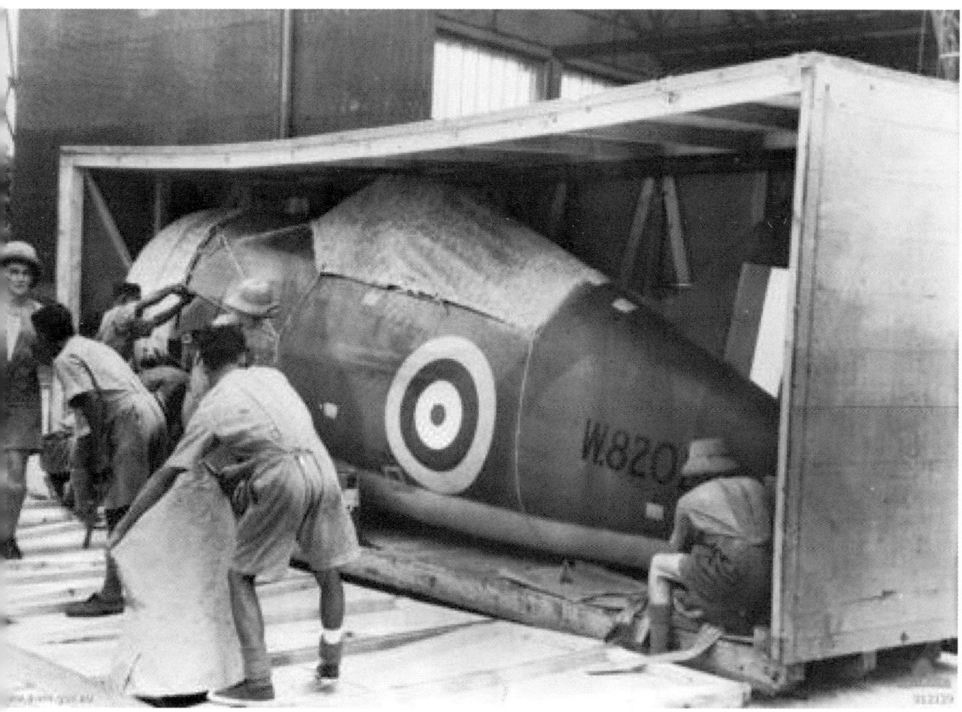

gure 10: Crated Buffalo aircraft being assembled by RAF mechanics in Singapore. Could the so-called urma Spitfires' be buried in similar crates. (Australian War Memorial Public Domain)

Figure 11: Flight 93 Memorial and burial site of the aircraft wreckage (Ron Shawley CC BY-SA 3.0)

Figure 12: a) Wreck of Hawker Hurricane P3179 in Tangmere Aviation Museum (HJ Mitchell CC BY-SA 4.
b) Engine and parts recovered from a North American Mustang III that crashed at RAF Coltishall on 4
July 1945 (Alan Wilson CC By-SA 2.0)

igure 13: Joint Prisoner of War and Missing in Action (POW MIA) Accounting Command (JPAC) unfurl SA flag at site of B-17 Flying Fortress that was shot down during the Second World War (US Department Defense Public Domain)

gure 14: Underwater wreck of Blenheim Bomber, Malta (Photo Courtesy of Mike Peters)

Figure 15: Mitsubishi G4M1 ('Betty') bomber wreck in Truk Lagoon (Clark Anderson CC BY-SA 2.0)

Figure 16: Operation Colony Glacier recovery team members cross glacier ridge looking for debris of 19[illegible] crash site, Alaska (Sgt. Don Hudson, USAF - U.S. Department of Defense, Public Domain)

igure 17: Diagram
llustrating the oceanic pole
f inaccessibility (Timwi
ublic Domain)

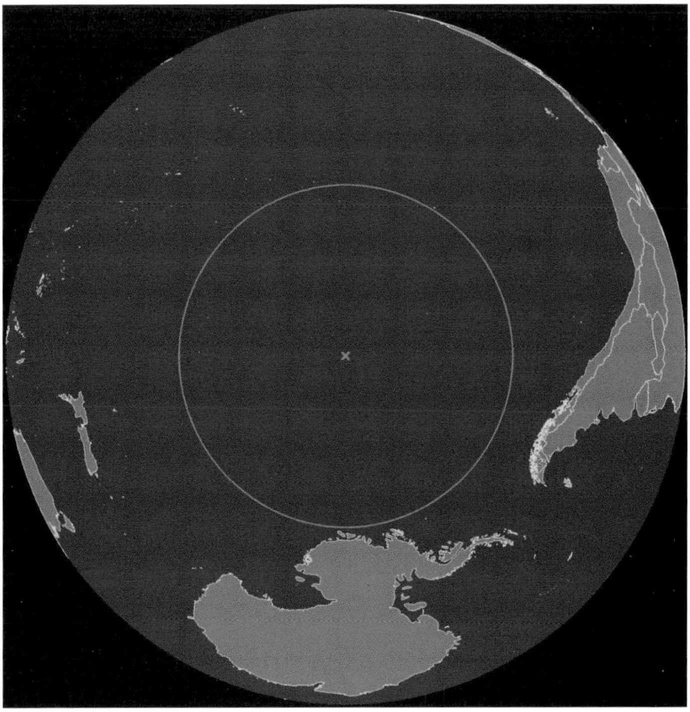

igure 18: Honouring the fallen, Djibouti, Africa May 2011 (Sgt. Dawn M. Price Public Domain)

Figure 19: Wreck site of Vickers Wellington bomber MF509, Carreg Goch, Wales (Image Author's Own)

Figure 20: Memorial to the Torino air disaster at the Basilica di Superga, Torino, Italy (Gianni Carred CC BY-SA 4.0)

gure 21: Soviet Pilots Cemetery, Estonia depicting aircraft tail fins as grave markers (Modris Putnas C BY-SA 3.0)

gure 22: Hindenburg Disaster Memorial, Lakehurst (Paxswill CC BY-SA.3.0)

Figure 23: a) Grave of László Molnár (Heroes Cemetery, Sopronbánfalva, Hungary (Fekist CC BY-SA 3.
b) MiG 15 tail fin grave of Senior Lieutenant Semyon Ivanovich Kharkhalup (Image Courtesy of M. Divovi

Figure 24: Captain Eric Lubbock Memorial, High Elms (Jwslubbock CC BY-SA 3.0)

igure 25: a) Burial of aircraft by artist Roger Hiorns (Sassliek CC BY-SA 3.0) b) The Boneyard Project - ma Open Air Museum (Alan Wilson CC BY-SA 3.0)

gure 26: a) Jumbo Stay Hotel, Stockholm Arlanda Airport (Barnfrend CY BB-SA 4.0) b) Boeing 727 otel Costa Rica (Gotanero CY BB-SA 4.0)

Figure 27: Boeing SB-307B N19904 The Flying Penthouse owned by Howard Hughes (SDASM Archiv
Public Domain)

Figure 28: Planes Plaza, Schiphol International Airport (Donald Trung CC BY-SA 4.0)

igure 29: Random MiG 21 aircraft in someone's front garden, Raduil, Bulgaria (BininGarten CC BY-SA 3.0)

Figure 30: Memorial stone commemorating the demise of JAT Airways Flight 367 in Srbaska Kamenice, Bohemia (Palickap CY BB-SA 3.0)

Figure 31: The Silver Spitfire on display in Japan during its round the world flight (Chang CC BY-SA 4.

Figure 32: Avro Lancaster B.VII NX611 LE-H 'Just Jane' (Alan Wilson CC BY-SA 2.0)

to a gravesite's formation. For example, perfectly straight or near-straight blades can indicate that the engine was not running at the time of ditching; propeller blades that have been bent backwards possibly indicate that the engine was just ticking over, which could indicate a deliberate ditching into the water. Blades which are normally bent forward, or have broken off from the aircraft entirely, suggest an uncontrollable and rapid descent or that the aircraft may have bailed out and struck the water at a shallow angle.[3] Once on the seabed, those areas carrying weight, being often a combination of ferrous metals and aluminium, are especially susceptible to galvanic corrosion. This can lead to parts, such as the engines, falling away from aircraft due to a lack of support from the underwater bottom. Interestingly, it has been shown that a combination of an aircraft's lower profile, compared to that of a sea/water vessel, and the direct environment, such as deep sand banks, can offer remarkable preservation qualities, as shown in the Dornier M17 recovered from Goodwin Sands by the RAF Museum in 2013. It had been submerged for over seventy years yet was still remarkably intact.[4] A deeper burial also mitigates the destructive effects of fishing nets and trawling lines upon sunken aircraft. The second factor to consider is the makeup of the aircraft, which can have a substantial effect upon their resistance to corrosion; for example, those aircraft deployed to aircraft carriers were built to have more protection against the salty sea air, namely in the addition of corrosive-resistant paint or with the bonding of pure aluminium onto duralumin alloys.[5]

What now follows is an exploration of several worldwide aviation underwater gravesites, many of which exhibit unique environmental conditions. We first begin with the waters around Malta, a small cluster of islands located just 80km (50mi) south of Italy, which is a rich site for underwater aviation burials, due to the role it played during the Second World War. During this time, it became an area of great strategic importance for the Allied effort, both as a fortress for their military campaigns in North Africa, and as a base from which to launch their mapped-out invasion of mainland Italy. After the fall of Crete in June 1941, the islands of Malta were the only prevalent Allied presence between Alexandria, on the Mediterranean shores of northern Egypt, and the Straits of Gibraltar, in the west.[6] At the outbreak of hostilities in the area, Malta's air force, if you can call it that, was virtually non-existent, consisting of just four ageing Gloster Gladiator biplanes. Albeit after intense modifications, such as the addition of armour plating, replacing the two bladed propellor with a three bladed alternative, and swapping out the Mercury XI engine for a Blenheim Mercury XV version, these ageing aircraft were considered superior in performance to that of the first Hurricanes to arrive on the island.[7] Despite concerns that Malta, far from Britain and close to Italy, could not be defended, in July 1939 the British decided to increase the number of anti-aircraft guns and fighter aircraft on Malta. By July 1943, Malta had become the base for more than 600 Allied fighters and bombers, subjecting it to a consistent aerial bombardment between June 1940 and November 1942, the so-called *Siege of Malta*. It is estimated that some 6,700 tonnes (7,385 tons) of bombs were dropped on the island, and surrounding seas, by Axis forces over a 154-day period. For a period in 1942, Malta was the most heavily bombed place on Earth, receiving a higher tonnage weight of bombs in March and April 1942 than London did in a twelve-month period, a timeframe that includes the Blitz.[8]

It is nigh-on impossible to fully quantify just how many aircraft crashed into the vast seascape surrounding the Maltese island chain. For Axis aircraft, estimates vary from 1,252 to 860, whilst for the Allies, estimates range from 840 aircraft lost to 707. Evidence suggests that Axis aircraft that came down over Malta usually did so due to being shot down and thus sustained significant damage. This, combined with the velocity in which they plummeted into the water, means that the chances of finding any intact Axis aircraft in the immediate waters around Malta are slight. However, for Allied aircraft, the situation is somewhat reversed, with those damaged in the skies above Italy or Malta undertaking an often-slower ditching into the sea. This goes some way to explaining the higher concentration of intact Allied aircraft wrecks found in Maltese waters.[9]

A number of these aircraft wreck sites are today under the protection of Heritage Malta's Underwater Cultural Heritage Unit, preserved in situ and recorded in minute detail, with the aim of protecting their structural integrity and their authenticity as historical sites.[10] Albeit this was not always the case. Three Second World War plane wrecks are of particular interest. The first is a German Junkers Ju 88 (1941), an aircraft that the

Luftwaffe relied on to inflict devastation upon the Maltese archipelago, particularly during the Siege of Malta, with 200 bombers attacking in waves ranging from 5 to 30 aircraft, the vast majority of which were Ju 88s. This Ju 88 aircraft was discovered in 2019, by a remote-sensing survey carried out by the University of Malta. The wreck sits at a depth of 106m (348ft), lying upright on the sandy seabed, approximately 6.9km (3.75 nautical mi) northwest of Marsaskala, a seaside town in the southern region of Malta, and is in rather good condition, with little damage to the glass nose and signs of damage to the port tail, which points to it being shot up from the rear, possibly in a dog fight with an Allied fighter.[11] How it came to reside in its final resting place is somewhat uncertain. On 1 January 1941, a Ju 88 is recorded as having crashed just offshore from Marsaskala Bay, resulting in the loss of its three-member crew. However, whether this is the same Ju 88 is indeterminate, especially as no human remains were uncovered during the 2019 survey. Although it is entirely possible that the crew ditched the plane upon hitting the waters, the aircraft drifted and subsequently sank a distance away from the initial impact point.[12]

In 2014, another wreck site was discovered by the University of Malta, utilizing the same remote-sensing, this time a Douglas A-1 Skyraider, designed by Ed Heinemann of the Douglas Aircraft Company.[13] Although the Skyraider played no part in the Second World War per se, it did feature in other military conflicts, including both the Korean and Vietnam wars. This particular model, serial code 09236, was part of the aircraft carrier USS *Midway's* air wing group, one squadron of which was composed of four Douglas A-1 Skyraiders, tasked with carrying mail between the USS *Midway* and the Royal Air Force Hal Far Airfield, the first permanent airfield to be built on Malta.[14] In December 1947, having just taken off from the Hal Far Airfield, the Skyraider suffered a total engine failure, and began deviating towards Bir˙zebbu˙gia, located approximately 13km (8mi) from the capital, Valletta, before it fell from the sky and struck the sea at an estimated speed of 75 to 90 knots (86 to 103mph). Hitting the water at a slight angle with the wheels and flaps up, the Skyraider floated for just a couple of minutes before sinking beneath the surface. The pilot, Lieutenant Robert H. L. Reeb, was fortunate to escape the sinking craft just in time before being rescued by a Sikorsky HO3S Dragonfly helicopter that had been dispatched by the USS *Midway*.[15] This was the first recorded account of a helicopter rescue in the Mediterranean. Today, the Skyraider's remains sit on the bottom of the sea floor and are in excellent condition, with the main fuselage, wings, tail, cockpit, nose, and propeller all intact.

The B24 Liberator has an unmistakable place in the history of American aircraft. An advanced heavy bomber designed by Consolidated Aircraft in San Diego, it's known for its size, versatility, and remarkable wartime service. One of the most historic missions undertaken by the B24 in the Second World War was during the bombing of Reggio Calabria in Italy in May 1943. Two waves of B-24s, totalling fifty aircraft, conducted a series of aerial raids targeting the Italian harbour, dropping 100 metric tonnes (110 tons) of bombs, causing extensive damage throughout.[16] Unfortunately, one of the B-24s developed engine trouble whilst conducting a raid and was forced to jettison its bomb load and head for the safety of Malta. Having attempted to land in Luqa, a small town in southern Malta, and failed, the pilot and crew were forced to ditch the plane into the waters below, where the aircraft overturned and sank beneath the surface. Nine members of a ten-man crew were rescued by the Royal Air Force, with one crew member lost.[17] According to a 2015 survey of the Liberator, it sits on the seafloor at a depth of 56m (184ft):

'It lies on a sandy seabed approximately a mile southwest of the traditional fishing village of Marsaxlokk. On its way to the seabed, the B-24 turned right side up, and on impact, one propeller detached itself. The visible part of the wreck is approximately 80 per cent intact, projecting prominently from the seabed. The entire wing structure is in exceptionally good state of preservation. The nose is destroyed, with the cockpit torn open, and the tail has collapsed under the main fuselage.'[18]

As part of protecting the integrity of Malta's rich aviation underwater graveyard, Heritage Malta has launched a virtual underwater museum entitled, rather imaginatively, 'Underwater Malta'. Through the creation of high-tech digital records, utilizing specialized high-resolution cameras that produce images for 3D conversion, the public can explore the wrecks for themselves using virtual-reality models with 360-degree rotation and zoom options. There are seventeen different sites, including the three aircraft featured above, whereby the viewer can read more information about this particular wreck, as well as watch videos of the dives and exploratory archaeological excavations.[19] Other aircraft resting in this remarkable graveyard include a Hawker Hurricane, which was discovered as part of the Malta Shipwreck Survey Project in 2020, and currently rests upright on the seafloor at a depth of 70m (230ft). There is also a wreck of a Supermarine Spitfire, which was discovered during a side-scan sonar survey in April 2021, just off the coast of Gozo, and is linked to Operation Husky, the Allied invasion of Sicily, Italy (10 July–17 August 1943). The aircraft is located upright on a sandy seabed at a depth of 70m (230ft), the rear fuselage folded forward as the aircraft ditched into the sea, and the tail can be seen upside down, just behind the port wing. The collapse of the rear fuselage suggests that the crash was somewhat violent. The propeller blades were made from wood, and these disintegrated upon impact. Sadly, the pilot was killed and remains missing. A Stuka Ju87, a German dive-bomber and ground-attack aircraft that formed a crucial part of Axis air-ground offensive tactics, was discovered in 2015 off the north-east coast of Malta during another planned Malta Shipwreck Survey Project, and can be viewed on the virtual-reality site; albeit the aircraft is badly damaged, and seems to have hit the water at an extremely fast rate. Located at a depth of 100m (328ft), iconic Stuka features, however, can be clearly seen, such as the empennage and the 'double-ended' glass canopy. Sadly, the whereabouts of the crew are unknown to this day. The site was also the subject of a National Geographic documentary entitled *Buried Secrets of World War II*. One of the most unique aircraft wrecks on 'Underwater Malta' is the Fairey Swordfish, a biplane torpedo bomber, developed by the Fairey Aviation Company in the early 1930s. The remains are located off the coast of Sliema, in eastern Malta, and are the result of catastrophic engine failure, whereby the pilot was forced to ditch the aircraft into the sea. The Swordfish now lies at a depth of 70m (230ft), with its position indicating a controlled ditch.[20] Only the steel skeleton remains, along with the engine, propeller and cowling, have survived intact. Only thirteen Fairey Swordfish exist today, so this wreck is of global significance.

As with its Mediterranean counterpart, the seas around Orkney, and Shetland to the north, were vitally important during both world wars. Orkney, an archipelago of around seventy islands located just off the northern coast of Scotland, is home to Scapa Flow, a large 312sq km (120sq mi) body of water, that forms a natural harbour with the Orkney mainland on one side and the islands of Graemsay, South Ronaldsay and Hoy on the other. It is arguably one of the most captivating bodies of water for those with an interest in all things military. Although the seas are predominantly connected to an inordinate volume of shipwrecks, after all, it was here, in June 1919, shortly after the end of the First World War, that the Imperial German Navy's High Seas Fleet was scuttled by its sailors whilst being held at Scapa Flow. It is also the site where the battleship HMS *Royal Oak* was regrettably sunk by a German U-boat, U-47, which had successfully slipped past the blockships and other defences guarding Scapa Flow. Nonetheless, it must never be forgotten that these waters have also become a perpetual mausoleum for many aircraft. During the Second World War, Orkney was a critical strategic location for defending the Scapa Flow naval base and beyond, operating four main airfields: RNAS Hatston (HMS *Sparrowhawk*), RNAS Twatt (HMS *Tern*), RAF Skeabrae, and RAF Grimsetter (HMS *Robin*). These bases hosted fighter squadrons, anti-submarine patrols, and carrier-based aircraft, playing a vital role in protecting the home fleet.

Unlike its Mediterranean counterpart, however, aircraft wrecks lying in the treacherous seas of the North are not so easily discernible. For example, the Spitfire wreck I am working on as of this writing, from Scapa Flow, just resembles a tangled mess of pipework. No propellor, no wings, just crumpled metallic leftovers. So, how are such wrecks found, you ask? In truth, much relies on local knowledge, combined with good fortune. What follows is the remarkable discovery and identification of an unknown Hawker Hurricane aircraft, carried out by Sula Diving (A.R.G.O.S.) in 2018. The full report, entitled *Investigation of Aircraft Wreckage, Scapa Flow, Orkney*, by Kevin Heath, can be viewed in full, including images, on the A.R.G.O.S. website.

In the summer of 2018, MV *Birsay Boy*, a fishing vessel operating in Scapa Flow, Orkney, recovered two artefacts from the seabed that appeared to be aircraft wreckage. The most significant of the two finds was an engine, which the fishing vessel returned to the seabed, and an aluminium tank, which was handed to my colleague Kevin Heath at SULA

Diving for A.R.G.O.S. Said artefact appeared to be an aircraft fuel tank, similar in construction to that installed in the wing of an aircraft. The approximate locations where each item was recovered, as well as the exact location of where the engine was returned to the seabed, can be seen in the official full report on the A.R.G.O.S website at www.crashsiteorkney.com. Funding from Historic Environment Scotland, with support from the JCCS/MoD, were obtained to carry out further investigations. These included a full side scan sonar survey, carried out on 1 February 2019, in the area where the engine was initially recovered, a drop camera survey, on both wreckage sites, conducted on 2 April 2019, and a dive survey, carried out on the same day.

The dive survey focussed only on the engine in its present location, just east of the Barrel of Butter (see report). The engine was found lying on its side, and on closer inspection was found to be a badly degraded 12-cylinder Rolls Royce Merlin engine, fitted with a three-bladed propeller. Of the original twelve cylinders, only eleven remained, the aluminium alloy cylinder block had completely corroded away. Some cylinder head bolts were still in place; the crankshaft was intact and all twelve connecting rods survived. Only one badly corroded propeller blade remained. Behind the propeller, the airscrew reduction gear was intact, as was the vacuum pump suction and the constant-speed airscrew governor unit. One-third of the aluminium crankcase casing was also present, but very corroded. From the initial description provided by the fisherman, it was initially thought that the engine was a Merlin engine, matching the type found in the Fairey Barracuda, one of which was reported to have ditched to the east of the Barrel of Butter in 1944. However, the dive survey showed that the engine had a three-bladed propeller, which discounted the Barracuda, as by 1944 this type of aircraft was fitted with the Merlin 32 engine that had a four-bladed propeller.

A small piece of the aircraft's fuselage, the starboard forward mounts for the engine, were still attached to the engine. The mounts comprise two plates made from stainless steel that bolt together through the tubular frame to make a joint. These specific components are often stamped with part numbers that would indicate the type of aircraft on which they were used, in effect the 'holy grail' for any aviation archaeologist. Remarkably, on 2nd May 2019, volunteer diver Lieutenant Jen Smith from the Royal Navy, diving from local dive boat MV *Jean Elaine*, provided evidence that the engine mounts were stamped with the numbers '72422,' which were preceded by a faint inverted 'v.' Above them was a small oval stamp, which contained the characters 'CCF 53'.

Research into the serial numbers/characters stamped on the engine mount bracket found that CCF was the stamp for Canadian Car & Foundry, a manufacturer of buses, railroad stock and, later, aircraft. The only aircraft built by CCF using Rolls Royce Merlin engines was the Hawker Hurricane aircraft, because of a contract made with the Royal Air Force in 1939, just before the outbreak of the Second World War. Over 1400 of these aircraft were built in Canada at the company's factories in Fort William, Ontario, and Montreal. Further investigation, including a discussion with Ray Polidano of the Malta Aviation Museum, found that the serial number was most likely A72422 (just the top of the "A" on the Scapa Flow engine was discernible), used to identify the "side outer starboard joint", according to p. 394 of the *Hawker Hurricane Parts Manual.* The page is titled "Power Unit Engine Mounting Mk I" (Appendix 1). The same component and part number are also used for Mk II Hurricanes. This identification was further confirmed by examination of the Hurricane aircraft exhibited by the Malta Aviation Museum (serial Z3055), which was recovered from the sea off Malta in 1993. The same component was present and stamped with "A72422". The evidence collected during the dive surveys therefore suggests that the engine is a Rolls Royce V12 Merlin engine that was fitted to a Canadian built Hawker Hurricane Mk I.

It is unlikely, although not impossible, that the aircraft belonged to the RAF. It is more likely that the aircraft is a Sea Hurricane, belonging to the Royal Navy Fleet Air Arm (FAA), which was unfortunately lost at sea due to some kind of incident, or deliberately dumped from an aircraft carrier. In his book *Fleet Air Arm Aircraft, 1939 to 1945* (1995), which has become my bible, author Ray Sturtivant lists the serial numbers and fate of all the aircraft used by the FAA. Sixteen Hurricanes were recorded as "Cat Z" (destroyed or lost) due to carrier accidents and these serial numbers were checked against a list of all Canadian-built Hurricanes. Eleven were discounted immediately, as the designated aircraft carrier was known not to be in Orkney waters at the time or were not built by CCF. Of the remaining five aircraft, one was discounted as lost off a land base, RNAS Machrihanish (HMS *Landrail*), at Campbelltown, Argyll and Bute. The remaining four aircraft were lost off two aircraft carriers, three off HMS *Argus* and one off HMS *Biter*. The logbooks for the two aircraft carriers were obtained to establish exactly where they were operating on the dates the aircraft were lost. Only one, HMS Biter, confirmed that a Hurricane AF963 was lost in Scapa Flow, the entry stating that the Hurricane was lost at a position 1.6 nautical miles from the Barrel of Butter on a bearing of 080°. True north was used for the purposes of this project; thus, the estimated position where Hurricane AF963 was lost occurred approximately 0.5 nautical miles away from the position where the engine was recovered, a relatively small distance from where she initially went into the water.

Regarding the aluminium tank, recovered in fishing gear north of the Calf of Flotta, research is currently ongoing. By its construction and shape, it is most likely to be an aircraft fuel tank, possibly sited in the wing. There were no immediate identifying marks or any maker's plates. The only fixture that was not aluminium was the small brass fitting for the fuel line. The only aircraft known to have crashed in this area is a Blackburn Skua L2883 of 771 Squadron, but this wreckage was reportedly recovered by Metal Industries in the days following the crash. Moreover, the fuel tank does not match Skua fuel tanks. Other aircraft known to have crashed in Scapa Flow were thoroughly researched, but no obvious matches for the fuel tank was found. Further discoveries regarding this fuel tank will be made public via the A.R.G.O.S website (www.crashsiteorkney.com).

As shown in the report above, unlike the seas surrounding Malta, and the remarkable examples within the Pacific, which will be discussed next, discoveries around the United Kingdom's northern seas, and further north are, often, purely coincidental, a chance lucky find by passing fishing trawlers. Entanglements with fishing gear and anchoring activity often result in wreckage being dispersed over wide distances across the seabed, and nowhere near the original point of entry. That's if said fishing boats report such incidences in the first instance. One must also consider previous salvage activity, primarily by divers. I am very fortunate that my fellow A.R.G.O.S. colleague, Kevin Heath, has amassed numerous contacts within both fields over the past thirty years, and is deemed the 'go to person' when it comes to aircraft/shipwrecks within this defined location.

Pacific Region Graveyard Sites

During the Second World War, the Pacific theatre of operations witnessed many air-naval battles, the remains of which now rest on the bottom of the sea. Chuuk Lagoon, also known as Truk Lagoon, a sheltered body of water within the eastern Caroline Islands, around 1,800km (1,100mi) north-east of New Guinea, is one such place. A constituent member of the 'Federated States of Micronesia', it consists of a series of low coral islands, surrounded by a protective reef, and in many ways it is the true definition of what many would deem a tropical paradise, with clear blue-turquoise seas and a vast array of marine life, such as sharks, manta rays, turtles and so on. However, if you look a little closer into the watery depths, at times only 15m (49ft) below the waves, your eyes will zero in on one of the world's largest underwater graveyards in the South Pacific.

At the start of the war, Chuuk Lagoon was Japan's main base of operations in the South Pacific region. Its location in the central Pacific made it an ideal staging and supply point for Japanese naval and air operations across a vast area, including critical campaigns in Southeast Asia and the South Pacific. It offered a perfect natural harbour to protect the Imperial fleet against Allied attack, who were operating in New Guinea and the nearby Solomon Islands, and allowed the Japanese Civil Engineering Department, together with the Naval Construction Department, to heavily fortify the surrounding ground, including the construction of roads, trenches, bunkers, five airstrips, a seaplane bass and a torpedo boat station, making it a formidable naval fortress, ideal for housing a significant portion of the Japanese Combined Fleet.[21]

Understandably such a frenzy of activity caught the attention of Allied forces, and recognizing Chuuk Lagoon's importance to the Japanese war effort, the United States launched a massive surprise attack. Codenamed Operation Hailstone, on the morning of 17 February 1944, American forces unleashed an assault on the Japanese base, employing five fleet carriers, seven battleships, submarines, destroyers and over 500 aircraft. In the midst of a bombardment from submarine, surface and air attacks, which lasted a full two days, more than sixty Japanese warships ended up on the floor of the lagoon, as did over 250 Japanese aircraft, many of which had just arrived from Japanese factories and had not yet been fully assembled. Tragically, most of the crew members also perished, sinking with their respective ships and aircraft.[22]

Over the following decades, the events at Chuuk Lagoon were largely forgotten, until the summer of 1971, when the wreck site became the subject of a major TV documentary, filmed by underwater adventurer Jacques Cousteau, entitled *Lagoon of the Lost Ships*. As Cousteau explored the wrecks, to his dismay he discovered that many still contained the corpses of Japanese sailors. Understandably, the public were horrified, and, consequently, the Japanese Government immediately began a recovery timetable, whereby large numbers of bodies were removed and returned to Japan for a formal burial.[23] Today, not only is Chuuk Lagoon regarded as one of the world's most extraordinary wreck-diving locations—after all the lagoon floor is a veritable underwater museum—but also a place of historical reflection and commemoration. The remains of hundreds of Japanese servicemen still lay entombed in the wreckage, and the site is now recognized as an official Japanese war grave.

Another aircraft graveyard, which receives a lot of attention, is sited in the Kwajalein atoll, a coral formation in the Ralik (western) chain of the Republic of the Marshall Islands, in the west-central Pacific Ocean. The string of some ninety islets has a total land area of 16sq km (6sq mi) and surrounds the world's largest lagoon, stretching some 1,722sq km (655sq mi). The area was, once again, a significant base of operations for the Imperial Japanese fleet during the Second World War, with a force of approximately 5,000 Japanese servicemen.[24] As part of the effort to win control of this crucial gateway to the Japanese empire, the United States decided to launch an offensive, commencing on 31 December 1944, consisting of 46,000 US soldiers. Three landing forces assaulted the islands. The Northern Attack Force led the attack on Roi-Namur Island; the Southern Attack Force led the attack on Kwajalein, whilst the Majuro Attack Group quickly discovered, upon landing, that the Japanese departed the island in November 1942! Both Kwajalein and Roi-Namur Island

Atolls were secured by 7 February, with 'mopping-up' operations lasting until a few days later. The 'Battle of Kwajalein', as it is referred to, was an overwhelming victory for the Americans, reportedly only 153 Japanese soldiers survived the onslaught.[25]

Interestingly, although a few aircraft did sink into the lagoon, this is not the reason as to why said atoll has become celebrated. After the Second World War, rather than ship surplus aircraft back to the United States, the authorities decided it was cheaper just to dump said aircraft into the sea. So, in September 1945, the United States Navy began disposing of approximately 150 military aircraft by throwing them overboard into the waters of the Kwajalein atoll. The list of unfortunate aircraft that were dumped into the sea include Chance Vought F4U Corsairs and Grumman F4F Wildcats fighters, Douglas SBD Dauntless dive bombers and Curtiss SB2C Helldivers, naval bombers Grumman TBF Avengers, eleven patrol bombers North American PBJ-1 Mitchells (the naval version of the B-25) and transport aircrafts Curtiss C-46 Commandos.[26] Brandi Mueller, a photographer, writer and Merchant Mariner licensed by the US Coast Guard captured some incredible photos of the sunken aircraft. Encrusted in coral, these nostalgic aircraft are now home to a colourful array of tropical Pacific marine life. 'They call it the "Airplane Graveyard" – they aren't war graves or planes that crashed. They were planes that were taken out over the reef and pushed off intact after the war ended', said Mueller, 'They should have flown more, lived longer, but they were sunk in perfect condition.'[27] The Kwajalein atoll is thus recognized as one of the largest aircraft graveyards of the Second World War.

Polar Region Graveyard Sites

In the summer of 2018, Latvian construction company, SPH Engineering, joined forces with non-profit organization Arctic Hot Point Solutions, led by Jim Salazar, Ken McBride, and the Fallen American MIA Repatriation Foundation in an expedition to Greenland, in search of several Second World War aircraft that had been originally abandoned on top of a glacier. Having been subject to over seventy-five years of Greenland's ever-shifting icesheets, however, the aircraft were now buried under approximately

100m (328ft) of ice. The aircraft in question, often referred to as the 'Lost Squadron', were six Lockheed P-38 Lightning fighter planes and two B-17 bombers that had left a US Army base in Greenland on 15 July 1942 to assist British forces. On that fateful day, due to adverse blizzard conditions, the entire squadron were forced to make an emergency landing on the glacier. Although all the crew members were rescued, nine days later, the aircraft were left behind.[28]

This was not the first group of intrepid explorers to go looking for the missing aircraft. In 1992, after years of searching and excavating, members of the Greenland Expedition Society, led by Project Manager Bob Cardin, successfully extracted one of the P-38s from the ice. They named her 'Glacier Girl'; her discovery is documented in an episode of the History Channel's *Mega Movers* series, titled *Extreme Aircraft Recovery*; and remarkably, she has now been restored to flying condition. Why, on 22 June 2007, Glacier Girl even made an attempt to fly across the Atlantic Ocean to Duxford, England, to complete the flight it had begun sixty-five years earlier. Sadly, however, a coolant leak in the number two (right) engine grounded the plane in Goose Bay, Labrador, and she never made it to Duxford.[29]

It now appears that this new search effort, led by Arctic Hot Point Solutions, has pinpointed the location of another P-38 aircraft, believed to be 'Echo', piloted by Lt. Col. Robert Wilson. Wilson's P-38 was the first to land wheels up after the first P-38, piloted by Brad McManus, flipped over when the front gear penetrated the ice on roll out and collapsed.[30] Hints of the aircraft were first detected in 2011 as the team combed the area with radar to search for objects under the ice. But it wasn't until 2018 that their efforts were rewarded. Initially the expedition team split up into two groups. The first began the search for the aircraft using an integrated ground penetrating radar (GPR) drone system, developed by SPH Engineering, which provides a fully automated surveillance of the glacier and precise location determination even in areas inaccessible or difficult to access for humans. In effect, it is very efficient at locating objects deep under the ice. Data from the system indicated that there was an object buried under more than 90m (295ft) of ice. The second group used a GPR antenna mounted on a sled, which produced very similar results, the comparable distance between the determined locations registered just 3m (10ft):[31]

> 'The search grid was established with the target point as the centre, and within one day, both of our radar teams located a substantial object approximately 64m (70 yards) from our target point. The radar data does not indicate what the target is, only that a substantial object reflected the radar signal back to the surface.'

Once the potential aircraft was detected, the search team used a heat probe, driven by a hot pressure washer system, to tunnel through the ice to touch the aircraft and confirm that it was indeed a plane. The steam probing operation required the full crew to melt snow, keep the filters clean, feed the generator and high-pressure pump motor with fuel, in addition to keeping the boiler running.

'Believe it or not, producing water on the ice cap can be a challenging proposition. Even though there is an unlimited amount of "water" there, melting enough snow to feed our steam probe for an excursion of more than 350′ down in the ice, uses a lot of water.'

Boring down the first two holes produced little results, but on the third, the probe stalled for a moment, before continuing. When the hose and probe were retrieved, from a depth of 104m (341ft), the team were surprised to find the end coated in a red-coloured oil, identified as 5606 hydraulic fluids used in US aviation, a sign that the object was indeed one of the missing P-38s: 'We pulled it up, and boy it was pretty dense, all over the place—our jackets, on the floor, all over our hands, and it was quite a surprise,' stated Jim Salazar, co-founder of Arctic Hot Point Solutions.[32] As of May 2025, the P-38 'Echo' has not been recovered, but future expeditions and attempts at extraction are planned for the summer.

In the heart of Europe too, as the effects of global warming gradually strip away the icy shroud of the land, a wide variety of aircraft are slowly resurfacing from the glacial waters, battered and torn. One such aircraft is a B-17 Flying Fortress, which began to emerge from the Eyjafjallajökull Glacier in southern Iceland in 2023. Some of you may recall the name Eyjafjallajökull, as this glacier is sited in the same location as the volcano that erupted in 2010, which unleashed a massive ash cloud into the atmosphere, disrupting European aviation for weeks. On 16 September 1944, the B-17 bomber had embarked on a departure from Meeks Field

(Keflavik Airport, Iceland) en route to England when it faced adverse weather conditions, forcing it to deviate from its intended course. Amidst turbulent weather and icing, the plane encountered a sudden downdraft and ultimately collided with Mt. Eyjafjallajökull, before coming to rest against a snowbank.[33]

Because of the collision, one of the plane's wings was violently ripped off, and the engines quickly ignited. Thankfully, all ten crew members managed to escape the carnage unharmed, and hid behind some adjacent rocks, waiting for the flames to subside. After which they re-entered the aircraft to salvage any remaining emergency flares to signal their presence, sadly to no avail. After two days waiting by the wrecked craft, they decided to climb down the glacier, a perilous journey by anyone's standards, avoiding crevasse and steep cliffs, tethered together by a line of parachutes. Having reached lower ground unscathed, after a thirteen-hour trek, all ten crew members embarked on crossing the Markarfljót River; six of the crew arrived in the town of Fljótsdalur, whilst the remaining four spent a very cold night outdoors. They were rescued by residents the following day. By the end of September, the US authorities had organized two salvage expeditions to the glacier. The first successfully reached the plane wreck, retrieving important documents etc., whilst the second group had to abort their mission due to the treacherous conditions, thus leaving the remains of the plane behind, which over time became engulfed by the glacier. It wasn't until 1996 that the USAF finally disclosed details of the crash.[34]

Climate change is having a devastating effect on the world's glaciers, especially in landlocked Switzerland, for example, where temperatures are rising much faster compared to those countries who benefit from the ocean's cooling effect. Since 1850 the Swiss glaciers have lost 60 per cent of their volume, with over 500 Swiss glaciers vanishing completely. As a consequence, objects once hidden from sight are now emerging as the ice retreats.[35] For example, in 2012, during a particularly hot Swiss summer, a US military transport plane, namely a C-53 Skytrooper, was found by three teenage hikers on the Gauli Glacier, located in the Bernese Alps, in western Switzerland.[36] Often referred to as a 'Dakota', the aircraft was flying from Austria to Italy in the winter of 1946, when the pilots became disoriented due to a snowstorm, and veered off course. Mistakenly believing they were in the French Alps, and not the Swiss, and having already avoided several mountain peaks, the plane suddenly experienced a violent downdraft, plunging the aircraft towards yet another mountain peak. In a brave move, the pilots dropped the plane from an altitude of approximately 3,353m (11,000ft), belly-flopping the fuselage onto the Gauli Glacier. It slid for a considerable time before hitting a snowbank, which caught the wing and fortunately kept the aircraft from plunging into a deep crevasse. All twelve people on board survived the impact. The only serious injury among the passengers was a compound fracture to the leg, and they were rescued five days later by the Swiss military, who sent eighty experienced mountaineers to the wreck site. The Dakota, however, was never recovered at the time, eventually buried by decades of glacial ice.[37]

Similarly, in 2022, the wreckage of a plane that crashed in the Swiss Alps in 1968 was discovered by a mountain guide on the Aletsch glacier, south-west of the Valais, near the peaks of Jungfrau and Monch.[38] 'Investigations have determined that the parts are from the wreckage of a Piper Cherokee, registration HB-OYL, which crashed at this location on 30 June 1968. Recovery work will be undertaken as soon as possible,' said a police statement. The passengers, a teacher, a doctor and his son, perished in the crash, and their bodies were recovered at the time, but not the wreckage, which was eventually engulfed by the glacier, and thus became hidden. 'At the time of the accident, more than fifty years ago, the technical means to recover aircraft wreckage in difficult terrain were limited,' the police explained. Due to the melting of the glaciers, particularly in summer, it is possible that other pieces of wreckage will soon be released from their icy tomb.[39] Whilst in 2020, a manager of a mountain hut found several newspapers on the retreating Bossons Glacier, located in the Mont Blanc massif, believed to have come from an Air India Boeing 707, which crashed above Chamonix, a commune in France. Dated 20 and 21 January 1966, they include copies of the Indian newspapers the *National Herald* and *The Economic Times*.[40] In fact, over the past fifteen years, a number of items from the crashed plane have been revealed by melting glacial ice, including another assembly of Indian newspapers, dated 23 January 1966, found by a climber in 2008; a diplomatic bag, upon which was stamped 'On Indian Government Service, Diplomatic Mail, Ministry of External Affairs', recovered by a mountain rescue worker in 2012; and a metal box containing a selection of precious stones, including sapphires, emeralds and rubies, worth between $158,000 to $312,500 (£117,000 to £230,000), discovered by a mountaineer in 2013.[41]

Alaska is one of the most heavily glaciated areas in the world outside of the polar regions. Approximately 59,570sq km (23,000sq mi) of the state are covered in glaciers—an area nearly the size of West Virginia. Glaciers have shaped much of Alaska's landscape and continue to influence its lands, waters and ecosystems. This remarkable climate and terrain, however, has contributed to numerous aircraft disappearances over the years, with many believed to have been buried in the glacial system. Now, because of climate change, scientists measuring the glaciers have discovered that they are shrinking in area, at an alarming rate. In fact, from 1985 to 2020, glacier-covered area in Alaska decreased by thirteen per cent.[42] This significant melting of the glacial ice has led to a significant discovery of both aircraft wreckage and remains.

Perhaps the most notable of these was the finding of a missing Douglas C-124 Globemaster II, which had crashed into Mount Gannett in 1952, killing all fifty-two US military service members onboard.[43] The wreckage, including a survival raft, was spotted by an Alaskan National Guard UH-60 Black Hawk crew in 2012, who were conducting routine training on the Colony Glacier, located in the Chugach Mountain range. The aircraft had originally departed from McChord Air Force Base in Tacoma, Washington, early on 22 November 1952, but never made it to its destination, Elmendorf Air Force Base. It was the third big Air Force transport plane to crash or vanish in Alaska that month. On the day of the crash, the weather was severe, with dense fog and swirling snow obscuring visibility, forcing the pilot to resort to an instrument approach to Anchorage. But with only a radio beacon receiver and stopwatch, for example, to navigate well, less than 97km (60mi) from its destination, the C-124 crashed into the side of Mount Gannett.[44]

Six days passed before a search team could survey the site of the crash; a twelve-member military team had tried three times previously but was thwarted by bad weather. When the site was eventually found, some 2.4m (8ft) of fresh snow covered the wreckage; the impact of the crash is thought to have triggered an avalanche that further entombed the debris. Over time, the wreckage slowly tumbled down the mountain, eventually freezing within the icy waters of the nearby Colony Glacier.[45] Every summer since its re-discovery in 2012, service members and civilians have searched the area in an effort to find the remains of the crash victims, identify them and bring them home. In what is officially called Operation Colony Glacier, in 2014, the US Department of Defense announced that seventeen of the lost service members had been identified and would be returned to their families for burial, with full military honours. By June 2017, the number of those identified was thirty-seven. As of June 2022, the operation's tenth anniversary, forty-four of the fifty-two service members had been recovered and identified. A unique video of the operation has been released by the US Department of Defense.[46]

Remarkably, only two weeks before the crash of the C-142, on 7 November 1952, a team of US Air Force and US Army service members were performing a routine training flight, known as Warm Wind, when their plane, a C-119 Flying Boxcar, crashed into Mount Silverthrone in the Denali mountain range, at an elevation of roughly 3.658m (12,000ft). All nineteen military personnel on board perished. Known by its radio call sign, Gamble Chalk 1, its intended flight path was to travel from Elmendorf Air Force Base in Anchorage to the Big Delta Army Airfield, in Alaska's interior region. Yet, the aircraft veered off course, for reasons unknown, and began to head west of its intended target, turning towards some of the tallest mountain peaks in Alaska, where it eventually crashed. The plane was spotted a few days later—but recovery was deemed too dangerous.[47] More than half a century would pass before it was ever seen again. Interestingly, a second aircraft, call sign Gamble Chalk 2, departed some twenty minutes later, also following the wrong navigation beacon. Thankfully, air traffic controllers, recognizing the impending calamity, were able to contact the plane and alert them of their mistake.

The wreckage would finally be found in 2016 by retired geologist, Michael Rocereta, on the Eldridge Glacier. Rocereta said his motivation to find the plane came from an 'unseen force that drives pilots together, especially in 'the midst of calamities'. 'We owe it to the families, and to the servicemen who gave their lives to their country, to get out there and find them and help recover them if we can,' said Rocereta.[48] Since the initial crash in 1952, the debris field had moved 8km (5mi) down the glacier. In August 2017, an NPS team went to the site, with a mission of documenting and evaluating the debris, but the only piece of debris recovered from the site was a plate with the aircraft's serial number inscribed upon it. Due to the hazardous terrain and extreme weather, the site is only accessible by helicopter, recovery efforts have been somewhat hampered.[49] On 3 August 2023, a recovery team, comprising members from the Air Force Mortuary Affairs Operations, Alaskan Command, Alaska National Guard, US Army Alaska, 673rd Air Base Wing, 3rd Wing, and Detachment 1, 66 Training Squadron hiked to the debris field in an effort to recover any remains and/or personal effects.[50] The search continues.

In July 1999, a pair of commercial pilots, Kevin McGregor and Marc Millican, finally found the wreckage of Northwest Orient Airlines Flight 4422, which had slammed into the side of Mount Sanford, in the eastern Wrangell mountain range, in 1948, killing all thirty men aboard.[51] Albeit the location of the crash site was known, the wreckage had become embedded in the mountain glacier and quickly covered by snow and ice. On one of their visits to the site, after locating the wreckage, they found a severed human arm complete with its hand embedded in the ice. After numerous attempts by experts to extract DNA for identification purposes, finally in 2007, the mummified arm was recognized as belonging to passenger Francis Joseph Van Zandt, a 36-year-old merchant marine from Roanoke, Virginia.[52] Another aircraft which is believed to have crashed in the Alaskan glacial wilderness is Canadian Pacific Air Lines Flight 3505, a Douglas DC-4 airliner enroute to the United Nations from Vancouver, Canada. After a stopover in Anchorage Airport, the flight was on schedule but then disappeared in deteriorating weather conditions and poor visibility. The USAF and Royal Canadian Air Force carried out an extensive search of the area but failed to find any trace of the aircraft or its thirty-seven occupants. The search was finally called off on 31 October 1951.[53]

So far, we have touched upon a few examples of aircraft buried in glacial deposits in the northern hemisphere. But there are some worthy of mention that are in the often-forgotten southern glaciers of this world. One such icy graveyard can be found in the Tupungato Glacier, in the

Argentine Andes, about 80km (50mi) east of Santiago, Chile. It was here on 2 August 1947 that *Star Dust*, a British South American Airways (BSAA) Avro Lancastrian airliner, crashed into Mount Tupungato, killing all those aboard. Built as constructor's number 1280 for the Argentine Ministry of Supply, *Star Dust* carried six passengers and a crew of five on its final flight, including first officer Norman Hilton Cook, who had been awarded both the Distinguished Service Order (DSO) and the DFC, and Iris Evans as flight attendant, a former chief petty officer of the Women's Royal Naval Service ('Wrens'). Having left Buenos Aires on the afternoon of 2 August, the Avro Lancaster sent a routine message in Morse code to the airport in Santiago at 5.41 pm, announcing an expected arrival of 5.45 pm. However, she never arrived, and no more radio transmissions were received by the airport. Although an extensive search was carried out by both the Chilean and Argentine authorities, no trace of the aircraft was ever found.[54]

That is until 1998, when two Argentine mountaineers climbing Mount Tupungato stumbled across a Rolls-Royce Merlin aircraft engine together with shreds of clothing in the Tupungato Glacier at a height of some 4,600m (15,000ft).[55] An expedition by the Argentine Army in 2000 found further wreckage, including some wheels and a propeller, as well as human remains. Damage to the propeller indicated that the engine was working normally at the time of the crash.[56] By 2002, the bodies of five of the eight British victims had been identified through DNA testing. Why the Avro Lancaster crashed some 50km (31mi) from the area where the aircraft was last reported is still a mystery, albeit the inclement weather, heavy snow and 'very cloudy weather' may have been contributing factors. It is thought she flew into an almost vertical snowfield near the top of the glacier, causing an avalanche that buried the wreckage. Over the following years, as the compressed snow turned to ice, the aircraft remains became incorporated into the body of the glacier, with fragments emerging many years later and much further down the mountain. Between 1998 and 2000, about ten per cent of the total expected wreckage emerged from the glacier, prompting several re-examinations of the accident, with more debris expected to emerge in the future as the glacier shifts and the ice melts. In 2000, an independent Argentine Air Force investigation cleared first officer Norman Hilton Cook of any blame for the Lancaster's crash. During the same year, on 2 November 2000, the BBC aired a Horizon documentary on the discovery of *Star Dust* entitled *Vanished: The Plane That Disappeared.*[57]

Another graveyard that is also worthy of mention, and is often overlooked, is the world's official spacecraft cemetery, known more formally as the South Pacific Oceanic Uninhabited Area. Albeit technically categorized as 'aerospace,' I believe it fits the criteria. Located in Polynesia, east of New Zealand, it is centralized at a spot known as 'Point Nemo', the so-called 'oceanic pole of inaccessibility', in effect an area that is the farthest from any landmass. Named after Captain Nemo, from Jules Verne's classic sci-fi novel *20,000 Leagues Under the Sea*, the spacecraft cemetery lies on the boundary between the bathyal zone and the abyssal zone, 4km (2mi) beneath the waves at 48°25.6' south latitude and 123°23.6' west longitude. Stretching approximately 3,000km (1,864mi) from north to south, some 5,000km (3,107mi) from west to east, away from international shipping lanes and human activity, it was the ideal place to dispose of spacecraft that have passed their sell-by date.[58]

Between the years 1971 and 2016, it is believed at least 264 spacecraft were disposed of in the cemetery, and it has been routinely used by multiple international space exploration organizations, including China and Russia. Entry into the graveyard is carefully coordinated. A few days before a spacecraft's de-orbit, the space agency who owns the spacecraft will notify aviation and maritime authorities in both Chile and New Zealand, who share responsibility for traffic in the remote stretch of ocean. They will inform the authorities about expected re-entry times, where debris is likely to fall and so on. After which, the craft can begin its controlled plunge through the atmosphere to its final interment in the ocean cemetery. The now defunct Soviet Union space station Mir, a 129.7-metric-tonne (143-ton) modular station, was deliberately crashed here in 2001, after spending fifteen years in low orbit. After entering Earth's atmosphere, it began to break up, some 95km (59mi) in the air, and by the time it had fallen to 85km (53mi), the space station's peripheral components had been ripped away, and its main structure had been to collapse. In the end, only 18 to 22 metric tonnes (20 to 25 tons) of Mir debris made it to the ocean cemetery, broken into approximately six main fragments. Six Salyut stations, the very first space station initiative undertaken by the Soviet Union, also entered the cemetery, as did 145 Soviet Progress autonomous resupply ships, making Russia the largest contributor of spacecraft in the graveyard with over 200 pieces. The spacecraft cemetery is also the final resting place of four Japanese HTV cargo craft and five of the European Space Agency's Automated Transfer Vehicles. The remaining pieces of debris belong to the United States and private organizations. At the end of its lifespan, the International Space Station is also slated to enter the spacecraft cemetery.[59]

Very few laws restrict the activity of nations within this area. There are some international treaties in place, but they do not assign clear responsibility to individual countries about liability for damages and pollution caused by re-entering space debris, even when the culprits are clearly defined. For example, the decommissioning of Tiangong-1, China's first prototype space station that orbited Earth from September 2011 to April 2018, was an unsuccessful targeted re-entry at Point Nemo. During an extended mission phase, the Chinese lost control of the craft, due to a power failure, which resulted in the spacecraft crash landing outside of the designated boundaries of the spacecraft cemetery.[60] There are two general agreements concerning space debris and marine pollution that are often expanded upon to govern the spacecraft cemetery. The first is the Outer Space Treaty, proposed by the United Nations, which states that countries are obliged to take action when disposing of registered spacecraft into the ocean when it causes damages to other parties.[61] Somewhat problematic as space debris is often left unclaimed and neither the spacecraft owner nor operator nor the launching state can be determined. Brian Weeden of Secure World Foundation said: 'Of the 500,000 estimated human-generated objects in orbit bigger than *1 cm*, we only know which country put it there for about 16,000 objects, and less than half of those 16,000 were registered with the UN.'[62] Moreover, deorbiting debris will often require moving the junk through lower orbits first, further aggravating the issue. The second is the United Nations Convention on the Law of the Sea, also known as Law of the Sea Convention (LOSC), previously mentioned in Chapter Two, which dictates that all states have the duty of protecting and preventing pollution of the marine environment. Hydrazine, a widely used rocket propellant that is highly toxic to living organisms, may occasionally survive re-entry, as do radioactive chemicals, and as any given spacecraft can scatter debris over huge swathes of ocean. For example, the Mir space station left a debris trail 3,000km (1,864mi) long and over 100km (62mi) wide; environmental concerns are growing.[63]

The Life and Death of Loyce Edward Deen

To end this chapter, I would like to briefly tell the story of one of the most remarkable and heart-wrenching burials I have encountered during my years as a professional archaeologist/historian, namely the demise and subsequent burial of Loyce Edward Deen, the only US Navy pilot to be buried at sea inside his aircraft. It is one that truly touches the soul. The reason why I say this is because the entire memorial service was captured on film, a rare feat, and can be viewed on YouTube (see Notes and References). It is an extraordinary piece of cinematic history.

Loyce Edward Dean was born in the small town of Sulphur, Oklahoma, to Grace and Allen Deen, one of eight children, at a time of deep economic depression. Because of this his parents, like many other native Oklahomans, packed up and moved west to the city of Altus in hope of a better life. Deen worked for a time with the Civilian Conservation Corps (CCC), later joining the Douglas Aircraft Company in Wichita, where he helped to build wing sets for the A-26 Invader attack bomber. But his dream was to join the navy. So, in October 1942, Deen did just that, first enrolling at the 'gunner's school' in San Diego, where he mastered the weapon's system aboard the Grumman TBF Avenger torpedo bomber, then on to Naval Air School in Fort Lauderdale, before joining the infamous 15th Air Group out of Westerly, Rhode Island. In April 1944, the 15th Air Group was stationed aboard the aircraft carrier USS *Essex*, based at Pearl Harbour.[64]

The 15th Air Group saw some of the most intense fighting it had ever encountered during the battle of Leyte Gulf on 24–25 October 1944, with Deen teaming up with Pilot Lieutenant Robert Cosgrove (24) from New Orleans, Louisiana, and Radioman Digby Denzek (20) from Grand Rapids, Michigan. Deen received a shrapnel wound to his foot in the battle, but rather than recovering on a hospital ship, he opted to stay with Cosgrove and Denzek. On 5 November 1944, Loyce Deen climbed into his gun turret for the last time:

> 'That day, Lt. Cosgrove received tail number #93 – a new plane just acquired in Ulithi Atoll a few days ago. Lt. Cosgrove's orders were to go after the Japanese cruisers in Manila Bay. After the briefing, Lt. Cosgrove joined his crew, Digby and Loyce, and they went topside to their plane. Loyce climbed into his gun turret for the final time. The VT-15 group took off mid-morning, and it would take about two hours to get to Manila Bay and release the ordinance.'[65]

During this mission, Lieutenant Cosgrove's Avenger came under savage anti-aircraft fire from a Japanese cruiser, with Deen receiving two direct hits from 40mm (1.6in.) anti-aircraft shells. He was killed instantly. In a 2001 History Channel documentary entitled *Battle Group Halsey*, Capt. Cosgrove recalls:

> 'Denzek told me over the intercom that Deen was hit bad. Then, Denzek came back up thru the small passageway to sit in the cabin behind me. He stayed there until we landed.'[66]

During the attack, the Avenger was so badly damaged that it took all of Cosgrove's considerable talents as a pilot to fly the aircraft through two thunderstorms and hours of open ocean back to the USS *Essex*. Sadly, Deen was dead, and what remained of his body was so crushed, that the decision was taken to leave him as is and bury him at sea with his aircraft. Covering his torso with a sheet, fellow shipmates first took his fingerprints and then carefully removed the dog tags. With the ship's complement assembled to pay their last respects, and a chaplain to read last rites, the shattered aircraft was tipped over the rear of the flight deck, and into the water, with Deen inside. Two Avengers flew overhead in salute as the torpedo bomber-turned-coffin bobbed in the waves. Finally, the Avenger went down, by the nose, into its watery grave and disappeared out of sight. Deen was just twenty-three years old when he died. His name is inscribed on the 'Walls of the Missing' at the Manila American Cemetery and Memorial in Manila, Philippines.[67]

Chapter 5

Lest We Forget

Across the world there exists a vast network of remembrance landscapes, in the form of gravesites, funerary architecture, memorial gardens, constructed cairns and so forth, that commemorate some kind of aviation mishap, whether that be down to mechanical failure, combat, adverse weather conditions or even terrorist activity. Touching both military and civilian aircraft alike, some are simple affairs, maybe a small, decorated stone honouring the fallen, a wooden cross or a simple plaque, whereas others are rather more grandiose constructs. Many aircraft, though, still lie where they fell, their metallic body and internal organs strewn across some inhospitable, barren terrain.

At times it is difficult to convey the emotional impact such commemorative remnants and/or structures have on the human psyche, especially in written format. A poignant example can be seen in Figure 18, which depicts a US Marine Corps soldier placing flowers on the wreckage of two downed CH-53 helicopters, located on the Godoria Range plateau, near the northern coast of Djibouti, in the Horn of Africa. No words can do justice to the sentiment portrayed within this image. Therefore, what follows is an attempt to offer just a taste of what still exists in the funerary landscape, taken from a plethora of personal notebooks, and incorporate as many graphics as deemed possible, considering the publication constraints. It became obvious very early on during the research process that such tributes ought to be subdivided into the following categories: a) large-scale aircraft wreckage; b) limited aircraft wreckage; c) aircraft wreckage with accompanying commemorative marker; d) commemorative structure demarking site of aircraft crash; e) commemorative marker near but not sited at exact location of air crash; f) commemorative marker constructed from aircraft parts; g) large-scale remembrance landscapes/constructs; h) small individual commemorative structures. Albeit somewhat broad, these subdivisions are not exclusive, and many examples could easily fall into more than one of the categories.

Large-Scale Aircraft Wreckage

This categorization concerns aircraft which, to the naked eye appear, relatively intact, with fuselage and/or wings still prominent and clearly noticeable. One such example, often referred to as *Miss Piggy*, is a Curtiss C-46 'Commando' twin-prop cargo aircraft, an image of which graces the cover of this very tome. Originally delivered to the US Army Air Forces in July 1945, as the Second World War was beginning to wind down, it was later sold to a variety of commercial enterprises. Its final owner was Lamb Airways Ltd, who purchased her in 1978 and utilized her as a freight aircraft servicing the remote areas of Northern Manitoba, Canada. The aircraft's demise commenced on 13 November 1979, shortly after take-off, when the pilot reported a mechanical issue in one of the engines and attempted to turn back to Churchill Airport from whence it had just left. Unfortunately, the aircraft could not hold altitude and thus crashed, landing several kilometres short of the runway, in a rocky outcrop of boulders. *Miss Piggy*'s largely intact wreckage, including the fuselage and broken wing, remain there to this day.[1]

Although subject to vandalism over the years, *Miss Piggy* has unexpectedly become a tourist attraction to those visiting Churchill to search for polar bears. Furthermore, in June 2017, her exterior became the canvas for a painted mural, as part of the Sea Walls Churchill Project, a public art initiative to bring attention to the struggles of those living in this remote town on the western edge of Hudson Bay. Painted by American artist Pat Perry, the mural is appropriately entitled *Mayday—EMERGENCY TRANSMISSION: 58°45'37" N 94°5'11" W*. and features a variety of skull and bone images surrounded by blooming flowers. It is intended as a statement to the economic decline and desolation of places like Churchill and the artist's hometown of Detroit, Michigan. Perry wrote: 'It is with my utmost humility that I ask for understanding and grace from the people of Churchill as to why I couldn't make something more cheery on the beloved Miss Piggy plane wreck, and it is my greatest wish that you find a sincere expression of solidarity in the artwork I've made.'[2]

The hulk of a US Air Force bomber, a B-24D Liberator, is also depicted on the cover of this book, which today can be found on Atka

Island, Alaska. It has led a relatively peaceful existence since its passing. Manufactured in 1941 by Consolidated Aircraft, this aircraft flew in at least eighteen combat missions and played a highly significant role in the Aleutian Campaign against the Imperial Japanese forces (1942–1943). Weighing approximately 16,329kg (36,000lb), and measuring 20m (67ft) in length, with an impressive wingspan of 34m (110ft), the B-24D was used primarily for bombing; however, at the time of this particular aircraft's demise, it had been removed from combat duty and was being used as a weather observation plane. On 9 December 1942, the plane was forced to make an emergency landing and crashed-landed in Atka, skidding along the ground.[3] A brief passage from the 11th Air Force History, 1941–1945, gives the following account:

> 'On 9 December (1942) Colonel Hart and Brigadier General William E. Lynd of General Buckner's staff, took off from Adak in a B-24 piloted by Captain John Andrews. The two officers wished to accompany the weather plane to make personal observations from Kiska and Attu. The plane reached Attu, circled over Holtz Bay, and then returned to Adak. Arriving back at Adak at 1600, the pilot found his base socked in by weather. He notified the tower that he planned to fly to the far end of Atka Island and attempt a crash landing. Atka, too, was closed in, and the plane was crash-landed . . . There was only one casualty. General Lynd sustained a fractured collarbone…'[4]

Although the tail broke off in characteristic B-24 fashion, the rest of the aircraft remains intact, minus the vertical tail fins, which are in the vicinity of the aircraft. It is now only one of two B-24Ds known to exist in the world.

Keeping with the theme of visual representations on the cover of this book, on the southern coast of Iceland, on the black sands of Sólheimasandur Beach, there sits the fuselage of a Douglas C-117D transport aircraft, once operated by the US Navy. On 21 November 1973, whilst flying from Hofn Hornafjördur Airport to NAS Keflavik, the plane unexpectedly crashed due to, what was believed at the time, severe icing conditions. It later transpired that the pilot had simply switched over to the wrong fuel tank! All seven crew members survived the crash and were rescued by helicopter, but the aircraft itself was 'written off'. The remains of the aircraft were thus left at the scene. As of 2025, the fuselage of the aircraft remains relatively intact, and like the aforementioned *Miss Piggy*, it has become a popular sightseeing destination, with official guided tours to its remote location available daily (weather permitting). The aircraft has even featured in the music video of Justin Bieber's 2015 song 'I'll Show You', as well as the Icelandic Netflix sci-fi drama *Katla.*[5]

Limited Aircraft Wreckage

Many aircraft gravesites have little to offer visually, bar the odd piece of metal scattered here and there. With regards to military aircraft, immediately upon the aircraft's demise, RAF Maintenance Units, or a country's equivalent, would appear on the scene and remove anything of worth. The rest was either left as is, or buried on site, after it had usually been set on fire. This scenario, however, often belies an intriguing probability. That being the remnants of the aircraft could, in fact, directly beneath your feet without your knowledge.

Aircraft Wreckage with Accompanying Commemorative Markers or Memorials

With little or no evidence of wreckage at most aircraft crash sites, the final resting place of Wellington Bomber MF509, at Garreg Goch (Red Stone), in the Brecon Beacons, Wales most certainly does not fall into this grouping. Located in a remote spot, about 520m (1,640ft) above the upper Swansea Valley, it was here on 20 November 1944 that Vickers Wellington bomber MF509, from 22 Operational Training Unit Wellesbourne, Mountford, on a cross-country nighttime exercise, suddenly developed trouble in the starboard Hercules XVI engine. Attempting to gain height to avoid the rapidly approaching mountain range, it flew directly into an accumulation of shower clouds, resulting in a heavy layer of ice developing on the wings. With insufficient power from engines, the aircraft rapidly lost height and tragically crashed into Garreg Goch, killing all six Canadian crew members: Sergeant Charles Hamel, pilot; Sergeant Jules Robert Rene Villeneuve, navigator; Flying Officer; William Joseph Allison, bomb aimer; Sergeant Joseph Paul Ernest Burke, air gunner; Sergeant Arthur Grouix, air gunner; Sergeant Gerard Dusablon, air gunner. The recovered bodies were interred with full military honours in the Canadian War Cemetery at Blacon, Chester, England.[6]

Today, there is a considerable amount of wreckage on view, as seen in Figure 19, with some strewn a considerable distance from the main point of impact. For instance, the main wheel is currently sited a very long way from the crash site, and one cannot help but be emotionally moved by the Canadian flag fluttering in wind, atop a stone and concrete memorial, with several adjacent poppy wreaths. These are accompanied by two commemorative plaques: an older one listing the names of the dead, and a more recent 2006 addition added by a visiting surviving relative. In 2005, the photograph of one of the airmen, found at the site in 1944, was placed on the Internet in an effort to identify him; the outcome was successful and some sixty years later the families of the dead crew finally discovered the fate of their loved ones. Mention should also be given to a new commemorative plaque that was added to the memorial in 2025 by the Ted Coningsby Squadron, complete with a model of the Vickers Wellington fashioned by model-maker extraordinaire Nick Ward. It reads: 'IN MEMORY OF THE CREW OF MF509 OF 22 OTU RAF - LEST WE FORGET, Donated by Ted Coningsby, Built by Nick Ward.'[7]

Staying briefly in the Brecon Beacons, just up the road from Wellington MF509, in Fan Ddu, the remnants of a crashed Supermarine Spitfire Mk.I X4588 No. 53 RAF, have been gathered in a small pile, alongside a commemorative cairn, marking the site of the crash. On 23 May 1942, the Spitfire was on normal flying practice from RAF Llandow, in the Vale of Glamorgan, when it entered some low-lying cloud and subsequently flew into a nearby hilltop at high speed, disintegrating on impact.[8]

The wilds of Scotland understandably have their fair share of crash sites where aircraft wreckage is still visible above ground. Some are even designated 'war graves', such as the crash site of Avro Anderson Mk.I M857 that ploughed into Ben More, located near Crianlarich, in the southern part of the Scottish Highlands, on 13 April 1941. The aircraft, from No.19 OTU RAF, was on a night cross-country navigation exercise from RAF Kinloss, in Moray, when it encountered bad weather. After turning onto a southerly track over Cape Wrath, the pilot attempted to climb above the clouds, but minutes later the following message was transmitted: 'Icing up…lost power import engine… losing height … descending through 3,000 ft.' The aircraft would never be heard from again. Over a month would go by before a local shepherd stumbled across the wreck site. The following day RAF personnel climbed to the scene of the tragedy and made the heartbreaking decision to bury the bodies of the crew on site; the graves being covered by a mound of peat and a stone cairn. The latter was rebuilt in 1985 with the addition of a memorial plaque and a tall metal cross. Around the cairn can be seen remains of the aircraft, including sections of the undercarriage assembly, various pieces of framework, wheels and tyres etc. The site is currently marked as a 'grave' on the relevant Ordnance Survey maps.[9] Similarly, the windswept landscapes of the Lake District, in Cumbria, conjure up some remarkable gravesites sites such as that of a Handley Page Halifax MkV LL505/FD-S aircraft from No.1659 HCU, RAF, arguably the most visited crash site in the vicinity. Located at Great Carrs, in the Furness Fells area, on the evening of 22 October 1944, whilst on a night navigation exercise from RAF Topcliffe in North Yorkshire, the crew became disoriented and slammed into the top of the mountain, disintegrating upon impact. Today, on the ridgeline, there sits a stone cairn mounted with a memorial cross complete with two adjacent main undercarriage assemblies. Most of the remains, however, including wing sections, propeller hubs and gear units, lie on the scree slopes of Broad Slack, where the bulk of the wreckage was dumped by the salvage team. In 1997, two of the engines were removed from the mountainside using a Chinook helicopter; one of which is displayed outside the Ruskin Museum in Coniston Village.[10] Another prime aircraft wreck area is the Peak District, which is also littered with aircraft parts, such as those from the demise of Vickers Wellington Mk IC R1011/ M: No.28 OTU RAF, which crashed near Birchen Bank Moss, Longdendale, Derbyshire, on the evening of 30 January 1943. It was one of three aircraft lost in the region that night due to the atrocious weather conditions; the other two crashed on private land lower down. A pile of small parts and sections of framework from the aircraft have been gathered at the site, complete with a commemorative ceramic plaque.[11]

Outside of the United Kingdom, well, the world is your oyster, to reference a popular phrase. One graveyard of wrecks, an image of which graces the back cover of this book, can be found on public land in Burma Rim, Oregon, Washington. Located on the remnants of a prehistoric shoreline, it is the final resting place of two notable aircraft wrecks, just 1.6km (1mi) apart, but separated by thirty years. The first, a Second World War Lockheed P-38 Lightning, crashed during a training flight in 1945, killing the pilot Second Lieutenant Max P. Clark outright. A few metallic remains are just about visible, and a plaque has been erected to mark the site.[12] The second crash occurred on 19 September 1973, when a Navy Grumman A-6 Intruder Bomber plummeted to the ground during a low-level night mission, killing both pilot Lieutenant Allan G. Koehler and navigator Lieutenant Commander Philip D. duHamel. The debris is spread over a mile across the high desert plain and has purposely been left as a permanent monument to the fallen, with accompanying memorial plaque.[13]

Commemorative Memorials Demarking Plane Crash

On the morning of 19 October 1964, a group of twenty-two Soviet dignitaries and veterans were flying from Moscow to Belgrade to take part in the twentieth anniversary ceremony for the Liberation of Belgrade, marking the Red Army's assistance in liberation of said city during the Second World War. The most notable figures in the group were Marshal Sergey Biryuzov and General Vladimir Zhdanov, two respected elders of the Red Army who aided in the expulsion of Germans from the Yugoslav region during the war. The plane was due to land at 11.30am at the Belgrade Batajnica Military Air Base, but by 11.34, it had disappeared from radar. It was then seen to mysteriously veer off course, at which point it crashed against the side of nearby Mount Avala. There were no survivors. The reasoning behind the aircraft's demise remains a mystery to this day; one theory lays blame at the challenging weather conditions; according to records it was very foggy on approach. Others point to possible faulty instruments; apparently there had been issues with USSR/Yugoslav unit conversions.[14]

Plans to commemorate the victims of the plane crash were initiated almost immediately after the disaster, and in the spring of 1965, Belgrade City Assembly organized a design competition whereby thirteen prominent sculptors and architects were invited to submit proposals for a suitable memorial. They included some of the most significant names in Serbian art and architecture, including world-renowned sculptor Olga Jevrić and architect Bogdan Bogdanović, but it would be a proposal put forward by native Belgrade sculptor Jovan Kratohvil, who interestingly was also an accomplished shooter and Olympian athlete, that would catch the eye of the selection committee. The official press release of 1965, announcing the competition winner states:

> 'The author of this award-winning project constructed an obelisk from an airplane's wings. By breaking the wings and building up the structure of the object, Kratohvil managed to suggest the tragedy of the event, while also monumentalizing it at the same time.'[15]

Opened to the public on 19 October 1965, to commemorate the first-year anniversary of the plane crash, the location chosen for the memorial was the crash site itself, Mount Avala, which today is accessed via a pair of grand stone staircases. A 5m (16ft)-tall monolith composed of 70sq m (753sq ft) of brass and iron, the commemorative structure rests on a marble pedestal overlooking the Serbian countryside. When interviewed about his creation by Sarajevo newspaper *Oslobođenje,* the artist remarked: 'It is appropriate to associate broken airplane wings, or wings in general, as symbols. Four such surfaces merge into one rhythm that suggests tragedy.' An engraved slab of white marble at the base of the stairs reads:

> 'This is the place of a plane crash on the morning of Oct. 19th, 1964, where Soviet heroes, our war friends and comrades, died. In Oct. of 1944, they were fighting for the freedom of Belgrade. In Oct. of 1964, they entered the city's legend and became the symbol of war-time brotherhood and camaraderie.'[16]

Devastation is an apt term that can be applied to our next example. For on 4 May 1949, an aircraft carrying the entire Torino football team (popularly known back then as the Grande Torino), was thrown off course due to adverse weather, and subsequently crashed into the hillside of the Basilica of Superga, which stands on the outskirts of Turin, in northwestern Italy. All thirty-one people onboard perished. In the aftermath, at the request of rival teams, Torino were proclaimed winners of the 1948–49 Serie A Football League season, whilst on the day of the funeral, half a million people took to the streets of Turin to give a final farewell to the players. The memorial is sited at the back of the Basilica, and comprises a cross-bearing stone arch, a banner depicting the full team, and numerous individual offerings from football supporters, see Figure 20.[17]

The next example also comes from Italy. A stone monument, embedded with aircraft parts, bears witness to a double-tragedy that occurred between 19–21 July 1957 involving two American Lockheed P2V Neptune aircraft. On 19 July 1957, during a flight transfer to Istrana, which is located approximately 22km (35mi) northwest of Venice, the first P2V Neptune crashed into the south wall of the Italian Dolomites mountain range, 2,650m (8694ft) above sea level, near Trentino. All eleven crew members perished. Two days later, the second P2V Neptune, which had taken off from Aviano NATO base, located approximately 80km (50mi) north of Venice, was on a search mission for the initial missing P2V Neptune when it too crashed, its left wing colliding with a tree, exploding on the rocks of Mt. Granero. Incredibly, two of the ten crew members survived, albeit one died a few hours later.[18]

Here in the United Kingdom, the barren landscapes are not averse to the odd tribute in memory of a fallen aircraft. Scotland, understandably, is awash with commemorative structures in many varied guises. For example, at Loch Skerrow, in Dumfries and Galloway, there exists a plinth into which a Typhoon propeller hub has been cemented. It marks the crash site of fighter jet JR439 of 440 Squadron, which came down in bad weather on 18 March 1944, whilst taking part in a unit move from RAF Ayr to RAF Hurn on the South Coast of England. The Canadian pilot, K.O. Mitchell, was killed instantly, and his remains are buried in Ayr Cemetery, whilst the aircraft's Napier sabre engine now resides with the Dumfries and Galloway

Aviation Museum.[19] In Dunbeath, in the Scottish Highlands, a stone cross marks the spot where Sunderland W4026 of 228 Squadron crashed on 25 August 1942, killing all fourteen crew and passengers, one of which was the Duke of Kent, who became the first son of an English sovereign to be killed on active service for more than 500 years. The aircraft was on its way from Invergordon to Iceland when it crashed for reasons unknown. The memorial bears the names of the crew and passenger and the dedication: 'In memory of Air Commodore HRH the Duke of Kent KG KT GCMG GCVO and his companions who lost their lives on active service during a flight to Iceland on a special mission the 25 August 1942. May they rest in peace.'[20] Still in the Highlands, at the east end of a small loch near Gairloch, in north-west Scotland, a bronze plate has been attached to a rock and reads as follows: 'USAAF. In memory of the crew and passengers of a B-24H Liberator bomber serial number 42-95095 which became lost while returning to the USA on June the 13th 1945 and crashed at this place with the loss of all on board.' The Liberator had taken off from Warton, Lancashire for Iceland and is believed to have struck Slioch, a mountain some 21km (13mi) away before breaking up in mid-air.[21] Whilst in the harsh, peat-bog infested terrain of Yell, in Shetland, there stands a 3m (9ft) stainless-steel cross, airlifted to the site by helicopter in September 1991, which marks the crash site of a Catalina flying boat z2151 of 240 Squadron, who were based at Stranraer. The flying boat crashed into the hillside on 19 January 1942, at night, whilst trying to alight at RAF Sullom Voe. Seven crew members were killed instantly, whilst three survived. The final example, the downing of a Boulton Paul Defiant Mk.I T4042 of No.60 OTU, RAF, has the unique honour of being one of the few true war graves where the aircrew lie buried at the site of impact.[22] The aircraft crashed on Hunt Law, near Lauder, on 29 August 1941, and the Australian pilot, Sergeant ADC La Gruta, sadly could not be recovered from the deeply embedded wreckage, so his remains were left in situ. There is a concrete square monolith, atop of which is a gravestone inscribed with the following: 'To the memory of AUS 400719 Flight Sergeant A.D.C. La Gruta RAAF who rests here where he died on active service 29.8.41. Aged 23 years.' Interestingly, a few wreckage remnants sit adjacent to the stone memorial;

however, these were disturbed and removed when the concrete foundations for the memorial were being dug.[23]

Wreck sites throughout the rest of the United Kingdom, within this sub-division, typically fall into the stone/cross/plaque variety. For instance, in a random field in Mugginton, Derbyshire, a stone surmounted with a cross marks another war grave, erected by the RAFA to commemorate the loss of aircraft Whitley BD230 of 42 OTU RAF, Ashbourne, a training flight that crashed into the ground whilst returning to base on 24 July 1944. The aircraft was entombed so deeply that it was impossible to recover three of the crew.[24] In Seal, Kent, a stone also marks the crash site of a Hurricane aircraft, N2401, that was shot down by enemy fighters on 27 September 1940, killing the pilot Flight Lieutenant Lionel H. Schwind. Whereas in the Preseli Mountains, Pembrokeshire, in September 1985, a memorial plaque was placed at the site of a crashed Consolidated Liberator, G.R. Mk.VI EV881 547 Squadron, by the Pembrokeshire Aviation Group. The aircraft had departed from RAF St. Eval in Cornwall during the evening for an anti-submarine exercise, codenamed Oasthouse, when it drifted from its designated flight plan, flew into a hilltop and caught fire.[25] There are a couple of examples, however, that pleasantly deviate from the norm. In Marden, Kent, for instance, near what is Little Cheveney Farm, there exists a solitary apple tree that was planted by the landowner in 1940 to mark the crash site of a Hurricane aircraft, from 111 Squadron based at Croydon. The pilot, Flight Lieutenant Michael Ferris, had collided with a Dornier DO17 that he was attacking; both aircraft fell a short distance apart with no survivors. Touchingly, subsequent generations made efforts to preserve this special tree, albeit its current condition is unknown, despite enquiries.[26] In Ashley Combe, near Porlock Weir in Somerset, a memorial has been built into the side of a rock bank, commemorating the demise of a Handley Page Halifax B. Mk.V Srs.I EB 132 that struck the hillside, bursting into flames, in 1943.[27] Whilst on the banks of the Leeds Liverpool Canal, in Bradley, Skipton, North Yorkshire, at Bridge 183, a rather impressive memorial, comprising a mounted bronze eagle was unveiled in September 2008 to commemorate the demise of a Vickers Wellington Mk.XI HZ251/38 No.6 (C) OTU RAF and its crew. The aircraft had suffered a devastating structural failure before diving into the ground, killing all its Polish crew onboard; one of whom, Flight Lieutenant Jozef Wolnik, a navigator, who had completed forty-six missions over enemy territory and received the Virtuti Militari, Poland's highest military decoration. A smaller memorial demarking the actual site of the crash site sits adjacent to the towpath.[28]

Commemorative Markers Not Sited at Exact Location of Crash

A truly remarkable memorial can be found in the 'Museo per la Memoria di Ustica' (Museum for the Memory of Ustica), located in a disused tram depot in the northern outskirts of Bologna, Italy—the reconstructed remains of Itavia Airlines DC-9 flight 870. Having departed Bologna Airport on 27 June 1980 with seventy-seven passengers and four crew onboard, an hour into the flight, at 20.59, as the DC-9 was about to commence its descent to Palermo; the plane completely disappeared off radar screens. It wasn't until dawn the next day that the DC-9's wreckage and floating bodies were spotted off the island of Ustica, near Sicily. Sadly, there were no survivors. Initially, the cause of the crash was assumed to be either mechanical failure or, more disturbing, by a terrorist bomb. However, a few weeks later reports began to circle that NATO jets had been seen in the area on the day of the accident. These reports were quickly followed by the discovery of the burnt-out remains of a Libyan MiG fighter jet, in the remote mountainous region of southern Calabria. Could Itavia Airlines Flight 870 have been the victim of a secret military operation? Oddly, all attempts to acquire the truth, by the families of the victims and their representatives, were met with a wall of silence.[29]

It took eight years for air accident investigators to recover the wreckage from the seabed and, having reconstructed the remains around a metal frame, their conclusion was that the plane had most definitely been brought down by an internal explosion. Accordingly, in 1999, a 5,500-word report released by the Italian authorities concluded that the plane was indeed likely to have been downed by a NATO missile and that there had been a criminal cover-up by the Italian military and security services to hide the truth. Nine people, four of them generals, were subsequently accused of destroying and withholding evidence, high treason, and perjury. Unsurprisingly, they were all later acquitted.[30] In 1994, a book claimed that Israel was responsible for the downing of Flight 870, whilst in 2023, in an interview with *La Repubblica*, former Italian prime minister Giuliano Amato accused a French jet of having fired the missile. In July 2024, in an article in *Il Resto del Carlino* newspaper, the blame was clearly laid at the doorstep of the Palestinians. Regrettably, for the victims' families, it is doubtful that the truth will ever be known.[31]

After the crash investigation had concluded, the families of the victims did not want to see the wreckage of the plane simply disposed of. After all, for many it was the only thing that connected them to their missing loved ones. Consequently, in 2007, the wreckage of Itavia Airlines Flight 870 was transported to the Museo per la Memoria di Ustica, in Bologna. There, renowned Parisian artist, Christian Liberté Boltanski, well-known for his memorials that tackled themes of death and trauma, was commissioned to create a suitable commemoration.[32] In a huge hall, created by knocking together three large tram sheds, in an excavated trench several feet below ground level, there now sits the huge, shattered hulk of Itavia Airlines Flight 870—all 2,500 pieces painstakingly jig-sawed together to create a fitting memorial. Positioned on a bed of stones to replicate the sea floor, the axis of the aircraft forms a cross. Several recovered effects, which include a crumpled shoe and rusty camera, a snorkel and flipper, a bra and broken tennis racquet, a life jacket and radio, are carefully placed inside nine black boxes and arranged around the twisted fuselage to signify eternal shrines. Overhead is stationed eighty-one bulbs that pulsate to the rhythm of breathing, each bulb representing a crash victim, whilst on the walkway surrounding the aircraft, eighty-one pitch-black mirrors with hidden speakers quietly whisper the last powerful thoughts, as visualized by Boltanski, of those who sadly perished.[33]

Monuments sited within a 'spiritual' environment, that being a church or a churchyard/cemetery/graveyard, are understandably abundant and can take on many forms. For example, in the village church of Cardington, Bedfordshire, there hangs the tattered and scorched RAF ensign from the airship R101, which crashed at Beauvais, France, killing all those onboard. Underneath is a tablet with the inscribed words: 'In remembership of those who died when HM Airship R101 was wrecked at Beauvais in France on October 5th, 1930, in attempting the first airship flight to India.' Across the road, in the small cemetery, is the communal grave of the forty-eight officers, airmen and civilians who died in the disaster; twenty-two of the bodies are unidentifiable.[34] A white stone sarcophagus, complete with RAF insignia, sits atop the mass grave. Furthermore, in Kesgrave, Suffolk an entire church was built a year after the disaster to commemorate Squadron Leader F. Michael Rope, who was killed in the previously mentioned R101 airship. Rope was Assistant Chief Designer at the Royal Airship Works at Cardington, and responsible for the design of dirigible prototypes. Metallic remnants from the wreckage of the airship were incorporated into the church structure, whilst inside, an incense burner in the shape of the airship has been suspended from adjoining pillars.[35]

In the village church of Woodchester, Gloucestershire, there is a stained-glass window incorporating the Royal Flying Corps insignia that marks the demise of a 3 Squadron BE2, which suffered structural failure and crashed near Netheravon on 11 March 1914. Its captain, Robert W. Allen, was killed on impact and his remains are buried in the adjacent churchyard.[36] Whereas in the churchyard wall of Aberedw, Powys, Wales there exists a stone and a wooden style with an attached plaque that reads: 'In memory of Flight Lieutenant Ian Hill, RAF, killed in an aircraft crash at the Pantau, Aberedw 24th of June 1987.' The local villagers are to this day convinced that Flight Lieutenant Hill deliberately stayed at the controls of his malfunctioning Jaguar XZ386 to avoid hitting the village, thereby sacrificing his own life.[37] A wooden board has been erected in the churchyard of Theberton, Suffolk, commemorating the demise of a Zeppelin airship, which bears the following inscription: 'Here were buried 16 German airmen crew of Zeppelin L48 17th June 1917. Who are thou that judgest another man's servant. To his own master he standeth for falleth. Romans XIV LV verse.' Inside the church is a glass case containing a piece of the airship structure, whereas the site where the airship fell is still known as Zeppelin Field.[38]

Continuing with the cemetery theme, in Babaoshan Revolutionary Cemetery, Beijing, China, there stands a mausoleum-style stone structure in memory of flight ČSA Czechoslovak Airlines Ilyushin Il-12B, an international scheduled passenger flight from Zürich to Prague, which crashed on 24 November 1956, killing ten members of the Chinese National Opera.[39] Meanwhile, in the city cemetery of Chachapoya, located approximately 644km (400mi) north of Lima, Peru, an imposing looking monument has been erected commemorating the demise of TANS Peru Flight 222, which crashed on 9 January 2003 in jungle-covered mountains. Encompassing a large triangular stone monolith, atop of which stands a metallic angel, a plaque has been attached inscribed with information about the crash and a full list of the victims.[40] A less grandiose memorial to commemorate the Kegworth Air Disaster has been constructed at the top of Kegworth village cemetery in Leicestershire. In January 1989, a British Midlands Airways Boeing 737 Flight 092, enroute to Belfast, crashed onto the motorway embankment between the M1 motorway and A453 road near Kegworth while attempting to make an emergency landing at East Midlands Airport. The memorial consists of several engraved stones listing the names of those who perished, and a small surrounding garden, utilizing soil from the actual crash site. Around the back of the stones there is also a seating area, for private contemplation, out of sight to those folks who may be visiting the main cemetery.[41]

Other categories of tributes are less distinct, and could be easily missed by a passer-by, such as a plaque on the clifftop between Clovelly and Hartland Point, in North Devon, commemorating the demise of Wellington ZA721, from 172 Squadron, which flew into the cliffs on 13 April 1942 whilst en route from RAF Chivenor to RAF St Eval. All the crew sadly perished. Said memorial is only visible to those hiking this section of the South-West Coastal Path. Similarly, a small metal plaque on the Cross Seminole Trail marks the crash of an A3D2 Skywarrior, in January 1962, which struggled to maintain height during take-off and subsequently hit the ground, bursting into flames upon impact. All aboard were killed.[42] Even more remote are the three pristine alpine lakes in Canada's Alberta Rocky Mountain region, named in memory of an accident that resulted in three different plane crashes. Close to the Ribbon Creek Trail, on 6 June 1986, a Cessna aeroplane carrying wildlife biologist Orvall Pall, who was tasked with monitoring bighorn sheep populations, crashed into a forested section of Mount Kidd, killing both him and his pilot. Only hours after the initial crash, having realized the Cessna had not returned, friends of the pilot took off in their own Cessna aircraft to search for them. They too crashed into the side of the nearby Mount Lougheed, killing all three passengers onboard. Unbelievably, only eight days later, another search plane, this time a Canadian Air Force DHC-6 Twin Otter, crashed into nearby cliffs, killing all search personnel, and starting a forest fire, which severely hampered the search efforts on the ground. To commemorate this tragic sequence of events, the Alberta government erected a large brick cairn in honour of all who perished.[43]

Inscribed plaques are a popular form of tribute, such as the one attached to the side of an unassuming wall in the village of North Creake, Norfolk, which commemorates a Mosquito Fighter Bomber Mk VI Serial LR 329 305 Squadron RAF, which crashed whilst out on a night training exercise on 27 April 1944.[44] Another memorial plaque, this time in the shape of a maple leaf, the national symbol of Canada, adorns a tree alongside a series of fields in Hanley Swan, Worcestershire. The plaque is inscribed: 'Dedicated to the memory of seven Canadian airmen who lost their lives as a result of a mid-air collision between two Wellington bombers on the 11th of August 1944.' A large semi-circle memorial bench, together with a commemorative plaque, located in the Moormede Housing Estate, Staines, has been dedicated to the passing of British European Airways Flight 548 on 18 June 1972, which entered a 'deep stall' only minutes after take-off from Heathrow Airport, from which there was no recovery, and crashed to the ground killing all 118 people onboard.[45]

To end this sub-category, I leave you with this rather contentious memorial from West Africa that commemorates the demise of Dana Air Flight 0992, a Douglas MD-83 domestic passenger airliner enroute from Abuja to Lagos, Nigeria. On 3 June 2012, the aircraft suffered a dual-engine failure during its approach to Lagos Airport and crashed into nearby apartment buildings, killing all 153 people on board and six on the ground. A year later a commemorative cenotaph, dedicated to those involved in the tragedy, well almost all, was unveiled to the public. Composed of a large three-tier marble platform, above which has been set a somewhat crude—and some would even argue offensive—model of a broken aircraft, painted in red and white, the colours of Dana Airways, depicting the front-end fuselage torn and ruptured. On the bottom tier are inscribed the names of those who died, albeit for some strange reason the names of the crew have been omitted.[46] Although the memorial was well-received at the time, over the intervening years there has been much criticism, with one well-renowned Nigerian artist, Chika Okeke-Agulu, stating:

> 'Apart from the stupidity of creating the crashed plane, did it not occur to the artist that the use of the colour red on the monument reinstates the violence of the crash and reminds us of the blood of the victims' - Chika Okeke-Agulu 2013

Commemorative Markers Constructed from Aircraft Parts

In a secluded stretch of woodland adjacent to Estonia's Ämari Air Base lies an old Soviet pilot's graveyard; visually, one of my all-time favourite sites. From the time of its establishment during the Second World War up until the breakup of the USSR, the airfield was under the control of the Soviet Union; the airbase was known as the Suurküla aerodrome. Today, it hosts the NATO-backed Baltic air-policing mission, an air defence system put in place to safeguard the airspace over the three Baltic states of Estonia, Lithuania and Latvia. The graveyard is small in design and was purposely sited a short distance away from the base during the Soviet era, so as not to deflate the morale of the airmen stationed there. Built over the site of a former war cemetery, it primarily consists of several crude grave markers dotted throughout the trees. There are some, however, that are unique, even by Soviet standards—original aircraft tail fin tombstones, seconded from various Russian aircraft, see Figure 21.

Opinion differs regarding the tail fin grave markers. Whether they originate from the specific aircraft involved in the accidents that killed the aviators is unknown. Some historians are adamant they do, but there is no recorded evidence that any of these pilots died whilst in combat. Most fatalities occurred because of accidents and instrument failure during training exercises and/or reconnaissance missions, usually involving the Russian-designed Sukhoi Su-24, a supersonic medium-range bomber that is still in use today. In fact, the most devastating recorded accident happened on the ground and not in the air when, in April 1978, an aircraft overshot its taxi-stand and hit a stationary truck, bursting into flames and killing a total of sixteen men. Their names are carved upon a stone in the cemetery.[47] Along the same line, there is also no evidence to suggest that every aircraft tail represents the physical burial of a dead pilot, as Estonian resources suggest that it was the norm to return the remains of any deceased back to their homeland for burial. That is not to say a few dead Soviet servicemen are not interred underneath these remarkable tombstones, but in all probability, they are just memorials, erected in the graveyard to honour their memory.

One memorial that does have a more established backstory is that of Vickers Wellington IC R1646 JM-D, which disappeared on 19 January 1942, whilst on a standard training flight. The bomber aircraft took off from 20 Operational Training Unit (20 OTU) at RAF Lossiemouth, Scotland, but never returned. It would be many weeks before the mystery of her disappearance would be finally solved, in part due to the keen eye of a local stalker, James Wright, who had ventured into the hills on the Invercauld Estate, located near Braemar, Aberdeenshire, to check on the health of the deer stock, and caught the glint of a metallic object some way in the distance. He was certain that it looked like the tail section of an aircraft. Having reported the find to the local Braemar Constabulary, Wright then organized a search party to go up into the hills the very next day—members of which included Wright, Constable Gerrie and two of Wright's family members, namely William Brown and his fifteen-year-old son, Andy Brown. After a treacherous hike up snow laden paths, they eventually came across the crash site, all that was visible was the tail of the aircraft and glass from the rear gun turret. They found no sign of human life.[48] Upon returning to Braemar, Constable Gerrie telephoned police headquarters to confirm that they had indeed found the wreckage of an aircraft on the hillside in Dubh-chorie, Glen Clunie. The RAF were duly informed about the discovery and on 22 February, over a month after Wellington IC R1646 had disappeared, an official surveying unit was sent out to the scene of the crash to investigate. Over the next two months, the bodies of the eight crew members were recovered and buried in Dyce Old Churchyard, Aberdeen, each grave marked honourably with a wooden cross. Quite why Wellington R1646 crashed into a hillside in Glen Clunie is not certain. Initial searches for the missing aircraft were carried out at sea, the thought being that the aircraft had somehow become lost somewhere off the Scottish coast. Now known that it had crashed on the mainland, it was imperative that any parts of the aircraft deemed valuable or confidential should be removed as quickly as possible. So, despite the harsh winter conditions, by the end of April 1942 this task was skilfully accomplished by 56 Maintenance Unit, Inverness, with those parts of the aircraft deemed unimportant left on the hillside whence they fell.[49]

This, however, is not the end of the tale. For atop that snowy hillside a seed was sown in the mind of a young fifteen-year-old boy, namely Andy Brown, who believed the plight of flight R1646 should not be forgotten. As such, in 1999, Brown applied to the MoD for official permission to recover the Wellington's Pegasus engines, which had lain on the hillside for over fifty years, with the notion of using them to construct a memorial. Permission was granted. Nonetheless, recovering such heavy engines from a remote area of the Cairngorm Mountain range would not be an easy task. Especially as the engines had, by now, shifted from their original resting position and had rolled someway down the steep hill. A helicopter would be required to do the heavy lifting, and thus an RAF Sea King Helicopter, based at RAF Lossiemouth, was called upon for assistance. But before the lifting procedure could commence, the engines had to be moved back up the hill, to a more accessible area. Another shout-out was made to the Argyll and Sutherland Highlanders regiment, who were based nearby at Balmoral Castle, for a little helping hand. Ironically, it was this very regiment who were the official guard at RAF Lossiemouth in 1942 when the Wellington bomber went missing. Once safely recovered from the hillside, the two engines were taken to Brown's workshop, where the less damaged of the two was cleaned up and painted black to be incorporated into the memorial. Finally, after years of planning and preparation, on Thursday 21 August 2003, in the presence of HRH The Princess Royal, and invited dignitaries, including relatives of the deceased, the official memorial to Vickers Wellington R1646 was unveiled.[50]

A rather poignant aircraft memorial dating to the Second World War can be found in Simiane-La-Rotonde, in southeastern France, dedicated to yet another Vickers Wellington bomber (LP180) demise. As in the above example, all five crew members perished in the crash. This region of France, at this time, was home to the French Resistance group known as the 'Abbatteur' (Slaughterman) and comprised seven members, who were responsible for the 'Section for Landings and Parachutes', a subset established by Charles De Gaulle. On the night of 10 May 1944, the 'Abatteur' were preparing to receive a parachute drop of weapons from London, using a flat area of ground a short distance away from the hamlet of Chavon, in the hills between Simiane-la-Rotonde and Saint Christol, as the designated drop zone. At this very same time, a formation of British Wellington bombers had just taken off from Italy to carry out an attack on Valence, the site where the Germans were building the highly destructive V1 bombs. During the raid, one of the bombers was unluckily hit by anti-aircraft fire and was forced to return to Italy with severe damage. However, quickly realizing that the aircraft would never make it back to base, the pilot searched for a suitable alternative to make an attempted landing. Spotting the beacon lights below him, ignited by the Abatteur, and believing them to mark out an emergency landing zone by the Resistance, he turned the aircraft around to make the landing. Sadly, he was flying too low, and the aircraft hit the valley floor, exploding upon impact.

The Abatteur, who had been awaiting their pre-arranged parachute drop, rushed to the crash site, but there was little they could do. The following day they returned to the site to recover the bodies of the crew, together with sections of the Wellington bomber, and then proceeded to bury both in a nearby field, in an effort to hide the crash site from the Germans and to protect the integrity of the parachute drop zone. Following the end of the Second World War, the bodies of the crew were recovered from the field and re-interred in the Mazargues Military Cemetery in Marseille, whilst parts of the exhumed aircraft were assembled into a memorial sculpture and placed at the site of the crash to commemorate the events of that night. Included within the metallic structure were remnants of fabric recovered from the crash site.[51]

Albeit not a full-size aircraft, remnants of an American B-17G bomber, tail number 43-39035, are kept on top of Reigate Hill in Surrey. In a tragic tale of lost youth, on the evening of 19 March 1945, the aircraft from 384th Bomb

Group, 547 Bomb Squadron was returning to base at Grafton Underwood, in Northamptonshire, after a bombing operation near the German Czech border. Just after 5.30 pm, residents were alerted to the sound of aircraft engines revving up at high power. Moments later, the B-17 was observed entering a thick cloud, after which a terrifying explosion was heard. The bomber had crashed into Reigate Hill killing all nine crew members on board, including Pilot Second Lieutenant Robert S Griffin from Glendale, California, who was just three months shy of his twenty-fifth birthday. Griffin was the oldest officer on board. Others included co-pilot Second Lieutenant Herbert S Geller from Wayne County, a university student, Second Lieutenant Royal A Runyon, from Hancock County, Illinois; Staff Sergeant Robert Manbeck, who had completed more than fifty missions and had volunteered for a second tour; and Sergeant Thomas J Hickey, the most highly decorated of the crew, having been awarded the DFC. Several key eyewitnesses reported to the Wings Museum, in West Sussex, that one engine was trailing thick black smoke as it made its way at low level over the town, so it is highly probable that the aircraft returned from its mission with serious battle damage. The memorial itself, carved by sculptor Roger Day, was inaugurated in 2015 and depicts two wingtip housing pieces of the crashed aircraft fuselage within. Mark Richards, a representative from the National Trust, who are guardians of the land, stated: 'Its beauty and poignancy [is] striking in what is now known as the memorial glade.'[52]

Another recent memorial to a B-17 bomber, the so-called 'Man 'O' War' today stands proudly in the northern French town of Breuil. Funded by Monsieur Bertrand Boilly, the town's mayor, and inaugurated on 6 May 2023, the memorial is built from the B-17's propeller, mounted on a highly polished black, stylized metal support. The aircraft in question was partaking in its twentieth raid over Germany, in a mission to destroy the Fock Wulf factories in Frankfurt, when on 20 March 1944 it encountered adverse weather conditions. Having lost contact with the aircraft formation, and unaware that the rest of the bombers had been ordered back to base, the B-17 carried on with its mission alone. Soon after dispatching its load, it came under fire from enemy fighters, encountering several direct hits, which killed two of the ten crew members instantly. With the aircraft's right wing in flames, and two of the four engines curtained off, the pilot ordered immediate evacuation; the B-17 thus collided with a tree and plunged into the marshes near the Vesle River.[53]

Other commemorative structures within this subsection, randomly chosen from a few of my personal notebooks, include a corroded Merlin engine mounted on a cairn, at the entrance to Esgair-Gawr Farm, in Henfaes, Gwynedd, Wales. An adjoining plaque reads: 'In memory of F/O M.O Slonski and Flt/Lt P. Riches, DFC who were killed on 9 February 1944 when their aircraft, a mark IX Mosquito, serial no. LR412 from Squadron 540, crashed on Aran Fawd-dwy.' The aircraft was on a cross-country exercise from RAF Benson in Oxfordshire when it flew into the mountain. This Mosquito aircraft had flown numerous operational photographic sorties, including ones over the skies of Berlin, Cannes, Munich Trondheim and Leipzig.[54] In Landsmeerderveld, Netherlands, some 5km (3mi) north of Amsterdam, as the crow flies, a memorial marks the crash site of a Vickers Wellington bomber that came down on the night of 29 September 1941, whilst on its way back to Britain from a bombing raid in Genoa, Italy. All those onboard perished. The memorial is constructed from parts of the aircraft that were found in adjacent fields.[55] On the bank of the River Avon, in Wasperton, Warwickshire, there is a brick plinth surmounted by a propeller with two twisted blades. An attached plaque reads: 'This memorial was erected by the Stratford Aviation and Militaria Enthusiasts to commemorate three separate air crash sites on this particular stretch of river in 1942 and 1943 respectively.' One of the aircraft involved was Wellington X9929 of 22 OTU, based at nearby Wellesbourne, Mountford. It crashed on the riverbank on the night of 25 August 1942, killing all five Canadians on board. The other was Whitley Z9167 of 24 OTU, based at Honeybourne, which crashed for unknown reasons on 23 July 1943 killing the five crew. The propeller incorporated in the memorial came from a third crash, that of Beaufighter X7920 of 96 Squadron at Honiley. It came down at Loxley, near Wellesbourne, on 7 November 1942, killing both crew members.[56]

Large-Scale Remembrance Landscapes and Constructs

Many large-scale state-sponsored memorials would arguably be best viewed from above to appreciate the sheer scale and majesty of their layout and structure. Some are even planned to incorporate the profile of an aircraft in their overall design, such as the official war memorial in Kranji War Cemetery, located some 22km (14mi) north of Singapore. Designed by a relatively unknown architect at the time, Colin St Clair Oakes, the war memorial was created to represent the three branches of the military, namely the Air Force, Army and Navy. The overall design resembles that of an aircraft complete with a 22m (72ft) central pylon, resembling the periscope of a submarine (Navy), together with a wing-shaped roof supported by twelve stone-clad pillars (Army). The pillars are inscribed with the names of over 24,000 Allied servicemen and women who died defending Singapore and Malaya against the invading Japanese forces during the Second World War. Oakes would later go on to become principal architect for the Imperial War Graves Commission, tasked with the design of numerous war cemeteries and memorials throughout Asia.[57]

Another remarkable example, and perhaps one of the most remote air crash memorials in existence, is located deep in the Tenere Desert, a vast arid region of the southern Sahara which borders the countries of Niger and Chad. Spanning an area of approximately 400,000sq km (154,440sq mi), at map coordinates 16°51'53.748"N 11°57'13.362"E, there exists a rather unique landmark, built in the shape of an aircraft to commemorate the victims of UTA Flight 772. On 19 September 1989, UTA Flight 772 was travelling from Brazzaville, in the Republic of Congo, to Paris, when it exploded over the Sahara Desert, killing all 156 passengers and fourteen crew members onboard. According to the investigation carried out by the International Civil Aviation Organization (ICAO), it was determined that the deadly explosion had been caused by a bomb placed in a suitcase which was stored in the forward cargo hold. In 1999, a French court found six Libyans guilty of the atrocity and, in their absence, sentenced them to life imprisonment.[58]

An earlier memorial was first erected at the crash site by oil workers from Exxon in remembrance of three of their colleagues who had perished in the explosion. Somehow, they managed to raise the remains of the starboard wing, entombed within the sand, adding a small plaque inscribed with the names of their three fellow workers. Unfortunately, the wing was poorly secured and with the ever-shifting desert sands, it eventually collapsed.

As such, the families of the victims decided to erect their own memorial, led by Guillaume Denoix de Saint Marc, whose father Jean-Henri had died on UTA Flight 772. A life-size silhouette of the aircraft was therefore created, the site some 10km (6mi) away from where the wreckage had originally fallen, to a) retain the sanctity of the crash site and b) to ensure that the memorial would be visible by those flying overhead. Denoix de Saint Marc stated that he was inspired by the 'Aeropostale', the pioneering company that delivered mail to French colonies in the 1920s by utilizing large stone circles to navigate their way across the vast Sahara landscape. He says: 'Everybody said: "Why build a memorial where nobody can see it?" he says. "But I thought - planes still fly over, the passengers can see it. So, I investigated how big it would have to be to be seen from the air.' It took 140 local men from Agadez, a city in north-central Niger, six weeks to construct the memorial, largely by hand. The form and dimensions of the aircraft they fashioned with black rock, the stones were carried by truck from some 70km (44mi) away, and placed, by hand, in a circle around the full-size silhouette of the plane. The remnants of the wing were then salvaged from the crash site and laid horizontally to represent a compass point; a commemorative plaque was then added inscribed with the names of all those who perished. Finally, the enclosure was surrounded by 170 broken mirrors, placed to symbolize reflections of the victims of the crash.[59]

Aeroplane memorials are not the only type of aircraft that would sometimes benefit from an aerial approach to appreciate their significance. In Lakehurst, New Jersey, there is a unique memorial to those who perished whilst travelling aboard the airship *Hindenburg,* one of two German-made and operated rigid airships that made transatlantic flights between Germany and the United States. The *Hindenburg* was a 245m (804ft)-long airship of conventional Zeppelin design, with a maximum speed of 135kph (84mph) and a cruising speed of 126kph (78mph). Though it was designed to be filled with helium gas, the airship was, in fact, filled with highly flammable hydrogen; the United States controlled the world's supply of helium and had banned its export, in part due to limited supply but also because of export restrictions by the United States against Nazi Germany. On 6 May 1937, whilst landing at Lakehurst, New Jersey, on the second of its scheduled 1937 transatlantic crossings, the *Hindenburg* burst into flames and crashed to the ground, killing thirty-five passengers and one ground-crew member. Although the surrounding area has now become a rather unassuming car park, the crash site itself is roped off and marked by a lone weathervane, in the shape of a Zeppelin, together with a large stone outline of the airship, symbolizing the *Hindenburg's* passing.[60]

Returning briefly to Africa, a relatively recent commemorative structure has appeared in KwaZulu-Natal, near the town of Winterton, in memory of a group of healthcare workers, whose Netcare 911 emergency helicopter tragically crashed in 2021, killing all those onboard. Following the incident, 2 hectares (5acres) of land surrounding the crash site was purchased by Netcare to not only preserve the integrity of the site, but also to erect a memorial in honour of those lost:

> 'We have erected this memorial to remember and to reflect on the exceptional lives of these individuals bearing witness to the extraordinary contribution that they each made in their own unique way. This space, this memorial, stands as a significant, and eternal symbol and reminder to all of us that these individuals lived and died as heroes.' (Dr Richard Friedland, Netcare Feb. 2022)

Assigned to Johannesburg-born artist Marco Cianfanelli, renowned for his work on South Africa's Freedom Park monument, as well as Nelson Mandela's fiftieth anniversary memorial, the design process involved excavating a series of earthworks, combined with targeted landscaping, to follow the flight path of the helicopter as the tragic events unfolded. Directly in front of the impact zone, the shape of the African continent has been gouged out of the land, echoing 'the remarkable and heartrendingly distinctive burn mark left on the veld when the helicopter wreckage set the grass ablaze'. The full effect is best appreciated from the specially constructed ramparts overlooking the site.[61]

Gardens of Remembrance

A garden of remembrance is a designated area that provides one with a quiet and contemplative space to reflect on the loss and the life of the departed. They often feature lawns, rose beds, ornamental trees, and other plant life, as well as memorial plaques, tablets, or dedicated plots to further personalize the remembrance. Those built to commemorate aviation disasters vary greatly in size, from the modest walled garden that commemorates the crash of TAM Airlines Flight 3054, a passenger jet that overran the runway at Sao Paulo, Brazil on 17 July 2007, killing all 187 passengers and crew on board, to the compact 'Grove of Memory' memorial in St Petersburg, Russia, dedicated to the 224 victims of Metrojet Flight 9268, that exploded in mid-air in October 2015 whilst enroute from Sharm El Sheikh, Egypt to St Petersburg. A large percentage of the aviation state-sanctioned gardens of remembrance are, for the most part, related to some form of major tragedy, often an act of terrorism. In this instance, several commemorative monuments, spanning many different countries, may be fashioned to memorialize a singular event. Two such examples, one in Lockerbie, Scotland, the other in the United States, perfectly demonstrate the requisite criteria.

Lockerbie, Scotland

On the evening of 21 December 1988, at three minutes past seven, Pan Am Flight 103, a Boeing 747 en route from London to New York, exploded in mid-air, killing all 259 passengers on board, as well as eleven people on the ground in Lockerbie, a small town in south-west Scotland, the latter hit by large sections of explosive aircraft wreckage falling from the skies. The Lockerbie Bombing or the Lockerbie Air Disaster, as it is sometimes known, remains the deadliest aviation incident ever to take place in the United Kingdom, as well as the most devastating act of terrorism on UK shores. With 189 Americans also killed, prior to the events of 9/11 it was also the deadliest act of terror against the United States. At first the tragedy was thought to be a horrific accident, but investigators soon discovered that the cause of the explosion was in fact a terrorist bomb, planted inside a radio-cassette holder, in a suitcase in the forward cargo hold. Having reassembled a large part of the fuselage to aid with the inquiry, in 1991, following a three-year joint investigation by Dumfries and Galloway Constabulary and the US Federal Bureau of Investigation (FBI), arrest warrants were issued for two Libyan nationals. This is a somewhat simplistic overview of such a catastrophic event, I admit; therefore, further details and sources can be found in Notes and References.[62]

Those killed include nationals of twenty-one different countries, with ages ranging from two months to eighty-two years old. Thereupon, to commemorate those lost, several significant memorials have been erected throughout the world. The focus for remembrance in Scotland lies just under a mile west of Lockerbie, in Dryfesdale Cemetery, where a formal Garden of Remembrance houses the official Lockerbie Air Disaster Memorial. This well-tended commemorative garden lies towards the far end of the cemetery and consists of a series of lawned areas, several flower beds and a number of paths leading past separate private and group memorials, such as the 1998 Memorial Stone, dedicated to Swedish diplomat and Assistant Secretary General to the United Nations Bernt Carlsson. The principal memorial is set into a wall and comprises three stone commemorative tablets, the large central one has the following inscribed upon it:

> 'IN REMEMBRANCE OF ALL VICTIMS/ OF LOCKERBIE AIR DISASTER/ WHO DIED ON 21st DECEMBER 1988/ (Names) Stone of remembrance: In/ Remembrance/ of/ all victims of/ LOCKERBIE AIR DISASTER/ who died on/ 21 st December 1988 Plaque: This garden of Remembrance is/ in memory of the 270 victims/ whose ages ranged from 2 months/ to 82 years from 21 nations./ The ages and nationalities of all/ victims are contained in the Book/ of Remembrance situated at/ Tundergarth Memorial Room.'[63]

Whereas the names of those who perished are inscribed upon the two adjoining stones, in six separate columns. In 2003, Dryfesdale Lodge Visitors' Centre, at the entrance to the cemetery, was opened to provide information about the air disaster and subsequent events. Here is kept the official Book of Remembrance.

Further memorials are scattered throughout the Lockerbie environs, including one at Tundergarth Church, near to where the nose section of Flight 103 came to rest, and one at Sherwood Crescent, the location where the ground fatalities occurred and where the wings of the fallen aircraft created a 50m (164ft)-long crater. Mention should also be given to a deeply personal Lockerbie memorial located in rural West Midlands, in the guise of a deciduous wood named after Flora Squire, one of the victims of the tragedy. It was planted by her family, who were also responsible for a copse of oak and beech trees nearby, which when in full leaf form a giant letter 'F' 'larger than the wingspan of a 747'. The family thought it would be fitting to have something that would be visible from the air. It is now officially referred to on Ordnance Survey maps as 'Flora's Wood'.[64]

Two Lockerbie memorials are based in the United States, the first is to be found in Arlington National Cemetery, Virginia, one of only two cemeteries that are maintained by the United States Army. Here, on 3 November 1995, the then-US President Bill Clinton unveiled a Memorial Cairn dedicated to the victims of the bombing. Built using 270 blocks of red Scottish sandstone from Corsehill Quarry in Annan, located approximately 13km (8mi) southeast of Lockerbie, it was financed entirely through private donations, a gift from the people of Scotland to the people of the United States.[65] On the cairn's base, it reads:

> 'On 21 December 1988, a terrorist bomb destroyed Pan American Airlines Flight 103 over Lockerbie, Scotland, killing all on board and 11 on the ground. The 270 Scottish stones which compose this memorial cairn commemorate those who lost their lives in this attack against America.'

Whilst on the side of the cairn, an attached bronze plaque reads:

> 'In remembrance of the two hundred seventy people killed in the terrorist bombing of Pan American Airways Flight 103 over Lockerbie, Scotland 21 December 1988. Presented by the Lockerbie Air Disaster Trust to the United States of America.'

The second Lockerbie memorial can be found at Syracuse University, New York state, as thirty-five of those killed on Pan Am Flight 103 were students returning home for the Christmas holidays from the University's London campus here in the United Kingdom. The memorial, located behind the gateway to the campus's Hall of Languages, features a semicircular Remembrance Wall made of limestone and granite, inscribed with the names of the victims. A circular stone bench also includes the names of Paula and Glenn Bouckley, a couple from Clay, New York, who were also on the flight.[66]

September 2001 Terrorist Attacks: American Airlines Flight 77

Following the tragic events on 11 September 2001, many cities, both in the United States and abroad, built commemorative structures to honour those affected, from families of the victims to survivors to first responders. These symbolic designs were often years in the making and ranged from large-scale installations to smaller (but no less poignant) memorials and gardens. We have already documented in Chapter 3 how the wreckage of one of the aircraft hijacked during the 9/11 attacks was formally buried in an atypical funerary service. As part of the same heinous attacks, at 09.37 EDT, American Airlines Flight 77, a scheduled Boeing 757-223 aircraft flying the domestic route from Washington Dulles, Virginia to Los Angeles, California, was hijacked by five Saudi men affiliated with al-Qaeda, and then deliberately crashed into the Pentagon, the headquarters of the US Department of Defense, killing all sixty-four people on board, including the five hijackers and six crew members, in addition to 125 people on the ground. The impact was so severe that a section of the Pentagon collapsed; it was rebuilt a year later.[67]

Two significant memorials mark the tragic series of events. The first is the official Pentagon Memorial itself. Designed by architect Julie Beckman together with her husband Keith Kaseman, the $22 million (£16.5 million) memorial consists of an 8,094 sqm (2-acre) park, decorated with maple trees and ornamental grasses, adjacent to where the aircraft initially hit the building. Here sits 184 individual cantilevered, stainless-steel benches, in remembrance of those who died, organized from the youngest victim to the oldest. Each bench is inlaid with granite, the end inscribed with the victim's name, sited over a reflecting pool of water, lit from below. The benches are cleverly positioned in such a way that visitors will have to face the sky simply to read the victim's name. The final inclusion is an 'Age Wall', a curved enclosure that cleverly increases in height to represent the age of those who perished, starting at 8cm (3in) to represent the youngest victim, rising to 180cm (71in) to represent the oldest. The second memorial can be found in Arlington National Cemetery, and consists of an octagonal shaped granite grave marker, approximately 1.5m (5ft) high, inscribed with the words 'Victims of Terrorist Attack on the Pentagon September 11, 2001'. Designed by Cemetery Superintendent John C. Metzler, Jr., a series of aluminium plaques, painted black, are also inscribed with the names of the 184 victims; those aboard Flight 77 are marked with a diamond in front of their name, whereas those for whom no remains could be identified are marked with a star.[68]

Small Individual Commemorative Structures

To conclude this brief look at commemorative monuments, I would like to share a couple of smaller markers dedicated to a single individual that exhibit aviation characteristics. For example, a particular favourite of mine is a simple white marble grave marker in Tomnahurich Cemetery, Inverness, crafted in the guise of a propellor blade. Dedicated to Sergeant Ian des E May, air gunner, RAF, said marker has been photographed numerous times by yours truly for a separate project. In fact, the use of propeller blades is often a common design theme, whether it be military or civilian, such as the distinctive mosaiced grave of Second Lieutenant Charles William Janes, a First World War RAF pilot, located in Abney Park, Stoke Newington. Janes was killed on 11 April 1918 when his Sopwith Camel B9210 aircraft went out of control at 61m (200ft) and crashed into the sea near Turnberry lighthouse, off the South Ayrshire coast of Scotland. In addition to being an accomplished pilot, Janes had also served as a soldier and is listed as a veteran of Gallipoli. He was only twenty-three years old when he perished.[69] By the same token, the grave marker of Second Lieutenant László Molnár, buried in the Heroes Cemetery in Sopronbánfalva, Hungary, is decorated with the twisted propeller of his downed fighter jet; the grave marker of decorated Russian pilot Ivan Antonovich Sollogub, located in Uspensky Cemetery, Chelyabinsk, was originally constructed by sawing two of his aircraft's propellor blades in half to form a cross. But perhaps the most heartbreaking image of all dates to the First World War and depicts a long line of pilot war graves from the Royal Flying Corps, where damaged propeller blades were used as headstones. This was before the Imperial War Graves Commission had erected their own standardized grave marker.

Aircraft are also a popular design for singular memorials, such as the visually impressive white marble gravestone that commemorates the bravery of Flight Sub-Lieutenant Reginald Alexander John Warneford VC, located in Brompton Cemetery, London. Warneford was a pioneering British aviator, best known for being the first airman in a heavier-than-air aircraft to shoot down a lighter-than-air German dirigible, earning him the prestigious Victoria Cross, the highest award for gallantry in the face of the enemy that can be awarded to British and Commonwealth forces. Tragically, only ten days after this encounter, Warneford would die in Paris, when a plane he was demonstrating crashed into the ground. With him was Henry Beach Needham, an American journalist, who was along for the ride. During a climb to 61m (200ft), the right-hand wings apparently collapsed, leading to a catastrophic failure of the airframe. Both occupants were thrown out of the aircraft, suffering fatal injuries. For Needham, death was instantaneous; Warneford died of his injuries on the way to hospital. Warneford's funeral, at Brompton Cemetery, was a splendid affair with over 50,000 in attendance. His coffin was carried through the cemetery on a gun carriage draped in the Union Jack, whilst the officers and men of the British Hospital in Paris sent a magnificent floral tribute in the shape of a plane. Warneford was only twenty-three years old at the time of his death.[70]

A small metallic sculpture of an aeroplane adorns the gravestone of Swiss military pilot Lieutenant Yves Domenjoz who died on 23 October 1943, whilst on active service during the Second World War, when his plane crashed in Saanen near Gstaad. Another renowned Second World War pilot, who fought numerous air battles against German enemy aircraft, is Senior Lieutenant Semyon Ivanovich Kharkhalup, who died on the morning of 30 June 1941 when his plane crashed on the outskirts of his native village whilst fighting the enemy. After the war, his remains were reburied in the centre of Konstantinovka, Moldavia, where he was endowed with an impressive monument in the shape of a MiG-15 tail, like those on display in the Ämari Pilots Cemetery, Estonia. The accompanying inscription reads: 'Those who lost their lives in the sky over the Motherland become the sky above it.'[71]

Keeping with the Soviet theme, only recently a secret graveyard has been revealed in Chinese territory, dedicated to Russian pilots who illegally flew MiG jets for North Korea during the Korean War (1950–53). For those unfamiliar with the Korean War, in short, it was an armed conflict on the Korean peninsula fought between North Korea and South Korea and their allies. North Korea was supported by the People's Republic of China and the Soviet Union, whilst South Korea was supported by the United Nations Command led by the United States. It was widely acknowledged that the North Korean army, the Korean People's Army (KPA), was obtaining its weapons from both China and the Soviet Union, with the former's direct participation in the war recognized by all. But precise Soviet involvement remained questionable. That was until several Russian veterans began to disclose to various news outlets about their illegal contribution to the war, specifically recalling engagements with American fighter jets. These revelations finally answered the burning question as to why North Korea pilots seemingly appeared to be so skilled in the air, especially as the Soviet pilots fighting for Korea were not your average airmen but came from Russia's elite Air Defense Forces (PVO). During the first two years of the Korean War, the Soviets began to build their own military cemeteries on Chinese soil, and those Soviet MiG pilots who were shot down and killed in Korea were thus buried in Soviet-occupied areas around Liaoning, in north-east China; albeit a few were also interred in colonial Russian cemeteries that dated from the early 1900s. In honour of their sacrifice, the Soviet Union validated each individual headstone with some form of aircraft emblem and/or the erection of an aircraft monument. Although, with the passing of time, a significant number of these cemeteries have fallen into disrepair, many of these aircraft memorials endure to this day.[72]

Perhaps one of the most remarkable grave markers currently sits in High Elms Country Park, Surrey, carved to honour the life of Captain Eric Fox Pitt Lubbock, son of Lord Avebury of the High Elms estate, see Figure 30. Lubbock was a renowned Royal Flying Corps pilot, who was awarded the Military Cross in 1915 for 'conspicuous gallantry and skill' shown in the theatre of war when he shot down an Imperial Albatross—a biplane fighter flown by many top German combat aces. Two years after this event, Captain

Lubbock was sadly killed in action when his Sopwith Camel biplane was shot down over Belgium on 11 March 1917. His grieving mother, Lady Avebury, commissioned a stone replica of his plane to be erected as his memorial in the family graveyard, alongside his brother and brother-in-law, who were also lost in the First World War. However, this is not the end of the story; after the First World War, as was the want of many aristocratic dynasties, the Avebury family fell upon hard times and were forced to sell their estate to the local county council. After decades of neglect by the local authority, which is not surprising in the least, in 1981 the family graveyard was disassembled, the gravestones were uprooted, and what was left was relocated into the nearby grounds of St Giles' Church. It was during this time that Lubbock's aircraft grave marker somehow went missing; some even believe that it had been stolen for profit. Unbelievably, it would turn up many years later at a stonemason's place of work in Hungerford, Wiltshire. According to Lyulph Lubbock, the fifth Baron of Avebury, it was being used to advertise the mason's services. He states: 'The mason wouldn't say how he got hold of it and refused to give it back. In the end my father had to buy it back at auction for £8,000.' And so, almost a century after its initial dedication, the memorial was placed back where it belonged, at High Elms Country Park. It was re-consecrated in 2010, complete with an accompanying plaque that reads:

> 'CAPT ERIC FOX PITT LUBBOCK/ KFC M.C./ SON OF JOHN BARON AVEBURY/ AND ALICE HIS WIFE/ BORN/ 16 MAY 1893/ KILLED IN ACTION 11 MAR 1917/ BURIED IN POPERINGHE/ BELGIUM'[73]

In 2018, to mark the centenary of the founding of the British Royal Air Force, Lubbock's stone plane was officially recognized by Historic England as one of fourteen war memorials dedicated to British airmen who fought during both World Wars.

Chapter 6

I Don't Believe It!

The bold, the beautiful, the nonsensical, and the downright audacious. What follows is an exploration into the world of 'aviation bizarre', a sepulchre of the unexpected, where the final resting place of some aircraft is outlandishly offbeat, to say the least. A case in point is the work of Turner-prize nominated artist Roger Hiorns, a man, it seems, who has a penchant for recycling and burying aircraft. Hiorns was born in Birmingham, United Kingdom, in 1975, a product of Goldsmiths College, University of London. Hiorns' first committal, in 2016, was that of a military passenger aircraft, a decommissioned Hawker Siddeley Dominie T1, in an undisclosed location in the east of England, near the River Orwell, just outside of Ipswich. The first in a network of submerged aircraft collectively titled A *Retrospective View of the Pathway,* he states: 'It's buried in a deep hole of chalk hillside on farmland. It's not publicly accessible, and in fact it's now a dense meadow.'[1] This was followed a year later by the burial of a MiG 21 in the grounds of the Eli Beamlines Laser facility in Dolní Břežany, Prague, a laser laboratory for physics and material research. The MiG 21 was the most widely used Soviet-produced jet fighter employed throughout the Eastern Bloc during the Cold War. Funded and co-organized by the Galerie Rudolfinum in Prague, Hiorns recalls:

> 'Burying a piece of Cold War history in the car park of an EU-funded laboratory is a loaded initiative,' says the artist: 'There are so many late post-Modern strands that interlink, it's an accidental collage of the networked reality, of layers. Burial is still a mystifying process, the separation of the world, and in the world is really jarring.'[2]

News of Hiorns' unusual artistic exploits soon garnered worldwide interest, from some rather surprising quarters, such as a preacher from a Christian church in Abuja, Nigeria, who was interested in the concept of burying a plane there, as he felt the ceremony might 'add to the connection between him and his congregation', whilst in 2018 a private Dutch art collector, from the city of Haarlem, located approximately 20km (12mi) from Amsterdam, commissioned Hiorns to repeat the burial exercise in his back garden, the entire process of which can be viewed on YouTube. The chosen aircraft, a British aerospace 1984 model obtained from a military airbase in East Anglia, was dismantled, reassembled and then buried.[3]

Why Hiorns chose to go down this artistic path is somewhat of a conundrum, even to himself: 'It's got something to do with taking something out of the air and putting it under the skin of the land.' He describes it as a motion towards changing the current parameters in our changing relationship to aircraft. In essence, the same sentiment I am aiming to achieve in writing this work. I would argue that if you purposely allow a plane to be buried then, in effect, you have created a new form of funerary rite. One that should be acknowledged and respected. The burial of the craft also acts as a conservancy for that landscape. As the owner of the land upon which Hiorns buried his first aircraft stated: 'It wasn't until we lowered the plane in and you could look at the nose, did something say to me: "Yeah, I can see it now."'[4]

Since then, Hiorns has revealed there are plans to bury not one, but a small fleet of planes around the world, stating that jetliners could be interred in the United States, South Africa, and the demilitarized zone between North and South Korea. One of his latest pursuits, in conjunction with the Tapestry Studio and the Ikon Gallery, Birmingham, was the burial of an entire decommissioned Boeing 737 on vacant industrial land beside the Old Canal, in the Port Icknield area of Birmingham. Although fully interred below ground, some 7m (23ft) down, the aircraft would have been fully accessible to visitors via a descending spiral staircase, whereby they could enter the cabin as you would on a regular 737, aircraft and sit viewing the earth around them. Jonathan Watkins, Ikon Gallery director, said: 'If you have a claustrophobic tendency, it may not be for you, but we think the plane will be a quiet place for reflection. The plane would be so incongruous, like a person in the future stumbling across Tutankhamun's tomb.' Unfortunately, for all those involved, Birmingham City Council did not endorse the idea and planning approval was rejected.[5]

The 'artistic' notion of an aircraft burial is not limited to Hiorns. For in 2020, Swiss artist Christoph Buchel announced that he too was looking for sponsors for his 'Terminal' project, a proposal to bury a decommissioned Boeing 727 in the Mojave Desert, west of Boron, California, a site located not far from the desert's established aircraft boneyard. The project's structural engineer, Derrick Roorda of Buro Happold, explains: 'the concept is to dig a great big hole, put the airplane in it, and fill it back up, leaving the surface of the desert above the burial looking just as it did before the dig'. Visitors will be able to experience the subterranean art project via an underground tunnel, some 122m (400ft) in length, connecting the plane to a parking area. Although the appropriate government body, namely Kern County, unanimously approved a permit for 'Terminal', way back in 2012, little has been heard since.[6]

Mention should also be made regarding The Boneyard Project, one of my favourite artistic endeavours that involves the reusing of dead aircraft. Conceived in 2010 by New York gallery owner Eric Firestone, and organized in conjunction with American cultural curator Carlo McCormick, the Boneyard Project revived a number of previously disused aeroplanes from the Boneyard at Davis-Monthan, now located in the adjacent Pima Air & Space Museum, and gave them to several renowned street artists. The first part of the Boneyard Project, entitled 'Nose Job', made its debut in the summer of 2011 with an exhibition of aircraft nose cones at the Eric Firestone Gallery in East Hampton, Long Island.[7] But having been convinced by Scott Marchand, Director of Collections and Aircraft Restoration at the Arizona Aerospace Foundation, to move the exhibition to the Arizona desert; the second instalment of the project, entitled 'Round Trip', saw a number of graffiti artists, such as Andrew Schoultz, Nunca, Retna, How & Nosm, Faile etc., travel to Pima Air & Space Museum to display their talents upon several chosen aircraft, including a Lockheed VC-140b Jetstar, a Beechcraft C-45 Expeditor, and a handful of Douglas Super DC-3s. What transpired was a cacophony of colourful imagery, including skulls, overlapping eyes, dark black Xs and Ys, fishtails, serpents, bird wings and alike. Artist Andrew Schoultz stated: 'I felt like I was doing some type of top-secret project, which felt special.... when one of the boneyard denizens is repainted it gets a brand-new life instead of being destroyed and becomes something to inspire.' Firestone anticipates that the third phase of the Boneyard Project will be to engage yet more artists, and to expand the project into new locations throughout the country.[8]

A fleeting display of mortality also befell a Sea Harrier and SEPECAT Jaguar aircraft in 2010, when they appeared in British artist Fiona Banner's exhibition at the Tate Britain, which featured the two decommissioned fighter jets as monumental sculptures within the neo-classical Duveen Gallery Hall. The Harrier was suspended nose-down from the ceiling. Mimicking its namesake, the harrier hawk bird, the aircraft's surface was reworked with hand painted graphic feather markings: the cockpit, the eyes; the nose cone, the beak; 'evoking both a fallen creature and dramatic sculptural presence'. The Jaguar lay on the gallery floor, polished to a mirror-like finish that 'reflected its surroundings and the viewers themselves'. Banner states:

> 'It's hard to believe that these planes are designed for function, because they are beautiful. But they are absolutely designed for function, as a bird of prey is, and that function is to kill. That we find them beautiful brings into question the very notion of beauty, but also our own intellectual and moral position. I am interested in that clash between what we feel and what we think.'

Having been fortunate to view said exhibition, I must say the overall effect was awe-inspiring. According to the 'official blurb', Banner's piece was meant to 'explore the themes of masculinity, war, beauty and the spectacle of technology'. By transforming these 'engines of destruction' into objects of art, Banner blurred the lines between 'fascination and repulsion, awe and anxiety - inviting reflection on the seductive power of warfare and the narratives we build around it'.[9]

A begrudging mention should also be made with regards to the more recent 'The MiG-21 Project', which opened in The Museum of Flight, Seattle, on 21 June 2025, just as I was about to deliver this manuscript to my publisher. In what I can only describe as an 'abomination', South African artist Ralph Ziman has 'transformed' a Soviet MiG-21 fighter jet into, and I quote, a 'stunning work of art entirely covering the jet in tens of millions of colourful glass beads'. He states: 'The aim of "The MiG-21 Project" is to take the most mass-produced supersonic fighter aircraft and to turn it from a machine of war into something that looks beautiful, changes the meaning of it.'[10] Moving swiftly on . . .

Aircraft are increasingly being repurposed into a variety of establishments, including holiday rentals, restaurants, cafes and even coffee shops. Not only do these conversions offer a unique experience for the aviation enthusiast, but they also offer the aircraft a distinctive final resting place, away from the inevitable demise. What follows is a brief exploration into the world of aircraft resurrection. Over the past few years, especially with the rise of the Airbnb phenomenon, a worldwide necropolis of dead aircraft has been miraculously reborn into forms of holiday accommodation. Some are basic in nature, whilst others offer a far more luxurious experience. A few even boast a historic association to past aviation glories, such as the 6m (20ft) Lynx helicopter, decked out in camouflage and providing private facilities for two, together with the ex-military Jetstream aircraft, expertly transformed into a sleek, stylish glamping pod for couples and small families. Both are sited on the now defunct RAF Wainfleet Airbase, in Friskey, Lincolnshire, a former weapons range, dating back to 1890, that was used by the Dambusters throughout the Second World War.[11] Another 'glamping' site, Pinewood Park, located some 3km (2mi) from Scarborough, North Yorkshire, offers the aviation enthusiast a unique night's stay in one of their two Sea King helicopters, one of which served in the Falklands, whilst the other was piloted by none other than Prince William.[12] A 1982 Westland Lynx XZ676, once used by the Army Air Corps, now sits, awaiting guests, in Ream Hills Holiday Park in Preston, Lancashire. Kitted out in full camouflage attire, it is just big enough to house a living area, a kitchenette and a double bed, with the former cockpit area transformed into a meal prep area. A similar set up can be found near Stirling, Scotland, when, in 2016, a local Stirling farmer, Martyn Steedman, purchased a 17m-long (56ft) Sea King from the Royal Navy helicopter for just over £6,000 ($8,000). ZA127 was first commissioned in 1980, serving on HMS Illustrious during the Falklands War in 1982. Decommissioned in 1994, it now features a large bedroom, designed to sleep six guests, a kitchen and even its own shower room.[13] As an aside, Steedman has recently purchased a 1950s Scottish Twin Pioneer CC2 RAF XT610 aircraft, which is currently undergoing renovation, to add to his accommodation empire. He says:

> 'G-APRS, or Primrose as she is affectionately known by those who flew her, was one of last flying Twin Pioneers in the world. She faithfully served on civilian and military missions for nearly 50 years, before being retired because of her ageing wing struts. We're delighted to be bringing her back home to Scotland where we'll convert her into a first-class glamping experience. We're sure that like our Sea King she'll attract tourists and aviation enthusiasts alike, which is great news for the rural economy and local jobs.' - Visit Scotland 2018[14]

Moving on to passenger aircraft, in Brislington, Bristol, in Skyline Park, there sits a somewhat ostentatious PYTCHAir Private Jet, a former 727 passenger airliner, rumoured to have belonged to Middle Eastern royalty and/or the Colombian drug lord Pablo Escobar, depending on what source you read. Converted into a private jet in the 1980s, today the inside comprises sleek walnut panelling, two lounge areas, a full kitchen with gleaming crystal detailing throughout, and a gold-plated shower and toilet! Local Bristol entrepreneur Johnny Palmer stumbled across the jet in an old aircraft graveyard and spent two years refitting the aircraft, adding new lighting and plumbing, before it entered the Airbnb market.[15] In Dolgellau, Gwynedd, Wales, you can book a night in a 1970s Hawker jet, which was previously used by an oil company to ferry employees. Complete with the original cockpit, features include two bedrooms, a fully functioning kitchen, a bathroom with a shower, and outdoor seating area.[16] Whilst in the heart of the Hampshire countryside, at Marwell Mile High Airbnb, you can stay in a converted Boeing 737-200, complete with an in situ cockpit flight simulator. In 2022, the entire renovation project was featured on George Clark's *Amazing Spaces* TV programme.[17] Then there is the somewhat unorthodox site of Apple Camping, in Pembrokeshire, Wales, some ten minutes' drive from the popular holiday destination of Tenby. In the company of an unidentified flying object (UFO), an igloo and a witch's hat, you will also find the original fuselage of an ex-Etihad A320 Airbus sympathetically converted into a self-contained accommodation unit, complete with two single beds, a fully-equipped kitchen, plus a range of original aircraft features, such as operational cabin doors, Etihad and Air France-branded storage, and aisle dolly trolleys. The enterprising couple who own the site saved the plane from being scrapped and ingeniously turned it into a charming holiday spot for travellers. In addition, there is also a luxury JetStar unit on site, once the height of sophistication during the 1970s; the renovated aircraft boasts a gaming cockpit, an illuminated bar area, a large king-size bedroom as well as the original front and rear entrances.[18]

Near Arlanda Airport, Stockholm there once existed an airliner hotel, Jumbo Stay, a spacious Boeing 747-212B jumbo jet, first produced in 1976 and last operated by Transjet, a Swedish airline that went bankrupt in 2002. Owned by hotelier Oscar Diös, who found the aircraft abandoned at Arlanda, the aircraft hotel was equipped with thirty-three rooms, which could accommodate seventy-six guests at any one time. There was also a communal breakfast room, a kitchenette and numerous bathrooms, plus several original features, such as cabin windows and emergency escape hatches. Unfortunately, as of March 2025, Jumbo Stay has permanently closed its plane door and is looking for a new buyer.[19] In contrast, a 1960s Ilyushin 18 aircraft based at Teuge airport, Netherlands, a plane for East German government officials, including its then leader Erich Honecker, has been converted into a single luxury suite for two guests, and features a Jacuzzi, separate shower, infrared sauna, mini bar, and three flat screen televisions.[20] In Alaska, working pilots and flight instructors Stephanie Blanchard and Jon Kotwicki successfully converted a 1956 Douglas DC-6 cargo plane into a liveable two-bedroom home, which they rent out to guests on Airbnb. It took them six months to find the 32m (104ft) long and 36m (117ft) wide aircraft, which had originally been used for hauling cargo and fuel around Alaska. Starting with an empty shell, the aircraft now sits on a set of pillars, with one of the plane's wings converted to provide an outside balcony area. Kotwicki explains:

> 'Before I started the conversion process, I thought it would be easy because the plane already had walls and was completely enclosed

> like a house," Jon says. "But it wasn't easy. It took me five months to finish.' The full step-by step renovation process can be viewed on the *Tiny House Giant Journey* YouTube channel.[21]

For nature lovers, Punteranes in Costa Rica offers adventurous folk the opportunity to spend a night in the '727 Fuselage Home', a stylishly refurbished vintage 1965 Boeing passenger aircraft perched upon a 15m (50ft)-high platform on the edge of one of Costa Rica's national parks. With panoramic views of the jungle on one side, and ocean scenery on the other, the 727 now comes with teak panelling, hand-carved Indonesian furnishings, a comfy living area with flat screen TV, plus a handy kitchenette and dining space, as well as an observation deck, surmounted to the aircraft's wings.[22] Whereas on a small campsite on Napa Thiraphirom Beach, Phuket, Thailand, visitors can not only pitch a tent by the sea on the final approach to Runway 36, but can also spend the night inside the cabin of a former Royal Thai Navy C-47 Skytrain, which has been converted into a hotel room complete with a sea view from the cockpit windows.[23] Yet for pure unadulterated splendour, nothing compares to the converted Boeing 737 villa in Uluwatu, Bali, Indonesia, perched upon a clifftop, overlooking Nyang Nyang Beach. Purchased for an undisclosed amount by Russian entrepreneur Felix Demin from the now-defunct company Mandala Airlines, the disassembled aircraft was about to be sold to China as scrap metal. It officially opened in December 2023. Denim spent two years renovating the interior space, which features a kitchen and living area, including an opulent dining space, direct access to an al fresco Wing Lounge—a terrace built directly onto one of the plane's wings—an infinity edged pool and a cockpit Jacuzzi.[24]

One of my all-time favourite stories is 'Man Converts World War II Navy Plane into Class A Motorhome', where Michigan-based Air Force veteran, Gino Lucci, spent an entire year converting a 1943-era plane into a Class A motorhome named *The Fabulous Flamingo*. Lucci revamped the flooring, using materials from an aviation warehouse, whilst installing a bathroom and kitchen faucets, light switches, an intercom system, and a decorative, nonfunctional co-pilot's yoke from parts from other planes. The plane's cockpit was also converted into the vehicle's dashboard. To function as a recreational vehicle (RV), a truck engine and frame acted as the substructure. Small enough to fit on the roads as a vehicle, Lucci was able to register his RV as a Class A motorhome and is now legally allowed to drive it throughout the United States.[25]

Living in a requisitioned or abandoned plane is a unique lifestyle choice that offers plenty of space, safety, and a touch of aviation history. As such, there are some folks who have chosen to make an aircraft their full-time home. One such fellow is former electrical engineer Bruce Campbell, from Oregon, United States, who decided to transform a Boeing 747 into a unique liveable space. According to Campbell the plane once belonged to Olympic Airways in Greece and was even used to transport the remains of the airline's magnate owner, Aristotle Onassis, in 1975. Having bought the plane in 1999 for £78,300 ($100,000) from an aircraft graveyard close to Hillsboro Airport, Oregon, he then forked out a further £94,000 ($120,000) to move the plane to his desired location in Portland, some 35km (22mi) away. Since the aircraft already had connection ports for water and sewage, very few modifications had to be made. In fact, Campbell did little renovation to the internal structure, preferring to keep the craft as is. Bar the additions of a bathroom, kitchen and living space, which doubles as a bedroom, the flight deck has been restored to its original glory and access to the home is via the original, retractable staircase that sits beneath the plane.[26] He says:

> 'I would never live in a conventional home. No chance. If Scotty beamed me to inner Mongolia, erased my fingerprints and forced me to live in a conventional structure, I'd do what I have to do to survive – but otherwise, it's a jetliner for me anytime.'[27]

Project Freedom is another example, the design process by which Texas-based Joe Axline fulfilled his dream of living in an aircraft too. Having looked for a suitable craft in the Arizonian boneyards, he found the costs were just too expensive: 'I started out with the big idea of buying a Boeing 747, and I was able to find one for around $150,000 (£114,570) but the shipping costs would have been around $500,000 (£369,000)' he said. So, he purchased two front ends instead, one from a Spirit Airlines DC-9-41 aeroplane that had been on display in a shopping centre in Florida, and a second 18m (60ft)-long McDonnell Douglas MD-80 passenger aircraft from Arkansas. Both were shipped to Brookshire, Texas, the MD-80 was converted into three bedrooms, a bathroom, a living room, a dining room, a kitchen and an office; whereas the DC-9-41 was to become a theatre, an arts, crafts and music room, with a gourmet kitchen built into the wings.[28] Axline states:

> 'Before I started my project, I carried a book around for a year, full of ideas. A lot of my friends told me not to do it because it was a waste of money, they told me to buy a house with cash and be done with it. I could have done that, but what's the point? Life is about the journey, not the destination.'

There are other notable examples of aircraft that have been converted to homes. For instance, American country singer and Nashville Hall of Famer Red Lane, who had a past as a plane mechanic, lived for decades in a converted DC-8 that he saved from the scrapyard in the late 1970s. One of the earliest examples is a Boeing 307 Stratoliner once owned by billionaire and film director Howard Hughes, who spent a small fortune remodelling the interior into the *Flying Penthouse*, complete with a bar, a generously-sized lounge, bunk beds in the rear, and a very spacious bathroom. The aircraft was then purchased, on lease, by Houston millionaire Glenn McCarthy, who renamed her *The Shamrock*, flying celebrities to and from the famous Shamrock Hotel, the grandest hotel in Texas when it was built, the largest outside of New York or Los Angeles, and a mecca for Hollywood's most famous. When McCarthy defaulted on payments, Hughes got the plane back.[29]

Having suffered extensive damage during Hurricane Cleo in 1964, whereby she was deemed no longer flight-worthy, the *Flying Penthouse* was saved from the scrapyard by a Mr Ken London, who renamed her the *Londonaire* and remodelled her into a motorboat vessel—for example, twin V8 engines were supplanted onto the original aircraft controls for aided propulsion. The original interior layout of the aircraft was maintained. The craft was finally purchased in 1981 by Fort Lauderdale resident Dave

Drimmer, who saw a classified advertisement for a 17-m (56-ft) boathouse for the sum of $8,500 (£6,255). When he went to view the yacht, he found that it was, in fact, a plane that floated. Against all advice, he bought it at a discount, for $7,500 (£5,519). Renaming her *The Cosmic Muffin*, at first Drimmer was unaware of the Howard Hughes connection. But when he discovered the backstory, Drimmer began to restore the aircraft's original elements, which included the corner bar, seats in the lounge, as well as the cockpit, which still had the original aircraft controls and pilots' seats. He lived in the plane-boat hybrid for twenty years before eventually donating it to the Florida Air Museum in 2018.[30]

Utilizing an aircraft as a form of lodgings is not the only avenue whereby an aircraft may end its days. The food service industry has provided many decommissioned aircraft with a somewhat less than distinguished final resting place. Probably the most famous is Taupo's McDonalds in New Zealand, where you can eat your Happy Meal in the comfort of a DC-3 passenger plane. Originally used as a promotional tool for Taupo's local car dealership, when the company dissolved and the site location came up for sale in 1990, McDonald's bought the entire plot, including the DC-3 aircraft, renovating the interior to provide extra seating for diners, plus decorating the walls an extensive history of the DC-3's previous life. McDonalds even kept the original cockpit in situ but protected behind a visible panel.[31] The award for the most ingenious restaurant moniker must go to 'Steaks on a Plane' in Bolton, Lancashire, a Boeing 737 that has been turned into a no-frills eatery and takeaway. Opened in 2015, diners can either reserve a table in the cockpit area or order their food through a window in the fuselage.[32] In contrast the Runway 1 restaurant, located at Rohini heliport, Delhi, India, offers their clientele a more sophisticated dining experience, in the heart of an old Air India Airbus A320. Opened in November 2018, Runway 1 has two elegant dining options: one inside the fuselage, the other an open-air section atop one of the aircraft's wings. In true aviation style, diners are required to obtain a designated boarding pass, after which they will be shown to their chosen seats, whilst the cockpit houses a fully operational 3D flight simulation game.[33]

For the full 'aviation' dining experience, it doesn't get any better than the Airplane Restaurant, a converted 1953 Boeing KC-97 tanker, that now sits in Colorado Springs. Opened in 2002, the former Texas Air National Guard refuelling aircraft was uniquely embedded into the side of the restaurant building, with the port wing and the engine left poking through the walls. The fuel tank was then removed, providing a large 275 seat interior dining space, whilst the cockpit and the tail of the KC-97 were left pretty much intact, allowing diners the experience of the 'pilot's chair'. The tables are covered with old aviation maps and charts, the aircraft wings serve as a display space for aviation-related memorabilia, and a full-size mannequin, dressed in 1950s aircrew attire, is located at the tail end of the aircraft, demonstrating the mechanics of refuelling another aircraft mid-flight.[34] An aircraft graveyard sitting next to Lake Victoria, Uganda, was once the location of Entebbe Airport. Now called Aero Beach, comprising also a bar and a restaurant, visitors to the lake can partake in a few refreshments besides or even inside the aircraft. Delights on offer include several fighter jets, such as the MiG-17 and MiG-2, as well as a Boeing 707 and a Sud Aviation Caravelle.

For interesting backstories, one cannot compete with the C-123 Fairchild cargo plane that now shapes the El Avion Restaurant and Bar in Quepos, Costa Rica. Designed by Chase Aircraft and built by Fairchild Aircraft for the US Air Force, this aircraft is the sister plane of an additional C-123 that was shot down during the Iran-Contra affair, one of the biggest political scandals of the 1980s. In brief, Ronald Reagan's United States-led administration had orchestrated a network of arms sales to Iran, designed to win the release of US hostages held in Lebanon, whereby the profits from these hugely inflated sales would then be funnelled to Nicaraguan counter-revolutionary guerrilla fighters, commonly referred to as the 'Contras', who were fighting the Cuban-allied Sandinista government. When the CIA-owned sister plane was shot down over Nicaragua in 1986, the sole survivor, Eugene Hasenfus, was captured by the Sandinista army; through his testimony, the whole sordid affair was exposed. The C-123 that gave birth to El Avion Restaurant and Bar was thus found abandoned in San Jose International Airport in 2000, subsequently purchased for the sum of $3,000 (£2,500), dismantled and shipped to its current location; the fuselage was too wide for Costa Rican railroad bridges, thus was shipped via an ocean ferry. The aircraft now sits atop Manuel Antonio Hill, adjacent to the local national park, where patrons can enjoy drinks in the fuselage, a meal under its wings or experience the cockpit at firsthand.[35]

Staying with the food and beverage theme, Sky Coffee Buenos Aires is the name of a coffee shop in Miami, which opened on 30 November 2023; housed in the front of the fuselage of a retired McDonnell Douglas MD-88. Painted a rather swanky metallic black, the Delta aircraft was in operation from 1990 to 2019, after which it was retired. Offering the customer a full 'aviation experience', leading up the path to the aircraft is a full-size airport metal detector and two sets of stairs: one lets you walk through a small part of the cabin, with cockpit and seating still intact, whilst the other one just lets you order from an exterior window without going through the aircraft cabin.[36] Relocating to the Far East, Thailand is world-renowned for its love of extracting aircraft from their eternal slumber and breathing new life into them. Just outside its capital city, Bangkok, for instance, there sits an old Airbus A330 that has been lovingly converted into an up-market coffee shop. Named 331 Station Coffee War, the Airbus A330 was originally part of the Thai Airways fleet before it was decommissioned in 2015. Thereafter, it was purchased by former Royal Thai Navy officer, Damri Sangtang, for ten million Thai baht, approximately £250,000, and shipped to its current location in Sattahip, around 160km (100mi) south-southeast of central Bangkok.[37] A former Angel Air Cambodia Lockheed TriStar 1 XU-700 (c/n 193A-1055) has recently been added to the 331 Station Coffee War portfolio, as has another Boeing 737-4D7 HS-TDD. Another flamboyant coffee shop entitled 747 Café, housed in a Boeing 747, can be found in Lat Krabang, near Bangkok's Suvarnabhumi International Airport. To enter the aircraft, which has been carefully stripped back to expose the metal framework and aeroplane skin, visitors must pass through a designated 'departure check-in desk' before purchasing a boarding ticket.[38] The similarly themed MD-82 Café lies at the other end of the Lat Krabang district and makes use of the beautifully decorated HS-MDL (c/n 49853). Further south, on the Bang Na Expressway, parked by a Caltex fuel station, is Coffee 123, a coffee bar inside a C-123K Provider, an aircraft that was used throughout the Vietnam War, and has since been repainted from its striking black and yellow livery into grey USAF markings.[39] Whilst in Chiang Mai, in northern Thailand, some 700km (345mi) from Bangkok,

Air Diamond operates the up-market Black Canyon Coffee shop in a decommissioned ex-Thai Airways Airbus A330. Customers can tour the aircraft, visit the cockpit and sit in the passenger seats, whilst experiencing some of the best coffee on offer, in my humble opinion.[40]

Converting old aircraft into an educational facility has become a 'thing' over the past few years too. For instance, St Helen's CE Primary School in Alveston, near Bristol, was looking for a unique space to create an engaging learning environment when the pupils decided to name their new houses after planes. Deputy Headmaster Richard Adams explains: 'There is a great history in the area with the link to planes and after a school trip, they came up with a "great idea" to rescue a plane that had finished its useful service from a plane graveyard.'[41] A fuselage of a scrapped BAE-146 that had been built in 1993 in nearby Filton, was thus purchased and positioned onto the school field by a large crane in January 2023, whereby it was converted into a library and outdoor classroom. It officially opened on World Book Day on 7 March 2024.[42] A similar library facility was created in the cockpit and fuselage of an Airbus 319 at Five Acre Wood (FAW) School in Kent. As well as reading materials, the library also has audio stations and a mocked-up cockpit, complete with buttons and flight panels.[43] Whereas Milton Hall Primary School, in Westcliff, purchased an entire Cessna Citation Bravo 550, minus the wings, to provide much-needed teaching space. Claire Reynolds, business manager at the school, said: 'It was the idea of our media manager John Baker. We're always short of space at the school and he had the idea of revamping an old jet. It will be an interactive learning base, a sensory room for children with special needs. It will also be used for creative writing and reading and all the children will have access to it.'[44]

An old Soviet-era Yakovlev Yak-42 aircraft was turned into a kindergarten in the Georgian city of Rustavi. Opened in October 2012, headteacher Gari Chapidze bought the defunct but fully functional Yakovlev Yak-42 from Georgian Airways and refurbished its interior with educational equipment, games and toys, including the cockpit instruments, which had been left intact.[45] Whereas students in Ogden, Utah, with an interest in science and technology, will be able to take classes inside a converted C-130, an old Vietnam era cargo plane, attached to The Hill Aerospace Museum. Ghanaian artist Ibrahim Mahama, whose artwork has sold for millions of pounds worldwide, used funds from his artwork to purchase six planes, and convert them into classrooms at his Red Clay Studio in Tamala, Ghana. Open to the local community, and offering a variety of free lectures and workshops, the aircraft space is used to teach flight physics, computer science and basic engineering. Mahama views the aircraft as a way to inspire the next generation and create a lasting legacy: 'For me this is not separate from my work, this is the core of my work. I invest everything that I make from my work into it. I am interested in building an institution that uplifts many generations.' In doing so, the Red Clay education campus (which also features Mahama's studio) now welcomes 100,000 visitors a year to its programme of exhibitions and screenings. This includes 2,000 pupils a week during term time, who travel from rural schools on buses, which Mahama pays for.[46]

To the north of Bangkok, Thailand at the Rajamangala University of Technology Thanyaburi, an ex-PC Air A310-222 HS-PCC (c/n 419) has been repurposed as a conference centre and training facility, resplendent with a luxurious cabin complete with brown leather sofas and ornate light fittings.[47] By contrast, a mighty Soviet Tupolev Tu-124, a sibling of the Tu-104, the world's first successful jet airliner, now sits just off the main road of Čačersk, a small town in Belarus. How and why it arrived at its final resting place is somewhat of a mystery, as the nearest airport is roughly 100km (62mi) away. With a seating capacity of fifty-six, and parachutes in case of an emergency, these planes flew the skies throughout the height of the Cold War, from 1962 to 1980. Since those lofty days this particular Tupolev Tu-124 has become a stalwart of the Čačersk community, first utilized as a movie theatre, and then as the local cultural centre, hosting several artistic exhibitions and events.[48]

I am also reminded of a few eclectic retail/service outlets I have witnessed in my travels over the years. The first is to be found in Schiphol Airport, in the Netherlands, where an old KLM Mc Donnell Douglas DC-9-32 has been transformed into an airport gift shop. Divided into three parts, its nose, complete with original cockpit, was placed inside the airport terminal, with the wheels and one of its engines displayed adjacent.[49] In Carluke, Lanarkshire, an enterprising makeup artist, Amber Scott, has opened a hair and makeup salon in a 1950s Air

Atlantique aircraft that sits in her parent's back garden. Her parents had purchased the aircraft when Amber was in her teens, intending to convert it into a luxury Airbnb rental, but their idea never 'took off the ground'. Runway Studios Makeup Lounge opened in 2017.[50] In Malaysia, at the Freeport A'Famosa Outlet, Malacca, a former Lufthansa Boeing 747-200 has undergone a remarkable transformation into a branch of the American luxury fashion brand, Coach. Designed by Shanghai and Kuala Lumpur architects Spaceman, in conjunction with Coach, New York, the ambitious project encompassed the acquisition of the aircraft, its dismantling, relocation and then its skilful reassembly, all in the space of two years. Officially opened in June 2023, the Coach Airways Store and Café aim to provide the customer with a unique shopping experience, to 'transport visitors back to the opulent era of air travel during the 1970s'. To set foot into the store, first and foremost, customers are required to obtain a boarding pass-style entry card before walking down the sky bridge to enter the aircraft. Once inside they will find the front of the plane, which has been converted into a first-class cabin, serves as the main store area. An additional pair of cabins, namely retail-class cabin one and retail-class cabin two, are used as extensions of the main shop along with a small café located at the tail end of the plane.[51] In southern Thailand, in the holiday resort of Pattaya, better known for its drinking establishments and nightclubs, there are two significant aircraft transformations. The first is located at Terminal 21 shopping mall—well, directly outside, to be exact—a 37-year-old Continental Airlines 737-3T0 HS-BRA (c/n 23374), which has swapped its original Orient Thai livery for promotional Terminal 21 tags. Unsurprisingly, the aircraft-theme continues inside, with escalators leading to 'gates and each shopping level named after an international destination'. Why, the staff at the information desk even wear cabin crew uniforms. There is also a Legacy Air Saab 340A HS-LAA (c/n 340A-115) aircraft on display too.[52] By far the most spectacular is to be found in the very heart of Pattaya, located on Beach Road, at the Royal Garden Plaza mall, where a bright red Douglas EC-47P 43-49703, employed during the Vietnam War, has been installed directly into the side of the building, as if it has crashed. The aircraft forms part of the Ripley's Believe It Not entertainment centre.[53]

A Conspiracy Triumvirate

The site known as 'Area 51', located south of Nevada, some 134km (83mi) north-northwest of Las Vegas, is the common name given to a highly classified USAF facility within the Nevada Test and Training Range, thought to support the development and testing of experimental aircraft and weapons systems. Officially it is sometimes referred to as Groom Lake and/or Homey Airport. Acquired by the CIA and the US Air Force in 1955, it was the ideal location to secretly test the evolution of the new U-2 plane, developed to spy on the Soviet Union during the Cold War. Even though a secret 1992 internal CIA history of the U-2 programme was originally declassified in 1998, with countless heavy redactions, the CIA did not publicly acknowledge the base's existence until June 2013, following a Freedom of Information Act (FOIA) request.[54]

'While scant particulars on Area 51 have been discovered over the years through other declassified reports and books that contained interviews with people involved in the operative, this new report is the first time the government has openly referred to Area 51 as a government facility, according to Foreign Policy.'[55]

It was this secrecy, coupled with the lack of any official information, that gave speculation to claims that Area 51 was a location where alien spacecraft and extraterrestrial life were being kept hidden by the government. Since then, Area 51 has featured in countless related films and TV shows, such as *Independence Day* and the *X-Files*, contributing to the perception that the base is a secret hub for alien research and experiments. The secret testing of the U-2 plane in the 1950s, at altitudes much higher than commercial aircraft then flew, combined with its spacecraft appearance, provoked a tremendous increase in reports of UFOs. 'At this time, no one believed manned flight was possible above 18,288m (60,000ft), so no one expected to see an object so high in the sky,' note authors Gregory Pedlow and Donald Welzenbach.[56]

The public's fascination with Area 51 and aliens has successfully acted as a distraction to another one of its well-kept secrets, that being the existence of a secret aircraft graveyard. In 2001, journalist Keith Rogers, writing in the *Las Vegas Review*, documented the account of a former Groom Lake employee, who spoke anonymously, who witnessed the wreckage of a classified plane being buried in a large dug-out grave. The wreckage, having spent months hidden in a 'Scoot-N-Hide' hangar, a site off a taxiway where secret planes are kept out of view of orbiting satellites, was put on a flatbed truck and then dumped into the hole: 'They attached a cable to the aircraft and just pulled it off. The thing was shattered like an egg.'[57] Moreover, Peter Merlin, an aviation writer, also found evidence of the aircraft graveyard in declassified documents, he believed more than a dozen were buried at Groom Lake with the combined value of up to $1 billion (£740,000). Writing on the Urban Ghosts website, a blogger, who will only identify as 'Tom', writes that secret projects may contain either highly toxic material or technology of such a sensitive nature that the military is unwilling to risk having it ferried to a 'boneyard', so they are buried in the desert, never again to see the light of day.

'When – and if – secret planes are declassified, they're treated differently from other military aircraft, and the specifics of their hardware may remain under wraps for decades. One such fate that has befallen crashed, retired or failed projects over the decades is burial. Aircraft have literally been dragged into deep pits miles from public land, often near the enigmatic Groom Lake test site in Nevada, famously known as Area 51. Not only does Groom serve as a testing ground for the US government's most advanced programmes, but it also serves as the final resting place of many of its most secret aircraft.'[58]

Aircraft believed to have interred within the graveyard include: several 1960s-vintage A-12s, predecessors of the fast, high-flying SR-71 Blackbird spy planes; four U-2s from the 1950s; an F-101 chase plane that crashed in 1965; two Lockheed Have Blue airframes that were used to demonstrate technology for the F-117A; and the wreckage of a MiG-23 that crashed in 1984.[59]

Another location beloved by conspiracy theorists is the Bermuda Triangle, a loosely defined region in the North Atlantic Ocean, roughly bounded by the southeastern coast of the United States, Bermuda, and the islands of the Greater Antilles (Cuba, Hispaniola, Jamaica and Puerto Rico). A vast area, stretching between 1.3 to 3.9 million sq km (501,933 to 1,505,798sq mi) depending on your definition, a significant number of aircraft have 'mysteriously' vanished here without a trace. The earliest suggestion of unusual disappearances in the Bermuda area appeared in the *Miami Herald* newspaper in September 1950, written by Edward Van Winkle Jones. Two years later, *Fate* magazine published 'Sea Mystery at Our Back Door', a short article by George X. Sand, that was the first to lay out the now-familiar triangular area where the losses took place. The term *Bermuda Triangle* itself is believed to have originated in a 1964 article from the American pulp magazine *Argosy*. The article, authored by Vincent Gaddis, illuminated a pattern of disappearing planes and ships, yet without explanations as to their fate. The Bermuda Triangle legend had begun![60]

Despite conventional environmental explanations such as 'white squalls', intense storms that arrive without warning, waterspouts, tropical cyclones, hurricanes, tidal currents (in particular the Gulf Stream), large deposits of methane gas spewing up from the ocean floor and magnetic variation, many naysayers hypothesize that a parallel universe exists in the Bermuda Triangle region, causing a time/space warp that sucks objects into it. Others pin the blame on leftover technology from the lost city of Atlantis, whereby powerful energy crystals hamper navigational instruments; and, of course, alien interference, in their eyes, should never be discounted. Nonetheless, whether you believe in the existence of a Bermuda-centric 'triangle of death' or not, here are just some of the aircraft that have perished within its midst.

1945: 10 July, Thomas Arthur Garner, AMM3, USN, along with eleven other crew members, was lost at sea in a US Navy PBM3S patrol seaplane, Bu. No.6545, Sqd VPB2-OTU#3, in the Bermuda Triangle. They left NAS, Banana River, Florida, at 7.07 pm on 9 July 1945 for a radar training flight to Great Exuma, Bahamas. Their last radio position report was sent at 1.16 am, 10 July 1945, with a latitude/longitude of 25.22N 77.34W, near Providence Island, after which they were never heard from again. An extensive ten-day surface and air search, including a carrier sweep, found nothing.[61]

1945: 5 December, Flight 19 was a training flight comprising five TBM Avenger torpedo bombers that disappeared on 5 December 1945, whilst over the triangle. The squadron's flight plan was scheduled to take them due east from Fort Lauderdale for 227km (141mi), north for 117km (73mi), and then back over a final 225km (140mi) leg to complete the exercise. The training flight never returned to base; all five bombers had disappeared. The last hysterical radio transmission from Flight 19 said:

> 'We can't tell where we are... everything is... can't make out anything. We think we may be about 225 miles northeast of base..." For a few moments, the pilot rambled incoherently before uttering the last words ever heard from Flight 19. "It looks like we are entering white water... We're completely lost.'[62]

Incredibly, this was followed by the loss of one of the search and aircraft rescue aircraft, a PBM Mariner, that was deployed to look for Flight 19. It too vanished with the loss of thirteen crew. For five days, Coast Guard, Navy, and naval aviation personnel searched extensively in more than 647,497sq km (250,000sq mi) of Atlantic and Gulf waters, but nothing was ever found—no bodies, no wreckage, life rafts, or even an oil slick. Nothing. There is a report that Mariner may have exploded off the coast of Florida, but again no wreckage was found. The Navy launched an investigation into the incident; its findings were inconclusive.[63]

1947: 3 July, a Douglas C-54 crashed off the Florida coast after the pilot lost control in turbulence.

1948: 30 January, Avro Tudor G-AHNP Star Tiger was lost with six crew and twenty-seven passengers, en route from Santa Maria Airport in the Azores to Kindley Field, Bermuda.

1948: 28 December, Douglas DC-3 NC16002 lost with three crew and thirty-six passengers, en route from San Juan, Puerto Rico, to Miami, Florida. A Civil Aeronautics Board found there was insufficient information available to determine the cause of the disappearance.

1949: 17 January, Avro Tudor G-AGRE Star Ariel lost with seven crew and thirteen passengers, en route from Kindley Field, Bermuda, to Kingston Airport, Jamaica.

1963: 28 August, A pair of US Air Force KC-135 Stratotanker aircraft collided and crashed into the Atlantic 480km (300mi) west of Bermuda. Some writers say that whilst the two aircraft did collide, there were two distinct crash sites, separated by over 260km (160mi) of water.

However, Larry Kusche, author of *The Bermuda Triangle Mystery: Solved* (1975), showed that the unclassified version of the Air Force investigation report revealed that the debris field defining the second 'crash site' was examined by a search and-rescue ship, and found to be a mass of seaweed and driftwood tangled in an old buoy.

1965: 9 June, A USAF C-119 Flying Boxcar of the 440th Troop Carrier Wing missing between Florida and Grand Turk Island. The last call from the plane came from a point just north of Crooked Island, Bahamas, and 285km (177mi) from Grand Turk Island. On 18 July 1965, debris from the plane was found on the beach of Gold Rock Cay just off the northeastern shore of Acklins Island.

1965: 6 December, Private ERCO Ercoupe F01 lost with pilot and one passenger, en route from Fort Lauderdale to Grand Bahamas Island.

2005: 20 June, a Piper PA-23 disappeared between Treasure Cay Island, Bahamas and Fort Pierce, Florida. There were three people on board.

2017: 23 February, the Turkish Airlines flight TK183 (an Airbus A330-200) was forced to change its direction from Havana, Cuba to Washington Dulles airport after some mechanical and electrical problems occurred over the triangle.

2017: 15 May, A private MU-2B aircraft was at 732m (24,000ft) when it vanished from radar and radio contact with air traffic controllers in Miami. Plane wreckage was found later.[64]

The Alaska Triangle

The aforementioned 'triangle', I will admit, is not one I was familiar with at all, until I began my research into strange aircraft phenomena. Spanning thousands of miles of remote wilderness, including harsh tundra and jagged peaks, this new vortex of unnatural phenomenon, bordered on three sides by the cities of Anchorage, Juneau and Utiqiagvik, is little known outside Alaska. Disturbingly, not only have an extensive number of people gone missing but also aircraft, lots of them, without a trace. For instance, in 1972, the small plane that Congressman Nick Begich and House Majority Leader Hale Boggs were travelling in suddenly fell off the radar somewhere in the triangular area between Anchorage and Juneau. The weather conditions were good, visibility was high and, despite one of the largest search-and-rescue missions in US history, no wreckage was ever found.[65] Similarly, in 2005, an Alaskan bush pilot named Gary M, with over twenty years flight experience, was flying solo from Talkeetna to a remote hunting post when, midway through the trip, his instruments began to go crazy. His GPS lost signal, his compass began to spin out of control, in fact all the electronics on the plane ceased to function; the result being the aircraft fell from the sky. Miraculously, Gary M survived the crash, but strangely, the search team not only found him 483km (300mi) off course, but in an area in which Gary M is adamant he never flew toward. Furthermore, when found not only was his watch some five hours behind, but Gary M had no memory of what happened between the crash and the rescue. He refuses to fly over the triangle to this day.[66]

Long before Alaska joined the United States in 1959, according to local folklore, indigenous Alaskan tribes were already aware of the triangle's dark energy. They speak of the Kushtaka, a part-human, part-otter shapeshifter said to lure victims to their downfall with cries that mimic a loved one in distress, stories of which passed down through successive generations. Others believe the land itself is cursed, by some powerful spiritual force, earthbound or otherwise. Some physicists have even proposed that the Alaska Triangle may sit on an energy vortex—a theoretical location where Earth's electromagnetic field warps space and time.[67] Such occurrences would explain aircraft instrument malfunction, as numerous pilots report electronic interference right before disappearing. It may also help to clarify the numerous eyewitness reports of strange lights that dart across the sky and mountains that emit a low-frequency vibration. Cynics argue that Alaska's triangle is no more mysterious than its geography, and such disappearances are a consequence of the unforgiving terrain. Many, however, disagree and argue that if this was simply the case then why is so much airspace in the triangle restricted? Why do the FBI seize certain air crash records and never release them? And why are high-level researchers quietly sent in to investigate aircraft disappearances, then pulled out as quickly as they were sent in? Only time will tell, it seems.

I would just like to briefly return to the topic of memorials. Although covered in some detail in the previous chapter, there are certain monuments, made of full-size decommissioned aircraft, that appear in some rather odd places. For example, a decommissioned Russian MiG fighter jet stationed in a local park, surrounded by well-tended flower beds, manicured lawns and a rather splendid water feature, would meet this requirement. Whereas large-scale state-sponsored aircraft monumental structures, such as the UH-1 'Huey helicopter', on display at the Vietnam Helicopter Pilot and Crewmember Monument, Arlington National Cemetery, Virginia, would not. Neither would the AH-1 Cobra helicopter and Hawker Hunter aircraft, belonging to the Royal Jordanian Air Force, that are currently exhibited in the forecourt of the Martyrs Memorial in Amman, Jordan. These aircraft are attached to specific places of active commemoration, therefore they do not fit the bill, so to speak. Whereas the majority of those that follow appear to exhibit no real purpose. I'm sure they once did, but for many those days are long gone.[68]

- Several abandoned aircraft, including ex-French Air Force Dassault Mystere IVA, a MiG 24, ex-Belgian Air Force Lockheed T33A and an ex-East German Air Force Su-22, can be found at RAF Spadeadam, in Cumbria, the only electronics warfare tactics range in the United Kingdom.
- In the small village of Raduil, in rural Bulgaria, there is a Mikoyan-Gurevich MiG-21 Fishbed C on public display in someone's front garden.
- Hidden beneath some trees in a local park in Jakabszallas, Hungary is a MiG-15bis 1978; the serial number 657 and is just discernible underneath.
- In a service area just off the A1 southbound, near Bedale, there sits a Red Arrows BAE Hawk in pretty good condition. It was previously the gate guardian at RAF Scampton.
- In Hosozawa, Minobu-cho, Yamanashi-ken, Japan, a full-size F-104J 46-8594 sits on the roof of a private house.
- On industrial waste ground adjacent to a petrol station in Pythää, Finland, is a former Polish Air Force TS-11 Iskra bis-B 610.
- At an outdoor activity centre near Old Hutton, Kendal, Cumbria, there sits the remains of a F-27.

- In the city of Omurtag, Bulgaria there is not one, not two, but three aircraft displayed in various flying modes at the highway exit.
- The main Portuguese shooting range at Alcochete is guarded by an immaculate A-7P Corsair II.
- In the garden area of Salty's Restaurant, Montrose, Scotland, there sits a WG30 N116WG helicopter.
- In the Romanian village of Balaci, a MiG 21 jet fighter once belonging to the Romanian Air Force lies adjacent to some telegraph poles and a cross-grave marker.
- In Lazarevskoye, Sochi, Russia, a MiG-23 fighter jet sits abandoned in a neglected park surrounded by high-rise apartment blocks.
- A Harrier Jump Jet is prominently displayed outside the Dyson factory in Malmesbury, Wiltshire, United Kingdom. It's positioned in the car park to inspire Dyson's engineers and is a part of the campus's overall design and engineering focus. The Harrier is a repaired GR9 jump jet that had previously crashed.
- At a petrol station in Touwsrivier, South Africa, a brightly coloured crumpled old Yak-52, ZU-ARB, has been weirdly set into the side of the building.
- In the town centre of Ekzarh Yosif, Bulgaria, a Samolet L-29 has been arranged next to some old park benches and two cars of the same era. The entire display is guarded by a camel!
- In a park in Miastko, Poland, there is a MiG-17 jet fighter aloft a pole.
- Again, in a park in Leira, Portugal, parked among some trees is a Beech 18 aircraft, number D18S 2508, one of only twenty-five once operational.
- Several aircraft relics can be viewed from the Chocks Away Café at Hawarden Airport, Chester, once the site of a Second World War RAF air base.
- Directly positioned on a stone plinth outside a grocery store in Halli, Finland, is a SAAB J 35BS DK-201.
- A Grumman can be found displayed in a van hire yard in Ringwood, Hampshire.
- In a weed-infested car park of an Eastern European church in Ravnetz, a small city near the Black Sea port of Burgas, a MiG-21 has been stuck on a pole.

- In Ali Pasha's castle fortresses in Gjirokastra, Albania, there are the remains of a USAF T-33 on the roof! There are conflicting stories regarding how it arrived there. The US version is that they had to make an emergency landing in Albania in 1957, and the jet somehow ended up atop the castle ramparts.
- There is a XZ177 Lynx AH7 helicopter at a paintball site at Kegworth near East Midlands Airport.

These examples are just a fraction of aircraft uncovered during the research process, and though arguably many of them have been saved from the 'aviation rainbow bridge', as one person poetically described it to me, in many instances, their final resting place has a lot to be desired.

The ultimate 'I don't believe it' moment, however, is reserved for a horrendous event that occurred way back in 1972. For there are some monuments that belie an extraordinary backstory. One such memorial is displayed in an unassuming car park, upright amongst some trees, alongside road 25854 in Srbská Kamenice, northern Bohemia. It is a simple stone monolith, complete with commemorative plaque, honouring those who were killed aboard JAT Airways Flight 367, a McDonnell Douglas DC-9-32 aircraft (registration YU-AHT), which exploded in mid-air whilst enroute from Stockholm, Sweden to Belgrade, Yugoslavia (now Serbia).[69] Twenty-seven out of the twenty-eight passengers and crew aboard lost their lives. On 26 January 1972, it is believed a bomb exploded in the baggage compartment, ripping through the fuselage. As the aircraft broke apart from the force of the explosion, the wreckage fell to the ground, dispersing over several kilometres. The bombing is believed to be the work of Croatian nationalists linked to the Swedish far right organization Ustashe.[70]

Yet the bombing of JAT Airways Flight 367 is not remembered for this wanton act of extremist violence, but for the remarkable story of Vesna Vulović, the bombing's only survivor. As her fellow passengers plummeted to their deaths, remarkably, Vulović weathered the fall. Investigators believe her body had become trapped between a food cart and the fuselage, the food cart somehow acting as a seat belt, thus preventing her from being sucked out of the plane. The falling fuselage, with Vulović pinned inside, then landed at an angle in a heavily wooded and snow-covered mountainside, which cushioned the impact. Barely alive, after hitting the ground, her cries and whimpers were heard by a local villager, Bruno Honke, an experienced medic during the Second World War, who administered first aid on the spot. If it hadn't been for Honke's medical skills, Vulović would have most certainly died. Vulović spent days in a coma and was hospitalized for several months.[71] She suffered a fractured skull, three broken vertebrae, broken legs, broken ribs, and a fractured pelvis. These injuries resulted in her being temporarily paralyzed from the waist down. Whilst recovering in hospital in Belgrade, her room was placed under twenty-four-hour police protection because the authorities feared that the perpetrators of the bombing would wish to see her dead. No one was allowed in to see her except for her parents and doctors. Within ten months of her fall, Vulović had regained the ability to walk, albeit with a slight limp, and spent sixteen months recuperating in total.[72] In 1985, *The Guinness Book of World Records* recognized Vulović as the official world record holder for surviving the highest fall without a parachute, plummeting a whopping 10,160m (33,330 ft). Vulović passed away in Belgrade in 2016.[73]

Chapter 7

Resurrection

To conclude this all-too-brief foray into the world of aircraft gravesites, I would like to bring the subject matter full circle, completing a three-stage mortuary process—namely death, deposition, followed by the act of resurrection, a distinctive aspect of aviation history. Throughout the world there exists an army of individuals and groups who are determined to not only keep the memory of iconic aircraft alive, but to raise them from the grave, in a bold Lazarus-type move, thus breathing new life into them. I would estimate that around ninety per cent of said folk are volunteers, passionate about preserving aircraft, giving up their time and often aviation expertise for the cause. The remaining ten per cent have more money than sense! In the process of writing this book I have been privileged to speak to a number of people in regards to their tireless efforts in this matter, from The Buccaneer Aviation Group based at Cotswold Airport, whose aim is to preserve the history and memories of the Blackburn Buccaneer aircraft, to engineers working on the Wellesbourne Vulcan bomber, one of only three left in a taxiable condition, looked after by the 655 Maintenance and Preservation Society (655MaPS). One cannot overlook the heroic efforts of Ed Maloney, an aviation enthusiast if ever there was, and founder of the Planes of Fame Air Museum in Chino, California, which today is home to over 160 unique aircraft from around the world—many of them the last of their kind capable of flight or even in existence. Maloney physically witnessed the destruction of Second World War aircraft in the Californian boneyards and knew something had to be done.

'I was a senior in high school, and I used to drive down to the Cal-Aero Field where they were storing thousands of the old warbirds,' he recalled. 'I remember watching this 18-foot steel plate drop from a crane. It would snap a B-17 or B-24 in half just as if they were toys. It was almost sickening to watch.'

Furthermore, as I commenced writing these final pages, I was made aware that the model F-5 Tiger aircraft, gate guardian at RAF Alconbury, which has proudly watched over the main gate for almost fifty years, has avoided the aviation death dealers and has been kindly donated to the Sculthorpe Heritage Centre, in Fakenham, Norfolk, by the USAF. Way to go USAF! Albeit I should add that said aircraft is, in fact, a carbon-fibre model and not an actual working aeroplane. At Aerospace Bristol, a Bristol 170 Freighter Mk.31M (ZK-EPG) is currently under restoration in its conservation hangar, whilst private-collection wise, the lovely Neil and Heather Airey, aka Lakes Lightnings in Cumbria, have saved several important aircraft from an untimely death. Steve at Stoneykirk Aviation Museum, south of Stranraer, Scotland, also has an impressive array of historical cockpits, including an Avro Vulcan B1 XA903, that was once used to test the Concorde engine, an English Electric Canberra, and a Harrier Sea Hawk to name but a few. These examples are just the tip of the iceberg, with hundreds, if not thousands, of well-meaning folk pulling together what little resources they have available to them, especially financial ones, to preserve their respective nation's aviation heritage.

As such, what follows next is the story of five much-loved aircraft, protagonists of the Second World War, representatives of the many of their type that flew operationally over Europe, staunch defenders against tyranny and evil, and great crowd-pleasers on today's current airshow circuit. Sadly, only a handful of such aircraft are still in existence worldwide, thus their continual survival is imperative. Two are based at the Lincolnshire Aviation Heritage Centre; two Hawker Hurricanes, one of my favourite aircraft, are stationed at RAF Coningsby, with the Battle of Britain Memorial Flight; whilst the Silver Spitfire is based at Goodwood Airfield. Each aircraft experienced an eventful life, full of ups and downs, and some even saw combat—yet what they all have in common is that all five aircraft cheated death, quite literally, by the skin of their teeth! Indeed, few realize just how close these legendary aircraft came to either an undesignated gravesite, the fires of a cremation furnace, or being unceremoniously hacked to pieces in a scrapyard. Those within the 'aviation enthusiast community' will, I am sure, be familiar with the aircraft described below, so please forgive my indulgence.

Avro Lancaster Bomber NX611 *Just Jane* Lincolnshire Aviation Heritage Centre

The Avro Lancaster Bomber is, for some, the most iconic aircraft of the Second World War, most famous for dropping the bouncing bomb during the Dambuster's raid, an attack on German dams carried out on the night of 16–17 May 1943 by 617 Squadron. Operational from 1942, 7,377 Lancasters were produced over the course of the war; 3,249 Lancasters failed to return from missions; and over 200 more were destroyed or written off in crashes. The Lancaster's bomb bay was versatile and could carry a combination of loads and was the only aircraft to be able to carry the 22,000lb (9,980kg) Grand Slam bomb, the largest bomb to be carried by an aircraft in the war.[1] At present, there are only three working Lancasters in existence: Two are airworthy. One is based here in the United Kingdom, with the Battle of Britain Memorial Flight (BBMF) at RAF Coningsby; the other is located at the Canadian Warplane Heritage Museum in Hamilton, Ontario, Canada. The third Lancaster bomber, serial number NX611, is currently undergoing restoration at the Lincolnshire Aviation Heritage Centre. Her name is *Just Jane*, and she is magnificent!

Just Jane has a somewhat-chequered history. Built in April 1945 by Austin Motors in Longbridge, near Birmingham, she was one of the first 150 B Mk VII Avro Lancasters destined to become part of the RAF's Tiger Force in the Far East. But, with the early surrender of the Japanese Imperial Army, NX611 suddenly found herself surplus to requirements and, instead of seeing active service, Lancaster NX611 ended up in a storage facility at Llandow, in the Vale of Glamorgan, Wales. There she stayed until April 1952, when she was bought by the French government. Painted a striking midnight blue colour, she flew maritime patrol for the French Naval Air Arm. Ten years later, in 1962, she found herself in Noumeau, New Caledonia, with a fresh new coat of white paint, where she was utilized for air sea rescue and cartography. Then, in 1964, the French government presented NX611 to the Historical Aircraft Preservation Society, where she was overhauled before commencing the arduous journey back home to Britain. It took nine days to complete the 19,312km (12,000mi) journey back home, a full seventy flying hours, landing at Biggin Hill Airport on

13 May 1965. Temporarily grounded due to expiry of permitted flying hours, it wasn't until 1967 before NX611 flew again. Even so, the expense of keeping her airworthy meant that public appearances were fleeting. She was flown to Lavenham in Suffolk and in 1972, was put up for auction at 'Squires Gate' in Blackpool.[2]

In the interim, in Lincolnshire, two brothers, Fred and Harold Panton, had set their hearts on buying a Second World War bomber. The purchase was to commemorate the death of their brother Christopher, who was killed during the Nuremberg Raids in March 1944, and to honour the other 537 aircrew of bomber command who lost their lives in the same mission. Initially, the brothers had their eyes on a Halifax bomber, which was coming up for sale, but were quickly informed by their father who, in no uncertain terms, informed them that said aircraft would not be permitted on his farm. Many years would pass before the brothers' ambitions would be fulfilled. Now owning their own farm, when they saw some land for sale that included the now-defunct RAF East Kirkby airfield, they jumped at the opportunity and bought it. Albeit bar a few old buildings and some areas of concrete, there wasn't much left of the airfield to see. They set up part of the land as a poultry farm whilst, with the idea of owning a Second World War aircraft still foremost in their minds, they also began to renovate a separate area of the airfield, including building a new hangar where an original T2 hangar had stood during the war years.

During this phase of construction, the brothers found out about the 'Squires Gate' auction in Blackpool via an advertisement and immediately knew that a Lancaster could be the perfect memorial to their brother's memory. Regrettably, due to the reserve not being reached, the aircraft was withdrawn from the auction and later sold privately to the Right Honourable Lord Lilford. Over the intervening years, the brothers kept in contact with the Lancaster's new owner. In September 1983, whilst NX611 proudly stood as gate guardian at RAF Scampton, Fred and Harold Panton struck a deal with Lord Lilford's agent—the Avro Lancaster Bomber NX611 would finally become theirs. Four years later, after completing an agreed total of ten years as gate guardian at RAF Scampton, *Just Jane* was brought to East Kirkby, courtesy of the RAF.[3]

In 1993, the process to restore NX611 *Just Jane* commenced. At first, work began to rehabilitate one of her four engines, ably accomplished by two ex-RAF engineers who were specifically brought in to do the job. Accessing spare parts was arranged; both camshafts had to be replaced, although the engine cylinders were in good working order. The aircraft's propeller was then removed, stripped down and examined and, bar having to adjust the blade settings, everything appeared to be in working order. The engine's starter motor, magnetos, fuel booster pump and ignition harness were removed and checked, the fuel tank was pressurized and the fuel jettison system reset. When the throttle controls between the cockpit lever and the engine were uncovered, it was discovered that almost a third of the small control rods had to be replaced. Finally, local contractors were brought in to check the wiring and to replace where necessary. After approximately 700 man hours, and at a cost of £7,000 ($9,500), the engine was finally ready. Now, all four engines have been fully restored and NX611 *Just Jane* is at a fully operational taxiing standard.[4]

Today, the Lincolnshire Aviation Heritage Centre is currently working through a long-term programme of restoration with said Avro Lancaster NX611, the aim of which is to take her to an airworthy condition. This is not an easy, or cheap, process; the entire project is estimated to cost £4 million ($5.5 million), all of which is being raised through museum admission fees, public donations and a unique taxi ride encounter in the Lancaster itself. The latter, I am personally looking forward to experiencing in the not-too-distant future. According to their official website the restoration works are as follows: 1) Winter 2025: Rear fuselage of NX611 completed. Tailplanes of NX611 in restoration. Nose of NX611 in restoration. Port wing of NX611 in restoration. Rear-mid-fuselage of NX664 fitted to the jig and restoration started. 2) Winter 2026: Potential rear-mid-fuselage of NX611 removed and swapped with NX664. Port wing of NX611 completed and refitted. Potential nose of NX611 completed and refitted. 3) Winter 2027: NX611 rear-mid-fuselage restoration. NX611 tailplanes completed, NX611 fin post replacements and rudder work. 4) Winter 2028: Potential bomb door, undercarriage valance, cowling work. 5) Winter 2029: Potential starboard wing, cockpit, centre section work.[5]

De Havilland Mosquito NF Mk II HJ711 B.XVI PF498: Lincolnshire Aviation Heritage Centre

Situated in the main hangar, adjacent to *Just Jane*, is another absolute gem, a reconstructed wooden Mosquito aircraft, a multi-role combat aircraft that was introduced during the Second World War. Often referred to as the 'Wooden Wonder', as its airframe was constructed predominantly from wood, at one time said aircraft was one of the fastest aircraft in the world; for example, during its trials on 16 January 1941, a prototype outpaced a Spitfire at 6,000ft (1,800m). This model, HJ711, has been a labour of love for its owner, Tony Agar, for decades, a fascinating lifelong restoration. It is also unique as it is the only active Mosquito outside of a very small number of airworthy examples in Canada and the United States. HJ711 served with both 141 and 169 squadrons. Whilst at the latter, at Little Snoring in Norfolk, HJ711 made the squadron's first kill. The pilot, Squadron Leader J.A.H. Cooper, shot down a Messerschmitt BF110 whilst patrolling west of Berlin. What follows is kindly paraphrased from the Lincolnshire Aviation Heritage Centre website.

The entire restoration process has not been an easy one for Agar. Without any financial backing, he resorted to trolling through scrap yards, old airfields and industrial complexes, to obtain any parts that may be of use. Assistance from several aviation enthusiasts was also invaluable. Agar has truly achieved the impossible. Mind you, it was not without its challenges.

1970: Agar went on holiday to Blackpool and visited a small museum housing the Reflectaire Collection, then home to Lancaster NX611, along with a Mosquito cockpit displayed nearby identified as HJ711.

1971: Agar located the remains of B.XVI PF498 which consisted of a section of the wing and undercarriage assemblies only. Said aircraft had been allocated to Kirkham airfield on 6 October 1948, after which it went to the Civil Defence Unit, Royal Ordnance Factory, Chorley, Lancashire, where it was used for crash rescue training.

1972: The Reflectaire museum had experienced financial difficulties, and its assets were to be disposed of at auction. As such on 29 April Mosquito cockpit was purchased by Agar for £7, about £1,253.00

($1,500) in today's money. Also obtained was a rudder for just £2, (£6,000 - $8,100) aileron and rudder pedals. Returning to Chorley in search of the undercarriage assemblies and wing sections he had located the year previously, Agar was informed that their removal was required immediately otherwise the aircraft remains would be scrapped and burnt. A friend of Tony's discovered the port and starboard wing remains from a crashed Mosquito, T.III VA878, which had lain derelict in St. David's, South Wales, since 1956. On close inspection, Tony found the remains in a poor state but cut off the port wing section and duly transported it home. Now, with undercarriage, wings and cockpit, the task was to find a fuselage.

1973: Agar, along with its owner, Eddie Renolds, salvaged the fuselage remains of de Havilland Mosquito TT.35 RS715 from a deserted film lot behind the MGM Studios at Boreham Wood. RS715 had been used in the making of the film 633 Squadron but was abandoned and left to rot ten years after filming had ended.

1975: Jim O'Sullivan wrote to inform Tony that they had recovered an ex-141 Squadron Mosquito from a crash site near Kings Lynn, Norfolk. Thus, a pair of needle blade propellers, albeit bent from the crash, joined the Huntington hoard, as did tailplane elevators and other sundry items.

1978: Two Merlin 76 engines became available, from Mosquito NF.30 NI616, which had been scrapped at Cosford. Later, Agar was able to acquire the correct engines for HJ711, namely two Merlin 25s. Other parts began arriving from all over the country, including a pilot's seat from a scrap yard in Warrington.

1986: Yorkshire Air Museum offered Agar much-needed space to complete the restoration. A pair of radiators for the Merlin engines were acquired, and a trip to a Gloucestershire gravel pit produced several engine firewalls and general fittings, all in amazingly good condition. A visit to a derelict farm in the wilds of Lincolnshire uncovered several Mosquito wheels and tyres, whilst a good friend made the long journey to Glen Esk, Scotland, to bring back a very well-preserved engine nacelle and other smaller items from a crashed Mosquito. This was the former de Havilland Mosquito FB.VI HJ720.

1989: New Zealand was the source of another nose cone, cannon frames and escape hatch with the help from the De Havilland Heritage Centre. Later in the year, Agar made public his ambition to have his completed Mosquito out on the perimeter track at Elvington Airfield, York, in time for the fiftieth anniversary of the first flight of the De Havilland Night Fighter prototype in 1941. Agar felt it would not only be a worthy tribute to all the Mosquito personnel and aircraft that were lost during the war, but it would also honour the many thousands of ground crew who worked so hard, very often in such trying conditions, to keep the squadrons operational.

15 May 1991: Mossie Day, saw HJ711 on three wheels for the first time in over forty years, and exactly fifty years after the first flight of the Night Fighter Prototype Mosquito, W4052. The plane was wheeled onto the perimeter track at Elvington to greet the only flying Mosquito in the United Kingdom at the time, RR299, owned by British Aerospace at Chester. The latter crashed at an airshow in Manchester in 1996. Witnesses to the event included six pilots and navigators of 169 Squadron.

2017: After many years of residing at Yorkshire Air Museum, Agar made the decision to move HJ711 to the Lincolnshire Aviation Heritage Centre to further the restoration to a ground running condition.

18 September 2018: 18 HJ711 performs a first engine run (port-side), the first time HJ711 had been operational since the Second World War.

6 May 2019: Short taxi runs take place with both engines running. HJ711 is now the only serviceable (albeit taxiing) Mosquito outside of the United States and Canada.

2025: HJ711 continues to undertake taxi runs and is now an established crowd pleaser at the Heritage Centre's public open days.

I leave you with these words from Director Karl Kjarsgaard of the Bomber Command Museum of Canada:

> 'It is one of the finest overall restorations on the face of the planet. The Mosquito was literally in pieces when Tony first started with airframe sections from all over the UK! It is not only a tribute to our

> RAF and RCAF boys who flew in Mossies but also to the relentless and determined perfection by Tony of a flying machine that was a true sword of Freedom.'[6]

The Silver Spitfire

The Supermarine Spitfire is a British single-seat fighter aircraft that was used by the Royal Air Force and many other Allied countries before, during and after the Second World War. Designed as a short-range, high-performance interceptor aircraft, by R. J. Mitchell, the Spitfire was built in many variants, using several wing configurations, and was produced in greater numbers than any other British aircraft. It was also the only British fighter to be in continuous production throughout the war.[7]

The Silver Spitfire is a sight to behold, an object of abject beauty, that is currently wowing spectators at many a summer airshow. It is one of the most archetypal airworthy Spitfires in the world today. Originally built in 1943 in Castle Bromwich, United Kingdom; serial number: CBAF IX 970; historic registration MJ271. The Spitfire first entered service on 15 February 1944 with RAF 118 Squadron, predominantly flying escort duties for B-24, B-17 and B-26 bombers attacking V1 launch sites, as well as fighter sweeps over France. On 8 March 1944, MJ271 was transferred to 132 Squadron, following the squadron to RAF Ford in Sussex in April–May 1944, where it took part in twenty-eight operational sorties, which included escort for B-25 and B-26 bombers as well as the dive-bombing of targets on the French coast. She was given a shared victory on 26 April 1944 when a German Junkers Ju-34 was destroyed. A few weeks later, on 9 May 1944, she experienced an unfortunate 'wheels up' belly flop landing at RAF Ford and was forced to undergo much-needed repairs, after which the Silver Spitfire transfers to 39 Maintenance Unit, at RAF Colerne, on 19 August; 83 GSU, at RAF Bognor, on 19 September; and RAF Westhampnett (home today to the Boultbee Flight Academy at Goodwood Aerodrome) with 83 GSU on 4 November. The Spitfire then joined RCAF 401 Squadron in Volkel, Netherlands on 23 November at Volkel. Having taken part in ten dive-bombing missions, deformations were found to be present in her sheet metal, and on 24 December 1944, the Spitfire was sent to RCAF 410 Squadron, a designated repair and salvage unit.[8]

On 21 June 1945, MJ271 was delivered to 29 Maintenance Unit at High Ercall, where she was placed into storage, only to reappear a year later, as one of fifty-eight Spitfires allotted to the Royal Netherlands Air Force (RNAF). Crossing the North Sea on 25 November, she is stationed at Twente Airbase as part of the JVS (fighter plane school), receiving the designation H-8, later becoming 3W-8, the designation she would wear for some seventy plus years. Subjected to numerous test flights over the next couple of years, in 1951, MJ271 was finally accepted into the RNAF and stationed at Soesterberg as part of 322 Squadron. Her tenure would only last a couple of years, for on 29 September 1953, MJ271 made her final active flight.[9]

At first, the future, from this point onwards, looked bleak for MJ271. After all, the new jet engine aircraft were beginning to make their mark, and many of her compatriots were heading for the scrap yards. In 1956 the Spitfire was 'rescued' by 313 Squadron, a Czechoslovak-manned fighter squadron of the RAF, and placed near the crew room, with a TA-26 marking on the nose and the name *Opa*, meaning *Grandpa*, scrawled on the fuselage below the cockpit; in 1962, in a somewhat ghastly condition, the plane was dumped on the roof of Delfzijl Museum in the northeast Netherlands. Here she would have stayed, her carcass rotting in the elements, if Dutch Spitfire aficionado Harry van der Meer had not recognized her importance. Consequently, in April 1973, MJ271 was lifted off the roof in Delfzijl and transferred to the Anthony Fokker School, in the Hague for restoration, the process of which commenced some five years later. On 12 January 1982, with the restoration complete, MJ271 was revealed as 'MH424', H-53, in tribute to the Dutch servicemen who flew Spitfires in Indonesia. Her final home in the Netherlands would be in the National Aviation Theme Park Aviodrome, at Lelystad Airport, where she was put on display, beautifully illuminated, in her own hall, in commemoration for all the brave servicemen who gave their lives in the Second World War.

Unfortunately, as plagues many aviation museums worldwide, the museum began to struggle financially. As such, in 2006, it decided to sell some of its stock to balance the books, and MJ271 became a casualty of the sad situation. Despite objections, the Spitfire was sold and shipped back to Duxford, here in the United Kingdom, packed away in a crate and placed into storage. It would be ten long years before she would see the light of day again, when in 2016, Spitfire MJ271 was purchased by the Boultbee Flight Academy, now known as Spitfires.com, based at the Goodwood Airfield, in Chichester.[10] Their aim was to restore her and make her airworthy once more. Unlike other Spitfire restorations, however, decked out in the atypical camouflage paint job, Boultbee decided that MJ271 would have no exterior paint applied to her, except for the black anti-glare in front of the cockpit. Her propeller blades would be black, and her fabric would be covered with high-gloss aluminium paint. The Spitfire MJ271 would emerge altogether silver in colour and undertake its first post-restoration flight on 27 June 2019—the Silver Spitfire was born!

'The Silver Spitfire is a Mk.IX Spitfire finished in polished aluminium with the guns removed. By "de-militarising" the aircraft in this manner we aim to highlight the timeless beauty of its design - By presenting the aircraft in this beautiful "bare metal" state we aim to highlight the beauty of the Spitfire's timeless design, drawing attention to the unique and famous shape of the airframe.'[11]

Resurrected from an uncertain future, the Silver Spitfire was now to undertake an adventure of a lifetime when she, piloted by Steve Brooks and Matt Jones, would fly some almost 44,000km (27,000 nautical mi) around the world, taking in some of the most famous landmarks on the planet, from the Grand Canyon in the west to the snow-capped peak of Mount Fuji in the east. Entitled 'The Longest Flight', to which there is an excellent book available detailing the expedition, the Spitfire left Goodwood Aerodrome on 5 August 2019, returning four months later.[12] Touchingly, the last stop before the return to England was at Lelystad Airport, at the National Aviation Theme Park Aviodrome, the final place where Spitfire MJ271 was proudly displayed. Today, the Silver Spitfire is a much-loved addition to the airshow circuit, pleasing crowds wherever she performs, including yours truly. To hear those Merlin engines purring in the skies above, look up, and see the sun glistening off a Spitfire's metallic flanks, well, there is only one word to describe it—magical.

Battle of Britain Memorial Flight (BBMF)

In the years that followed the end of the Second World War, and as the RAF began the widespread adoption of jet-powered aircraft, serving pilots and the public alike still had a great affection for the more traditional fighters of the Battle of Britain. The aircraft became a popular feature of the annual Battle of Britain Victory Day flypasts, with either a Hurricane or Spitfire leading the formation. With many thousands of former wartime aircraft deemed surplus to requirements and scrapped, the idea arose of preserving a small number of historic aircraft for commemorative and ceremonial duties, from state occasions, such as Trooping the Colour, to major airshows and flypasts. The notion soon began to receive official recognition, with the inauguration of the RAF Historic Aircraft Flight, which consisted of three PR Mk XIX Spitfires and the RAF's last airworthy Hurricane, LF363, on 11 July 1957 at RAF Biggin Hill. Over the years, the Flight operated several Spitfires and Hurricanes and was based at several different RAF stations around the country—whilst at RAF Coltishall, the Flight received its largest and arguably most famous aircraft in the shape of Avro Lancaster PA474. In 1969, the flight changed its name to the BBMF. Today, the Flight operates five Spitfires, two Hurricanes, a Lancaster, a C47 Dakota, and two Chipmunk aircraft (primarily for training). Their mission statement is: 'to maintain the priceless artefacts of our national heritage in airworthy condition in order to commemorate those who have fallen in the service of this country.'[13]

The Hawker Hurricane

The Hawker Hurricane occupied a space between the last of the biplane fighters of the inter-war years and the modern monoplane designs that would feature so heavily during the Second World War. Taking much of its design and construction techniques from the tried and trusted manufacturing methods perfected since the end of the Great War, the Hurricane provided the RAF with an effective, reliable and easy to maintain fighting aeroplane when it was needed most. Although always overshadowed by the more glamorous Spitfire, the Hurricane was easier and faster to construct, could be effectively repaired in the field, and accounted for more enemy aircraft destroyed during the Battle of Britain than all of Britain's other defences combined. In fact, Hurricanes accounted for just over fifty per cent of all enemy aircraft shot down by British and Commonwealth forces throughout the Second World War.[14] The BBMF at RAF Coningsby currently owns two Hurricanes of historical importance: The first is Hawker Hurricane Mk IIC LF363, believed to be the last ever Hurricane to enter service with the RAF, and Hawker Hurricane PZ865, the last of 14,533 Hurricanes to be built and rolled off the production line.[15] Both have somehow survived the trials and tribulations normally bestowed upon aircraft of their genre.

Hawker Hurricane LF363

Hurricane LF363 was built as a cannon-armed Mk IIC at the large Hawker Aircraft factory at Langley, Slough, in Berkshire, during the latter part of 1943. The aircraft's maiden flight, an air test, was on 1 January 1944. LF363 is unique in RAF history, as she has been in continual service from 28 January 1944, when she was delivered to 5 Maintenance Unit at Kemble, Cirencester—albeit this does include periods of storage and restoration. LF363 served operationally with the RAF during the Second World War on coastal shipping protection and air defence patrols off the east coast of Scotland. LF363 flew with 63 Squadron, based at Turnhouse, west of Edinburgh; and 309 Squadron, at Drem, North Berwick. As we have already documented, after the conflict ceased, LF363, as with many wartime aircraft, faced an uncertain future. In 1948, she was sent back to the Hawker factory in Langley, no doubt for scrapping, and left in open storage. Thankfully, a hero stepped up to the plate, so to speak, in the guise of Air Vice Marshal Sir Stanley Vincent CB DFC AFC, who spotted the languishing Hurricane and immediately recognized its historical significance, thus securing the aircraft's future.[16]

LF363 would spend the next few years under the care of the RAF, receiving regular maintenance, unofficially, and flying on numerous ceremonial occasions. Between 1949 and 1956, the Hurricane was passed around a few front-line squadrons and went on to feature in several films and BBC productions including *Angels One Five* in 1951, *The War in the Air* in 1953 and *Reach for the Sky* in 1955. Her most significant role came in 1969 in the classic film *Battle of Britain*. In July 1957, after a major refit at the Hawker factory, LF363 became a founding aircraft of the RAF Historic Flight, the forerunner of the BBMF, when the Flight was inaugurated at Biggin Hill. As the official RAF website states: 'It is probably no exaggeration to state that without this Hurricane the BBMF would probably never have existed.'[17]

Hurricane LF363 would go on to have her first major mishap, ironically not during times of conflict, but in September 1991 when, en route to an airshow in Jersey with the BBMF, she developed serious engine trouble and had to divert to the nearest available airfield, in this instance RAF Wittering. Tragically, whilst attempting to land, the engine failed completely, causing the aircraft to stall and crash onto the runway, and burst into flames, causing monumental damage. Thankfully, the pilot, Squadron Leader Allan Martin, managed to escape relatively unharmed. The wreck was thus transported back to RAF Coningsby, where she lay broken in a hangar for three years, until a decision could be made with regards to her future. Finally, due to her historical importance, it was decided that she would be restored to an airworthy condition. To illustrate just how little respect and gratitude, outside of the service, is afforded such aircraft, from the powers that be, the BBMF was forced to sell one of their prized Spitfires (PR Mk XIX PS853) just to raise the necessary funds for the Hurricane's rebuild. In 1994, the remains of LF363 were moved to Historic Flying Ltd at Audley End, Essex, where a painstaking restoration was carried out to bring the aircraft back to life. On 29 September 1998, Hurricane LF363 flew again for the first time in seven years, subsequently re-joining the BBMF team. She continues to serve to this day.[18]

Hawker Hurricane PZ865 (Mk IIC)

Hawker Hurricane PZ865 was the last of 14,533 Hurricanes to be built and rolled off the production line at the Hawker factory, Langley, Slough, in July 1944. Inscribed with 'The Last of the Many' on both her port and starboard sides, her first flight was on 27 July 1944. A month later she became the centrepiece of an official 'christening ceremony' where officials from Hawker, the Air Ministry and the RAF gathered to wax lyrical about the Hurricane's impressive combat history and to honour its many accomplishments. After which, Hawker purchased PZ865 back from the Air Ministry to preserve the final Hurricane ever built.[19] The following decades would be rather venturesome, with PZ865 first undergoing a brand-new dark blue colour scheme complete with gold lettering. As well as a communications and testing aircraft, she also entered several air races. In 1950, she achieved second place in the King's Cup Air Race; became the chase plane during the early development of the Hawker Harrier jet; appeared in the well-known 1952 film *Angels One Five*, for which it was painted back into military colours wearing the serial number P2619 and the code 'US-B' to represent an aircraft of 56 Squadron; and had a leading role in the cinematic air sequences of the *Battle of Britain* film.[20] In the 1960s, Hawker Hurricane PZ865 was changed back to her wartime camouflage scheme, appearing in several air displays around the country. Alas, as we have seen, like so many before her, a combination of limited financial resources and hangar space forced Hawker to reconsider the future of their historic aircraft collection, and PZ865 was threatened with being permanently grounded. Once more, up stepped another hero, this time Hawker Siddeley's Chief Test Pilot Duncan Simpson OBE, who, through intense negotiations behind the scenes, gained permission for the Hurricane to be donated to the BBMF. So, in March 1972, Hawker Hurricane PZ865 was given back to the RAF BBMF, transferring to the unit's base, which was then housed at Coltishall in Norfolk.[21] In 2010, Hawker Hurricane PZ865 was rebuilt and a new paint scheme applied, representing Hurricane Mk IIC HW840, coded 'EG-S', of 34 Squadron, Southeast Asia Command. As of 2026, she resides alongside the rest of the BBMF team, at RAF Coningsby, and is a much-loved inclusion to the air show circuit.

The above five examples are arguably the pinnacle of aviation resurrection. I have many more examples that are not. Regardless, one has immense admiration for the efforts made by all such people to preserve aviation heritage. It can be a thankless task. As I am quickly discovering. One of the main aims of *Boneyards of Steel* was to introduce the subject matter of aviation gravesites, aircraft final resting places and the basics of aviation archaeology, to the uninitiated. I hope in some small way I have succeeded. When it became known that I had taken over A.R.G.O.S.

(Aviation Research Group Orkney & Scotland), I received an email from a young archaeological student, who had no idea that the topic of aviation archaeology could possibly be a career choice, asking where they could gain hands on experience, a prerequisite of any archaeological qualification. So, for those reading this who may also be interested, my advice would be to see if your area has an aviation heritage group, as I am certain they would be delighted to hear from you. As would many provincial aviation museums, who are always on the lookout for new helpers. By volunteering one's time, not only will you have an opportunity to 'get up close and personal' to some rather legendary aircraft, ranging from Second World War stalwarts to RAF icons, but the people volunteering beside you often have firsthand experience in either flying said aircraft or they were once acting maintenance crew or former RAF engineers, tasked with keeping these glorious machines alive and skyward bound.

The search for hidden deposition sites has just begun. With the advent of new, updated technology I do believe that there is still much to be uncovered, as demonstrated by the recent discovery of a Hawker Hurricane aircraft and its pilot, Squadron Leader George Morley Fidler, that was shot down over northern France some 86 years ago. On a smaller scale, I could also add the custodian of a world-famous museum who was completely unaware that they had a Merlin engine in one of their outbuildings from a Spitfire aircraft deposition site I am currently working on. It's arguably all relative. I also believe collaboration with like-minded folk is the way forward. Although, having read about the historical exploits of other aviation groups, I fully comprehend how challenging this may be. Nevertheless, I will endeavour to try. If truth be told, *Boneyards of Steel* has only just begun. . .

Per Adua Ad Astra – Through Adversity to the Stars. . .

Notes and References

Chapter 1: Where Planes Go to Die

1. Chinnery, P. *Desert Boneyard*, Davis-Monthan AFB Arizona, Airlife Publishing Ltd, 1–2, 1987.
2. Ibid.
3. Kingman AAF Boneyard and Kingman Airport (IGM) in Arizona, www.airplaneboneyards.com/kingman-arizona-airplane-boneyard-storage.htm.
4. Ibid.
5. Ibid.
6. Ibid.
7. History of Walnut Ridge Army Airfield in Arkansas. www.airplaneboneyards.com/walnut-ridge-arkansas-airplane-boneyard.htm
8. Military Aeroplane Boneyards and Scrapping Depots After World War II www.airplaneboneyards.com/post-wwii-military-airplane-boneyards.htm.
9. Ibid.
10. Ibid.
11. Albuquerque Airport-Oxnard Field 1928-1930, www.cavalcadeofwings.com.
12. Chinnery, P. *Desert Boneyard*, Davis-Monthan AFB Arizona, Airlife Publishing Ltd, 1, 1987.
13. Davis-Monthan History, Davis-Monthan Airforce Base Website www.dm.af.mil/Newcomers/Welcome-to-DM/History.
14. Davis-Monthan Air Force Boneyard in Tucson, www.airplaneboneyards.com/davis-monthan-afb-amarg-airplane-boneyard.htm.
15. Chinnery, P. *Desert Boneyard*, Davis-Monthan AFB Arizona, Airlife Publishing Ltd, 6, 1987.
16. Ibid.
17. Ibid, 67.
18. Ibid, 10.
19. Strategic Arms Reduction Treaty, AMRAC Experience wwwamracexperience.com.
20. Ibid, 2–3, 1987.
21. Davis-Monthan Air Force Boneyard in Tucson. www.airplaneboneyards.com/davis-monthan-afb-amarg-airplane-boneyard.htm.
22. Chinnery, P. *Desert Boneyard*, Davis-Monthan AFB Arizona, Airlife Publishing Ltd, 14, 1987.

23. Davis Monthan Airforce Base, www.dm.af.mil/Media/News/, 2025.
24. Chinnery, P. *Desert Boneyard*, Davis-Monthan AFB Arizona, Airlife Publishing Ltd, 19, 1987.
25. AMARG Processes - Process In, AMRAC Experience wwwamracexperience.com.
26. Steele, G Master Sgt. 'Resurrection of the Ghost Rider' Barksdale Airforce Base www.barksdale.af.mil/News/Article/634812/resurrection-of-the-ghost-rider.
27. Tirpek J. A. 'Living Boneyard', *Air and Space Forces Magazine*, February 2013.
28. Southern California Logistics Airport (SCLA) in Victorville www.airplaneboneyards.com/california-airplane-boneyards-storage.htm.
29. Mojave Air and Space Port, www.mojaveairport.com.
30. Craven S. 'Pinal Air Park: Once secretive aircraft boneyard slowly opens its gates', *AAHS Flightline*, 2015.
31. Jim Petty in conversation, Pinal Air Park.
32. Ibid.
33. Smith, Dale. 'BAS Part Sales Buys Competitor, Enters Bizjet Market', www.ainonline.com/aviation-news/business-aviation/2023-03-13/bas-part-sales-buys-competitor-enters-bizjet-market, March 2023.
34. Personal Correspondence Air Historical Branch (RAF), March 2025.
35. Research Results Example www.nationalarchives.gov.uk, November 2024.
36. www.apas.com.au.
37. Ibid.
38. Ibid.
39. Bailey, A. 'Aircraft Storage in Alice Springs, Australia', August 2024 https://simpleflying.com/alice-springs-australia-aircraft-storage-guide.
40. Maszczynski, Mateusz. 'Cathay Pacific Brings Home its Last Airplane from the Australian Desert After Nearly Four Years in Storage', *PYOK Magazine*, June 2024.
41. Teruel Airport Airliner Storage & Maintenance Facility, www.airplaneboneyards.com/teruel-airport-spain-airplane-boneyard.htm.
42. Tarmac Aerosave, www.tarmacaerosave.aero.
43. China Aircraft Leasing Group Holdings Limited, www.calc.com.hk.
44. web.archive.org/web/20120209204905/http://www.cotswoldairport.com/history.
45. Air Salvage International, https://airsalvage.co.uk.
46. Ibid.
47. Aircraft End-of-Life Solutions, https://aels.nl.
48. EirTrade Aviation, https://eirtradeaviation.com.
49. Mojave Air and Space Port (MHV), www.airplaneboneyards.com/mojave-desert-california-airplane-boneyard.htm.
50. Nelson, Jake. 'Rex accused of stealing planes from aircraft boneyard', *Australian Aviation*, australianaviation.com.au/2024/09/rex-accused-of-stealing-planes-from-aircraft-boneyard, September 2024.

51. Kucove, 'Abandoned Forgotten & Little-Known Airfields in Europe', www.forgottenairfields.com/airfield-kuecovee-1255.html.
52. 'NATO completes modernisation of a major airbase in Albania', www.nato.int/cps/en/natohq/news_223351.htm, March 2024.
53. 'What Happened with Moscow's FIRST Airport?' *Russia Beyond*, May 2020.
54. Richter, D. 'MiGs, Stars & Magic Books: A Brief History of Trespassing in Moscow', *EX-UTOPIA*, August 2015.
55. Hohenhaus, P. 'Monino Central Air Force Museum', *Dark Tourism*, www.dark-tourism.com/index.php/1227-monino.
56. Google Map Imagery of Russia's Gromov Flight Research Institute, https://virtualglobetrotting.com/map/m-m-gromov-flight-research-institute-zhukovsky-ramenskoe-air-base/view/google.
57. Prisco, J. 'Concordski: What ever happened to the Soviets' spectacular rival to Concorde?' *CNN Edition*, July 2019.
58. 'Collection of Russian and Soviet Experimental Aircraft', Gromov Flight Research Institute, Russia, Weird Wings 2020.
59. Kolomeits, A. 'The Abandoned Vozdvizhenka Air Base & Aircraft', *Abandoned Spaces*, July 2018.
60. Conversino, M. *Fighting with the Russians*, University of Kansas Press, 1991.
61. Museum of Long-Range Aviation, Poltava.
62. Shootdowns and Accidents During the Russian/Ukraine War, https://en.wikipedia.org/wiki/List_of_aviation_shootdowns_and_accidents_during_the_Russo-Ukrainian_War.
63. Boneyards Outside the US, www.airplaneboneyards.com/airplane-boneyards-outside-usa.htm.
64. Richter, D. 'A Latvian Aircraft Graveyard', *EX-UTOPIA*, March 2016.
65. Dowling, S. 'The secrets of the desert aircraft "boneyards"', *BBC Future*, September 2014.
66. Personal conversations with ex-USAF service personnel, January 2025.
67. Gordon, Y. 'Mikoyan MiG-19 Variants', *Wings of Fame*, Volume 9, 1997.
68. Trevithick, J. 'Dozens of United States-Bought Afghan Air Force Aircraft Are Now Orphaned at an Uzbek Airfield', *TWZ*, August 2021.
69. Drake, N. 'Creepy Soviet Space Shuttles Are Sitting in a Kazakhstan Desert', *National Geographic*, May 2017.
70. 'What You Can See by Taking a Walk in the Countryside in Hungary: A Fighter's Cemetery', DefenseandAviation.Info, March 2018.
71. Steven, P. 'Military Photography in Bulgaria', *Target Aviation Photography*, April 2010.
72. Zruc Senec Air Park, https://airpark.wz.cz.
73. Deano 'Serbian Air Force "Boneyard" at the Belgrade Aeronautical Museum', *Aces Flying High*, March 2016, acesflyinghigh.wordpress.com. Serbian-air-force-boneyard-at-the-belgrade-aeronautical-museum, March 2016.

74. 'On Museum Night 2025, Kapela becomes the center of the Croatian Air Force', LiveCamCroatia.com, January 2025.
75. Oyebade, W. 'Nigeria: The making of the world's largest aircraft cemetery', *The Guardian*, April 2021.
76. Guttery, Ben R. *Encyclopaedia of African Airlines.* Jefferson, NC: McFarland & Company, 1998.
77. Personal conversation with former airport employees, April 1999.

Chapter 2: Aviation Archaeology

1. Burgess, A. 'Underwater Aviation Archaeology: What Is Its Place and Value Within Archaeology, and in Particular Maritime Archaeology', Master Thesis, University of Southampton, 7, 2013.
2. McLachlan, I. *Final Flights: Dramatic Wartime Incidents Revealed by Aviation Archaeology*, Patrick Stephens Ltd, 1989.
3. Christian, T. 'Development and Application of a Standardised Methodology to Second World War Aircraft Sites in Scotland', PhD Thesis, University of Glasgow, 1–3, 2014.
4. Bédoyère, de la G. *Battle Over Britain: The Archaeology of the Air War*, Tempus Publishing Ltd, 2000.
5. www.gov.uk/guidance/aviation-archaeology.
6. McLachlan, I. *Final Flights: Dramatic Wartime Incidents Revealed by Aviation Archaeology*, Patrick Stephens Ltd, 1989.
7. Protection of Military Remains Act 1986, gov.uk/guidance/aviation-archaeology.
8. Ibid.
9. Ibid.
10. Ibid.
11. www.gov.uk/guidance/aviation-archaeology.
12. Ibid.
13. Ibid.
14. Ibid.
15. Joint POW/MIA Accounting Command (JPAC), www.15wing.af.mil/About-Us/Fact-Sheets/Display/Article/376358/joint-powmia-accounting-command.
16. Frythens Farm, St. Erth, Cornwall, 'Archaeological Investigation of a WW2 Spitfire Crash Site', Cornwall Archaeological Unit, Cornwall Council, 2017.
17. Ibid.
18. Ibid.
19. Ibid.
20. Ibid.
21. Ibid.
22. Freedom of Information Act, 2000 communication with the Ministry of Defence.
23. Ibid.

24. Ibid.
25. Roberts, P. 'Throop residents slam souvenir hunters visiting crash site of Red Arrows pilot Jon Egging', *Bournemouth Daily Echo*, August 2011.
26. Red Arrows crash, 'Souvenir hunter in eBay sale claim', *BBC News*, August 2011.
27. Roberts, P. 'Throop residents slam souvenir hunters visiting crash site of Red Arrows pilot Jon Egging', *Bournemouth Daily Echo*, August 2011.
28. Bailes, K. 'Police release image in investigation of suspected looting from World War Two B17 bomber wreck at Sandwich Bay', *The Isle of Thanet News*, June 2021.
29. Ibid.
30. 'DIGGING FOR TREASURE-TONIGHT [Without an MoD Licence?]' thePipeline, September 2022. https://thepipeline.info.
31. Ibid.
32. Ibid.
33. Ibid.
34. Christian, T. 'Development and Application of a Standardised Methodology to Second World War Aircraft Sites in Scotland', PhD thesis, University of Glasgow, 7–11, 2014.
35. Ibid.
36. British Aviation Archaeological Council, www.aviationarchaeology.org.uk.
37. Ibid.
38. Christian, T. 'Development and Application of a Standardised Methodology to Second World War Aircraft Sites in Scotland', PhD thesis, University of Glasgow, 7–11, 23–25, 2014.
39. Ibid.
40. Ibid, 7, 23–25, 2014.
41. British Aviation Archaeological Council Guidelines, 2000a: Section 2.1.
42. Christian, T. 'Development and Application of a Standardised Methodology to Second World War Aircraft Sites in Scotland', PhD thesis, University of Glasgow, 23–30, 34, 2014.
43. McLachlan, I. *Final Flights: Dramatic Wartime Incidents Revealed by Aviation Archaeology*, Patrick Stephens Ltd, 234, 1989.
44. Taylor, T. 'Time Team Reports 99', Channel 4 TV, 61, 1999.
45. Christian, T. 'Development and Application of a Standardised Methodology to Second World War Aircraft Sites in Scotland', PhD thesis, University of Glasgow, 2014.
46. Mc Nee, J. *The Story of the Donegal Spitfire*, 2012, 2020.
47. See personal website www.lorraineevans.com.
48. Christian, T. 'Development and Application of a Standardised Methodology to Second World War Aircraft Sites in Scotland', PhD thesis, University of Glasgow, 75, 2014.
49. Wreckchasing: The Source for Aviation Archaeology Information, www.wreckchasing.com.

50. Silveri, G. 'Wreck Hunters: Uncovering the History of Unlucky Aviators', *The Flying Magazine*, October 2013.
51. Aviation Archaeology, www.worldofwarplanes.com.
52. The International Group for Historic Aircraft Recovery, www.tighar.org.
53. Christian, T. 'Development and Application of a Standardised Methodology to Second World War Aircraft Sites in Scotland', PhD thesis, University of Glasgow, 7–8, 2014.
54. McLachlan, I. *Final Flights: Dramatic Wartime Incidents Revealed by Aviation Archaeology*, Patrick Stephens Ltd, 1989.
55. Saunders, A. 'Aircraft Salvage in the Battle of Britain and the Blitz', September 2013, erenow.org/ww/aircraft-salvage-in-the-battle-of-Britain-and-the-blitz/1.php.
56. Bédoyère, de la G. *Battle Over Britain: The Archaeology of the Air War*, Tempus Publishing Ltd, 103, 2000.
57. Chaters, G. R. 'Aviation Archaeology: A Legitimate Branch of Archaeology? Its Development and Path to Professional Standards', War and Peat Conference Proceedings, September 2013.
58. Bédoyère, de la G. *Battle Over Britain: The Archaeology of the Air War*, Tempus Publishing Ltd, 96, 2000.
59. US Air Force Civil Engineer Support Agency, 153, 2006.
60. Christian, T. 'Development and Application of a Standardised Methodology to Second World War Aircraft Sites in Scotland', PhD thesis, University of Glasgow, 10, 2014.
61. McLachlan, I. *Final Flights: Dramatic Wartime Incidents Revealed by Aviation Archaeology*, Patrick Stephens Ltd, 1989.
62. Holyoak, V. *Out of the Blue: Assessing Military Aircraft Crash Sites in England, 1912-45*, *Antiquity 76*, 657–63, 2002.
63. Bédoyère, de la G. *Battle Over Britain: The Archaeology of the Air War*, Tempus Publishing Ltd, 2000.
64. Excavation of Spitfire X4273, Tracy Spaight, www.worldofwarplanes.com.
65. Bédoyère, de la G. *Battle Over Britain: The Archaeology of the Air War*, Tempus Publishing Ltd, 103–111, 2000.
66. Historic England, 'Military Aircraft Crash Sites: Archaeological Guidance on their Significance and Future Management', 2002, https://historicengland.org.uk/images-books/publications/military-aircraft-crash-sites.
67. Burgess, A. 'Underwater Aviation Archaeology: What Is Its Place and Value Within Archaeology, and in Particular Maritime Archaeology', Master Thesis, University of Southampton, 16, 2013.
68. Spraight, T. www.worldofwarplanes.com.
69. Underwater Archaeology, www.worldofwarplanes.com.
70. United Nations Convention on the Law of the Sea, www.un.org/depts/los/convention_agreements/texts/unclos/unclos_e.pdf.
71. Decreto legislativo 22 gennaio, no 42.
72. Constitution of Malta, Cultural Heritage Act, 2002.

Chapter 3: A Traditional Ending

1. Parker, D.D. 'Australians in Iraq 2003: The SAS in Iraq', Australian War Memorial, www.gov.au, 2003.
2. Rhem K.T. 'American Forces Unearth Hidden Aircraft in Iraq', *American Forces Press Service*, August 2003.
3. Ibid.
4. Leon Dario, 'Here's Why Australia Buried 23 F-111s After the Aircraft's Retirement', *The Aviation Geek Club*, July 2020.
5. Ibid.
6. Ibid.
7. Gibson, J. 'Russian-Built Mil Mi-24 Attack Helicopters Buried in Darwin Dump', www.abc.net.au/news/2019-10-29/russian-attack-helicopter-buried-in-darwin-dump/11637448, 2019.
8. 'Challenging the State: The Sandline Affair in Papua New Guinea', Anu Pacific Institute, http://hdl.handle.net/1885/132682, 1997.
9. Gibson, J. 'Russian-Built Mil Mi-24 Attack Helicopters Buried in Darwin Dump', www.abc.net.au/news/2019-10-29/russian-attack-helicopter-buried-in-darwin-dump/11637448, 2019.
10. Greene, A. 'Leaked Photo Reveals Dismantled Taipans Waiting in Warehouse for Burial, Reigniting Frustrations Not to Send Aircraft to Ukraine', www.abc.net.au/news/2024-02-13/leaked-photo-reveals-dismantled-taipan-helicopters/103456586, 2024.
11. Ibid.
12. Ibid.
13. 'Buried Secrets: The REAL Story of the Nazi Warplanes Found in an Indiana Field', *Daily Mail* Newspaper, March 2012.
14. The History of Freeman Army Airfield 1942–1946, Freeman Army Airfield Museum, freemanarmyairfieldmuseum.org.
15. Ibid.
16. Buried Secrets: The REAL Story of the Nazi Warplanes Found in an Indiana Field', *Daily Mail*, March 2012.
17. The History of Freeman Army Airfield 1942–1946, Freeman Army Airfield Museum, freemanarmyairfieldmuseum.org.
18. Bother, L. 'The Dig Story', Freeman Army Airfield Museum, September 2014.
19. Ibid.
20. Ibid.
21. Ibid.
22. Ibid.
23. Ibid.

24. Metcalfe T. 'Metal Detectorists Find Buried Second World War Aircraft in Ukraine While Disarming Wartime Bomb', livescience.com, July 2023.
25. Ibid.
26. Lend-Lease Act (1941), National Archives, www.archives.gov/lend-lease-act.
27. Metcalfe T. 'Metal Detectorists Find Buried Second World War Aircraft in Ukraine While Disarming Wartime Bomb', livescience.com, July 2023.
28. 'Recovering a WWII Bomber Hidden in a French Cave', *BBC News*, September 2013, www.bbc.co.uk/news/magazine-24159975.
29. Ibid.
30. Ibid.
31. Ibid.
32. Personal conversation with a Second World War veteran, who wished to remain anonymous, in January 2025, who has firsthand knowledge of the burial of aircraft, in particular Mosquito aeroplanes.
33. Personal conversation with Alan Withers, Orlando, November 2024.
34. Smith B. 'I Remember Clark Airbase', November 2019.
35. Personal conversations in WarbirdInformationExchange, February 2025.
36. Ibid.
37. Ibid.
38. Ibid.
39. Personal conversations, Sky Pilot, Key Aero, keyaero/forum/historic aviation.
40. Personal conversation with RAF personnel, February 2025.
41. Ibid.
42. Ibid.
43. Personal conversations in WarbirdInformationExchange, April 2025.
44. Personal conversations in WarbirdInformationExchange, January 2025.
45. Personal conversation with ex-RAF Maintenance Unit personnel, October 2024.
46. Burgess A. 'Underwater Aviation Archaeology: What Is Its Place and Value Within Archaeology, and In Particular Maritime Archaeology', University of Southampton, 2013.
47. Personal conversations in WarbirdInformationExchange, December 2024.
48. Personal conversation with scrap merchants responsible for the destruction of the RAF's Tornado fleet, who kindly provided me with photographic evidence from his own private collection. Said image I have posted on my website www.lorraineevans.com.
49. Stilwell, B. 'This Is What Happened to All the Old US F-14 Tomcats', We Are the Mighty, www.wearethemighty.com/popular/old-us-f-14-tomcats, May 2023.
50. *The Jerusalem Post* Newspaper, www.jpost.com/omg/article-840754, February 2025.
51. Ibid.
52. Ibid.

53. Ibid.
54. Walters, L. 'Auckland Underground: Missing Planes Mystery in North Head Bunkers', www.stuff.co.nz/auckland/67033079/auckland-underground-missing-planes-mystery-in-north-head-bunkers, March 2015.
55. Ibid.
56. Boyle, D. 'Turkish Military Enthusiast Has Claimed He Has Found the Final Resting Place of 50 German Second World War Fighters', *Daily Mail* Newspaper, October 2016.
57. Durgut, M. 'The Story of Turkey's First Aircraft Factory TOMTAŞ', aviationfile.com, June 2022.
58. Ibid.
59. Ibid.
60. Kline, S. 'Unearthing WWII Aircraft Buried in Kayseri', *Daily Sabah*, March 2019.
61. Ibid.
62. *Broken Wings: The Search for a Remarkable Legend*, brokenwings.com.au.
63. Brisbane Line: Australia War Memorial, www.awm.gov.au/articles/brisbane-line.
64. https://ww2aircraft.net/forum/threads/spitfires-found-still-in-crates.27986.
65. Ibid.
66. Ibid.
67. As of June 2025, awaiting response from the RAF. Any relevant communication will be uploaded to my personal website.
68. https://ww2aircraft.net/forum/threads/spitfires-found-still-in-crates.27986.
69. *Broken Wings: The Search for a Remarkable Legend*, brokenwings.com.au.
70. Historic Aircraft Recovery, worldofwarplanes.eublog/historic-aircraft-recovery.
71. 'Spitfires in Burma "Could Be Found"', www.bbc.co.uk/news/uk-politics-17710598, April 2012.
72. Davies, L. 'Dozens of Spitfire Planes to Be Excavated in Burma', *The Guardian* Newspaper, www.theguardian.com/world/2012/oct/17/spitfireplanesburma-excavation, October 2012.
73. Brockman A & Spaight T. *The Buried Spitfires of Burma: A 'Fake' History*, The History Press, 2020.
74. Ibid.
75. Ibid.
76. Fordy, T. 'The Mystery of Burma's Buried Spitfires: How an Urban Legend Became an Obsession', *The Telegraph* Newspaper, June 2020.
77. 'Spitfires in Burma', *British Airshows,* https://britishairshows.com/burmese-spitfires.
78. Ibid.
79. Brockman A & Spaight T. *The Buried Spitfires of Burma: A 'Fake' History*, The History Press, 2020.

80. 'Drug Plane Found in Northern Belize Buried Underground After Landing', *Belize News*, October 2020.
81. Fineman M. & Pyes C. 'A Plane Is Buried in Baja - And Drug Ties Unearthed', *LA Times* Newspaper, November 1995.
82. Ibid.
83. The Story of 9/11 and United Flight 93, flight93friends.org/flight-93-story.
84. Phone Calls from Flight 93, NPS, www.nps.gov/phone-calls-from-flight-93.
85. Pickels M. 'Flight 93 Memorial Work Set After 4th', *Pittsburgh Tribune Review*, July 2008.
86. September 9 Towers of Voices Dedication, Flight 93 National Memorial Pennsylvania, United States National Park Service, 2018.
87. 'National Park Service to Return the Remaining Flight 93 Wreckage to the Crash Site', Flight 93 National Memorial Pennsylvania, United States National Park Service, June 2018.

Chapter 4: A Watery Grave

1. Scoltock, J. *The Meltin' Pot from Wreck to Rescue to Recovery*. Stroud: The History Press, 57, 2008.
2. McCarthy, M. 'The "Black Cats" Report into the Feasibility of Locating, Raising and Conserving One of the Four Catalina Flying Boats Scuttled off Rottnest Island in the Years 1945\46', Report #125. *Western*Australian Maritime Museum*, 12, 1997.
3. Murashima, T. 'Pacific War Recovery', *After the Battle*, 38, 1980.
4. 'Air Crash Sites at Sea Scoping Study', *Wessex Archaeology*, 2008.
5. Wills, R. 'Dauntless in Peace and War: A Preliminary Archaeological and Historical Documentation of Douglas SBD/2 Dauntless', BUNo 2106, 1997.
6. Heritage Malta, Underwater Cultural Heritage Unit, www.heritagemalta.mt7. Thomas, Andrew. *Gloster Gladiator Aces*, Oxford: Osprey, 2002.
8. Burgess, A. 'Underwater Aviation Archaeology: What Is Its Place and Value Within Archaeology, and In Particular Maritime Archaeology', University of Southampton, pg. 44, 2013.
9. Ibid, 45–46.
10. Heritage Malta, Underwater Cultural Heritage Unit (UCHU), https://heritagemalta.mt/departments/underwater-cultural-heritage-unit.
11. JU-88 South, The Virtual Museum, Underwater Malta, Malta Tourism Authority, https://underwatermalta.org/discover/ju88-south.
12. Ibid.
13. Douglas A-1 Skyraider, The Virtual Museum, Underwater Malta, Malta Tourism Authority, https://underwatermalta.org/discover/skyraider.
14. Ibid.
15. Ibid.
16. B-24 Liberator, Heritage Malta, https://heritagemalta.mt/explore/b24-liberator.

17. Ibid.
18. Heritage Malta, Underwater Cultural Heritage Unit, www.heritagemalta.mt.
19. The Virtual Museum, Underwater Malta, Malta Tourism Authority https://underwatermalta.org.
20. Ibid.
21. Evans, Lorraine. *Burying the Dead: An Archaeological History of Burial Grounds, Graveyards and Cemeteries*, Pen and Sword, 2020.
22. Ibid.
23. Black, Annetta. 'Ghost Fleet of Truk Lagoon,' Atlas Obscura, July 2013.
24. 'Kwajalein Naval Base,' US Navy, Bureau of Yards and Docks, *Building the Navy's Bases in World War II* v.2, Alaska, and overseas. Washington, D.C., 1947.
25. Spenneman, D. 'Invasion of the Kwajalein Atolls,' National Museum of the US Navy, www.history.navy.mil.
26. 'WWII Airplane Graveyard in Pacific Ocean,' *Argunners Magazine*, June 2015.
27. Ibid.
28. 'SPH Engineering Helps Locate Aircraft Buried Under Greenland Ice With GPR-UAV Integrated Systems,' www.sphengineering.com, August 2018.
29. 'Glacier Girl: The Back Story,' airandspacemag.com, July 2007.
30. Allnutt, R.M. 'FOUND! Lost Squadron P-38 Piloted by Lt. Col. Robert Wilson,' *Vintage Aviation News*, July 2018.
31. Ibid.
32. Ibid.
33. Ferris, J. 'B-17 Wreck Exposed by Melting Glacier in Iceland,' Planet Historia, October 2013.
34. Ibid.
35. Jorio, L. 'Why Melting Glaciers Affect Us All,' March 2025, www.swissinfo.ch/eng/climate-solutions/why-melting-glaciers-affect-us-all.
36. 'Teens Find Famed 1946 Plane Wreck in Swiss Glacier,' The History Blog, August 2012, www.thehistoryblog.com/archives/18829.
37. Dennis, E.T. 'Heatwave Uncovers Second World War Plane Hidden in Glacier for 72 Years,' *The Independent* Newspaper, August 2018.
38. 'Wreckage of Plane That Crashed In 1968 Found on Swiss Glacier,' The Brussels Times Newspaper, August 2022.
39. Ibid.
40. 'Newspapers from Crashed Jet Found in Melting Glacier Ice,' *Planet Ski*, July 2020.
41. Ibid.
42. 'Alaska's Shrinking Glaciers', National Park Service: www.nps.gov/articles/000/alaskas-shrinking-glaciers.htm.
43. Mount Garnier Crash, en.wikipedia.org/wiki/1952_Mount_Gannett_C-124_crash.

44. 'Sacred Search: Operation Colony Glacier,' US Department of Defense, July 2023.
45. Ibid.
46. Ibid.
47. 'Crash of a Fairchild C-119C-22-FA Flying Boxcar on Mt McKinley: 19 Killed,' Bureau of Aircraft Accidents Archives.
48. Andrews, L. 'How a Retired Geologist Discovered a Long-Lost Air Force Crash in the Alaska Range,' *Anchorage Daily News*, July 2018.
49. Fernandez, G. '7 Decades Later, the Military Is Searching for the Remains of 19 Service Members,' *Alaska's News Source*, August 2023.
50. Ibid.
51. AirLine Disasters, www.airdisasters.co.uk/120348.htm.
52. Ibid.
53. Ibid.
54. Official Accident Report, www.pbs.org/wgbh/nova/vanished/sten_report.htm.
55. Dimri, B. 'What Happened to Star Dust? The Plane Taken by the Andes Historic Mysteries, October 2021.
56. Bowcott, O. 'DNA Clues Reveal 55-Year-Old Secrets Behind Crash of the Star Dust,' *The Guardian* Newspaper, September 2012.
57. 'Vanished: The Plane That Disappeared,' *Horizon*, BBC TV, November 2000.
58. Strickland-Smith, K. 'This Watery Graveyard Is the Resting Place for 161 Sunken Spaceships,' https://gizmodo.com, May 2015.
59. Ibid.
60. Slezak, M. 'Tiangong-1 Crash: Everything You Need to Know,' *The Guardian* Newspaper, March 2018.
61. 'Treaty on Principles Governing the Activities of States in the Exploration and Use of Outer Space, Including the Moon and Other Celestial Bodies,' United Nations Office for Outer Space Affairs, www.unoosa.org.
62. Ibid.
63. Ibid.
64. 'Loyce Edward Deen USNR WW II,' www.loyceedeen.org.
65. Ibid.
66. Stilwell, B. 'Aerial Gunner Loyce Edward Deen, Was Buried at Sea Inside His Aircraft', We Are the Mighty, April 2024. www.wearethemighty.com/popular/loyce-edward-deen-was-buried-at-sea-inside-his-plane.
67. Video of the burial of Loyce Edward Deen, https://youtu.be/FMWz10jaK0g?si=H4uSHGMwDF0uEiKB.

Chapter 5: Lest We Forget

1. Rose, S. 'Miss Piggy Plane Wreck', Atlas Obscura, 2023.
2. Ibid.
3. National Park Service, www.nps.gov/articles/atka-b24d-liberator.htm.

4. Ibid.
5. Rantor, H. 'The Story of DC3 or C-117 Plane Wreck on Sólheimasandur in Iceland', amazingiceland.is.
6. 'Crashed World War II Wellington Bomber, Garreg Goch', adventurebritain.com.
7. Courtesy of the Ted Coningsby Squadron, www.tedconingsby.com.
8. 'Ystradgynlais Aircraft Crash Site', www.ystradglynlais-history.co.uk/spitfirex4588.
9. Smith J. D. *Britain's Aviation Memorials and Mementoes*, Patrick Stephens Ltd, 162, 1992.
10. Halifax LL505 on Great Carrs, Lake District, www.yorkshire-aircraft.co.uk.
11. Clark Alan, 'Wellington Mk.IC R1011 / M of No.28 OTU RAF crashed on Birchen Bank Moss', Peak District Air Accident Research, 2023.
12. 'Every Day Is Memorial Day on Burma Rim', US Department of the Interior, Bureau of Land Management, May 2020.
13. Ibid.
14. Soviet War Veterans Monument, www.spomenikdatabase.org/avala.
15. Ibid.
16. Ibid.
17. Jennings P. 'The Plane Crash That Killed Serie A's Champions and Their English Coach', *BBC Sports Insight*, www.bbc.co.uk/sport/football/46788983, May 2019.
18. Shermet, W. & Maioni E. 'The Plane That Crashed on the Fradusta Glacier, Italian Dolomites', www.guidedolmiti.com, June 2009.
19. Smith, J. D. *Britain's Aviation Memorials and Mementoes*, Patrick Stephens Ltd, 171, 1992.
20. Ibid, 165, 1992.
21. Ibid.
22. Ibid, 176, 1992.
23. Ibid, 169, 1992.
24. Ibid, 98, 1992.
25. Ibid, 155, 1992.
26. Aviation Safety Network, https://asn.flightsafety.org/wikibase/217661.
27. 295 Squadron Halifax V EB132, https://aircrewremembered.com/tomkins-bl.html.
28. Clark Alan, 'Vickers Wellington Mk.XI HZ251 / 38 of No.6 (Coastal) Operational Training Unit, Crashed at Low Bradley on the 23rd of September 1943', *Peak District Air Accident Research*, 2016.
29. Turner Christopher, 'The Plane Crash That Made It into a Museum', *Apollo Magazine*, September 2024.
30. Ibid.
31. Ibid.
32. Ibid.

33. Ibid.
34. Smith J. D. *Britain's Aviation Memorials and Mementoes*, Patrick Stephens Ltd, 32, 1992.
35. Ibid, 70, 1992.
36. Ibid, 143, 1992.
37. Ibid, 147, 1992.
38. Ibid, 127, 1992.
39. Babaoshan Revolutionary Cemetery, Beijing, www.visitbeijing.com.
40. 'Peruvian Jetliner Carrying 46 People Feared Down in Jungle', *New York Times* Newspaper, January 2003.
41. Pendleton L. 'Kegworth Air Disaster 1989', www.kegworthvillage.com.
42. Cross Seminole Trail, www.seminolecountyfl.gov.
43. Desilets, X. 'Memorial Lakes', Atlas Obscura, June 2023.
44. Mosquito Fighter Bomber Mk VI LR 329, www.iwm.org.uk/memorials/106494.
45. Kershaw, R. 'Staines Air Crash 50 Years On', *The National Archives*, June 2022.
46. Ezeamalu, B. 'Governor Fashola, Victims' Families Unveil Dana Air Crash Cenotaph in Emotional One Year Anniversary', *Premium Times Nigeria* Newspaper, June 2013.
47. Grundhauser, E. 'Ämari Pilots' Cemetery', Atlas Obscura, 2015.
48. Duncan, L. 'Wellington R1646 - Glen Clunie', www.archieraf.co.uk, 2014.
49. Ibid.
50. Ibid.
51. 'A Memorial Amongst the Lavender', www.vauclusedteamer.com, December 2017.
52. 'B-17G Tail Number 43-39035', www.wingsmuseum.co.uk.
53. 'B-17 'Man O'War' (42-38033) Memorial', American War Memorials Overseas, www.uswarmemorials.org.
54. Smith, J. D. *Britain's Aviation Memorials and Mementoes*, Patrick Stephens Ltd, 150, 1992.
55. Vickers Wellington Monument, www.laagholland.com/vickers-wellington.
56. Smith, J. D. *Britain's Aviation Memorials and Mementoes*, Patrick Stephens Ltd, 136, 1992.
57. www.cwgc.org/find-cemeteriesmemorials/cemetery-details/kranji-war-cemetery
58. Venema Vibike, 'The Sahara Memorial Seen From Space', *BBC News*, January 2014.
59. Ibid.
60. Paone, T. 'Dealing with the Aftermath of the Hindenburg Disaster', National Air and Space Museum, airandspace.si.edu/stories/editorial/aftermath-Hindenburg, 2022.
61. 'Memorial to Healthcare Heroes Unveiled at Crash Site Near Winterton, KwaZulu-Natal', *The Witness* Newspaper, February 2022.

62. Pan Am 103 Bombing, Federal Bureau of Investigation, www.fbi.gov.
63. Lockerbie Garden of Remembrance, www.undiscoveredscotland.co.uk/lockerbie.
64. 'The Wood Where "Love Is Greater Than War"', www.thevillage.co, July 2010.
65. Pan Am Flight 103 Memorial (Lockerbie Memorial Cairn), Arlington National Cemetery, www.arlingtoncemetery.mi/monuments-and-memorials/pan-am-flight-103.
66. Remembering Pan Am 103, Syracuse University, www.syracuse.edu.
67. Pentagon Memorial, www.defense.gov/Pentagon-Memorial.
68. Ibid.
69. Lives of the First World War, livesofthefirstworldwar.iwm.org.uk/lifestory/2581628.
70. www.hertsatwar.co.uk/biographies/198663/reginald-alexander-john-warneford.
71. Grave of the pilot S.I. Kharkhalup, Konstantinovka village, tourismpmr.org.
72. Hanguk Staff, 'A Cold War Secret: Graves Discovered of Russian Pilots Who Flew MiG Jets for North Korea During Korean War', *Milwaukee Independent* Newspaper, October 2024.
73. 'Capt. E Fox Pitt Lubbock RFC MC', *War Memorials Register*, iwm.org/mem/43554.

Chapter 6: I Don't Believe It

1. www.bbc.co.uk/programmes/articles/he-man-who-buries-planes.
2. Ibid.
3. Harris, G. 'Lift off: UK Artist Buries Planes at Three Sites as Part of Growing Global Network', *The Art* Newspaper, 2018.
4. www.bbc.co.uk/programmes/articles/he-man-who-buries-planes.
5. Ibid.
6. Kudler, G. A. 'Take a Look at Artist's Proposal to Bury a 727 in Kern County', www.la.curbed.com, 2012.
7. 'The Boneyard Project: street artists paint aircraft at plane graveyard in Arizona', *Telegraph*, www.telegraph.co.uk, 2012.
8. Ibid.
9. Banner, F. 'Harrier and Jaguar', Tate Gallery 2010, www.tate.org.uk.
10. The MiG-21 Project, www.museumofflight.org, 2025.
11. https://rafwainfleet.co.uk.
12. www.pinewoodpark.co.uk/helicopter-glamping-breaks.
13. Petrauskaite, G. 'Royal Navy helicopter transformed into a hotel room', *AeroTime*, www.aerotime.aero, 2022.
14. www.visitscotland.com, 2018.
15. www.pytch.co.uk/pytchair-plane-office-bristol-private-jet.

16. Harries R & Fawcett E. 'A Disused Private Jet Has Been Turned into an Airbnb in the Welsh Countryside', www.walesonline.co.uk, 2025.
17. Marwell Mile High AirBnB, www.marwellmilehigh.co.uk, 2025.
18. The Jet Star, www.applecamping.co.uk, 2025.
19. Schlappig, B. 'Sad: Iconic Jumbo Stay 747 Hotel Stockholm Arlanda Closes', One Mile at a Time, 2025.
20. www.hotels-insolites.com/en/airplane-suite.hotel, 2025.
21. Noyce, E. 'I Bought Two Old Planes and Transformed Them into a Swanky £450-a-Night Airbnb', *Metro Newspaper*, August 2024.
22. The 727 Fuselage Home, www.costaverde.com/727-fuselage-home, 2025.
23. Grothe, D. 'Thailand's Crazy Airliner Conversions: An Illustrated Tour', Key Aero, 2023.
24. Griddell, S. 'A Boeing 737 was transformed into a luxury villa in Bali',Pettyjohn, www.businessinsider.com, 2024.
25. Charles, B. 'Man Converts World War II Navy Plane into Class A Motorhome', www.rv.com, 2021.
26. Miller, H. 'Meet the Man Who Lives in This Airplane in the Woods', www.livenowfox.com, 2023.
27. Fernandez, C. '73-Year-Old Pays $370/Month to Live in a Plane He Bought for $100,000 from a Salvage Yard: "I Have No Regrets"', www.cnbc.com, 2022.
28. Gorgon, E. 'Project Freedom: The Airplane Home with Deck, Garage, and a Second Plane for Entertaining', www.autoevolution.com, 2022.
29. Gorgon, E. 'Meet Cosmic Muffin, the Iconic Howard Hughes Boeing 307 Stratoliner Turned Plane Boat', www.autoevolution.com, 2022.
30. Ibid.
31. www.lovetaupo.com/en/operators/mcdonald-s, 2025.
32. www.facebook.com/Thesteakoutbolton/?locale=en_GB 2025.
33. 'Runway 1: This Old Aeroplane Is Now a Quirky Restaurant in Haryana', *India Times* Newspaper, 2018.
34. www.theairplanerestaurant.com.
35. Sarouhan, T. 'How a Plane Became One of Manuel Antonio's Most Popular Restaurants', www.govisitcostarica.com, 2015.
36. Schlappig, B. 'Sky Coffee: Miami's New Airplane Coffee Shop', One Mile at a Time, 2023.
37. Loh, C. 'A Look Inside Thailand's 331 Station Coffee War', *Simply Flying*, 2021.
38. Grothe, D. 'Thailand's Crazy Airliner Conversions: An Illustrated Tour', Key Aero, 2023.
39. Ibid.
40. www.blackcanyonthai.com.
41. Bassingham, A. 'Bristol Plane Fuselage Turned into Primary School Library', *BBC News*, 2024.

42. Ibid.
43. Gupta, T. & Field, M. 'School Turns Airbus 319 Fuselage into Library', *BBC News*, 2024.
44. 'Cessna Jet Classroom Opens at Westcliff-on-Sea School', *BBC News*, 2016.
45. 'Kindergarten Co-Pilots: Airplane Transformed into Kids' School', photoblog, www.nbcnews.com, 2012.
46. Fleur, A. 'Red Clay Studio - A New Art Space in Ghana', Africa Blooming, 2020.
47. Grothe, D. 'Thailand's Crazy Airliner Conversions: An Illustrated Tour', Key Aero, 2023.
48. Ulinskas, V. 'A Decommissioned Soviet Airplane Has Been Used as a Movie Theater and a Cultural Center', Atlas Obscura, 2017.
49. 'This Old KLM Airplane Cut into Three Parts Was Transformed into an Eclectic Airport Gift Shop', CoolCrab, Atlas Obscura, 2019.
50. Hind, S. 'See Inside Plane that Scots Make-Up Artist Has Converted into Stunning Beauty Salon', *The Daily Record* Newspaper, 2017.
51. Venu Das, M. 'Coach Launches New Air Travel Themed Boutique Inside Actual Airplane', *Marketing-Interactive*, 2023.
52. Grothe, D. 'Thailand's Crazy Airliner Conversions: An Illustrated Tour', Key Aero, 2023.
53. Ibid.
54. 'Area 51 'Declassified' in U-2 Spy Plane History', BBC News, 2013.
55. CNet.News, 2013.
56. 'The Secret History of the U-2 - and Area 51', The National Security Archive, nsarchive2.gwu.edu, 2013.
57. Urban Ghosts Media, www.urbanghostsmedia.com.
58. Newitz, A. 'The Mysterious Area 51 Graveyards Where Secret Military Technologies Go to Die', www.gizmodo.com, 2013.
59. Ibid.
60. Gaddis, Vincent, 'The Deadly Bermuda Triangle - Argosy', physics.smu.edu. 1964.
61. Cochran-Smith, M. 'Bermuda Triangle: Dichotomy, Mythology, and Amnesia'. *Journal of Teacher Education*, 54(4), SAGE Publications: 275, 2003.
62. Quasar J. G. 'Disappearance of Flight 19', web.archive.org, 2006.
63. McDonell, M. 'Lost Patrol', *Naval Aviation News*, 8–16, 1973.
64. Ibid.
65. Rukka N. 'America's Most Terrifying Mystery You've Never Heard About', vocal.media.com, 2025.
66. Ibid.
67. Ibid.
68. Further examples are detailed at www.lorraineevans.com.
69. 'Vesna Vulović: How to Survive a Bombing at 33000 Feet', *Aviation Security Magazine*, April 2002.

70. Ibid.
71. Ibid.
72. Kebabjian Richard, Planecrashinfo.com.
73. 'Vesna Vulović, Stewardess Who Survived 33,000ft Fall, Dies', *BBC News*, 2016.

Chapter 7: Resurrection

1. Avro Lancaster - Lincolnshire Aviation Heritage Centre, www.lincsaviation.co.uk.
2. Ibid.
3. Ibid.
4. Ibid.
5. Ibid.
6. Mosquito - Lincolnshire Aviation Heritage Centre, www.lincsaviation.co.uk.
7. Ethell, J. L. & Pace, S. *Spitfire*. St. Paul, Minnesota: Motorbooks International, 1997.
8. The Silver Spitfire, www.silverspitfire.com.
9. Ibid.
10. Ibid.
11. Ibid.
12. The Longest Flight, www.silverspitfire.com.
13. Battle of Britain Memorial Flight, www.raf.mod.uk/display-teams/battle-of-britain-memorial-flight.
14. Bader, D. *Fight for the Sky: The Story of the Spitfire and Hurricane*, London: Cassell Military Books, 2004.
15. www.raf.mod.uk/display-teams/battle-of-britain-memorial-flight.
16. Models and Military Aircraft, www.militaryplanes.co.uk/lf363-h.html.
17. Hawker Hurricane, www.raf.mod.uk.
18. Hawker Hurricane 75th Birthday, www.memorialflightclub.com/blog/hurricane-lf363-75th-birthday--1st-january.
19. 'BBMF Hurricane PZ865 Is 80 This Month', https://memorialflightclub.com/blog/bbmf-hurricane-pz865-80-month.
20. Ibid.
21. Ibid.

Select Bibliography

'Aircraft Crash Sites at Sea: A Scoping Study', Wessex Archaeology, 2008.

Balory, D. *The History of Aviation*, Hamlyn Publishing, 1999.

Bédoyère, de la G. *Battle Over Britain - The Archaeology of the Air War*, Tempus Publishing Ltd, 2000.

Bédoyère, de la G. *Aviation Archaeology in Britain*, Shire Archaeology, 2001.

Brockman A & Spaight T. *The Buried Spitfires of Burma: A 'Fake' History*, The History Press, 2020.

Burgess, Anthony. 'Underwater Aviation Archaeology: What Is Its Place and Value within Archaeology, and in Particular Maritime Archaeology?' Master's Thesis University of Southampton, 2013.

Chinnery, P. *Desert Boneyard - Davis Monthan AFB,* Arizona, Airlife Publishing Ltd, 1987.

Christian, T. 'Development and Application of a Standardised Methodology to Second World War Aircraft Sites in Scotland', PhD Thesis, University of Glasgow, 2014.

Clark, B. *The Archaeology of Airfields*, Tempus Publishing, 2008.

Col Zbyšek Nečas-Pemberton, *Beaufighter and Mosquito Operations in WWII*, Pen and Sword Aviation, 2024.

Critchell, A. *A Tale of Ten Spitfires*, Pen and Sword Aviation, 2018.

Ellis, K. *Aviation Museums of Britain*, Midland Publishing, 1995.

Ellis, K. *Wrecks and Relics*, Midlands Publishing, Leicester, 2024.

Freeman, R.A. *The Fight for the Skies*, Arms and Armour, London, 1998.

Fugere, J. *Inside AMRAC - The Aerospace Maintenance and Regeneration Center*, Tucson, Arizona, Airlife Publishing Ltd, 2001.

Gero, D. *Early Aviation Disasters: The World's Major Airliner Crashes Before 1950*, The History Press, 2011.

Grant, R.G. *Flight: 100 Years of Aviation*, Dorling Kindersley Ltd, 2002.

Guttery, Ben R. *Encyclopaedia of African Airlines.* Jefferson, NC: McFarland & Company, 1998.

Hoffen, G. *Restoration Force,* Grub Street, 2021.

Lepin, M. *The Avro Lancaster: WWII's Most Successful Heavy Bomber*, Sona Books, 2022.

McLachlan, I. *Final Flights: Dramatic Wartime Incidents Revealed by Aviation Archaeology,* Patrick Stephens Ltd, 1989.

McNab, C. (Editor). *Encyclopaedia of Military Aircraft*, Amber Books Ltd, 2024.

Military Aircraft Crash Sites: Archaeological Guidance on Their Significance and Future Management, Historic England, Arkle Print Ltd, 2002.

Mondey, D. *British Aircraft of World War II*, Chancellor Press, 1994.

Munro, A. *Fast Jets on the Frontline: Flying Phantoms, Javelins and Tornados in the Cold War,* Grub Street, 2025.

Nichol, J. *Spitfire: A Very British Love Story,* Simon and Schuster UK, 2019.

Robertson, B. *Epics of Aviation Archaeology*, Patrick Stephens Ltd, 1978.

Saunders, A. *Aircraft Salvage in the Battle of Britain and The Blitz*, Pen and Sword Aviation, 2014.

Shaw, P. *Discover Aviation Trails: Touring Britain's Aviation Heritage*, Midland Publishing, 1996.

Smith, D. J. *Britain's Aviation Memorials & Mementoes*, Patrick Stephens Limited, 1992.

Smith, D. J. *High Ground Wrecks and Relic*s, Midland Publishing, Leicester, 1997.

Sturtivant, R. *Fleet Air Arm Aircraft 1939 to 1945*, An Air-Britain Publication, 1995.

Thomas, A. *Gloster Gladiator Aces*, Oxford: Osprey, 2002.

Wotherspoon, N. *North-West Aircraft Wrecks*, Pen and Sword Aviation, 2006.

Wotherspoon, N., Clark, A. & Sheldon, M. *Aircraft Wrecks: The Walkers Guide*, Pen and Sword Aviation, 2009.

Wragg, D. *The Fleet Air Arm Handbook 1939 to 1945*, Sutton Publishing, 2001.

Wragg, D. *RAF Handbook 1939-1945*, Sutton Publishing, 2007.